Buddhist Philosophy

Buddhist Philosophy

A Historical Analysis

David J. Kalupahana
Foreword by G. P. Malalasekera

AN EAST-WEST CENTER BOOK
The University Press of Hawaii
Honolulu

Library of Congress Cataloging in Publication Data
Kalupahana, David J 1933–
Buddhist philosophy.
"An East-West Center book."
Includes bibliographies and index.
1. Buddhist doctrines.
2. Philosophy, Buddhist.
I. Title.
BQ4150.K34 181′.04′3 75-20040
ISBN 0-8248-0360-4
ISBN 0-8248-0392-2 pbk.

Filmset in Hong Kong by Asco Trade Typesetting Ltd.
Manufactured in the United States of America
Designed by Penny L. Faron

On the cover: Bodhisattva, presumably Śākya Muni, the Buddha. First or second century A.D. Red sandstone figure, 28 inches high; from the Katrā mound, Mathurā; now in the Mathurā Museum. Photograph by Prithwish Neogy, professor of art, University of Hawaii.

To Indrani

Contents

Foreword

I have much pleasure in writing a foreword to the present publication by Dr. D. J. Kalupahana, my friend and erstwhile student. Here we have a volume that fulfills admirably the purpose for which it was intended—to outline the development of Buddhist philosophy from the days of its origin down to the time of the development of Zen. Starting from the philosophical and religious ideas prevalent during the pre-Buddhist period, the author has extended his survey to the later schools of Buddhism.

One whole chapter is devoted to the Buddhist theory of causality, which forms the basic teaching of Buddhism and is its central conception. The author's chief endeavor is to prove that early Buddhism is empiricistic and antimetaphysical and that it does not accept anything which cannot be experienced either through the senses or extrasensory perception. This point of view he follows up with a later chapter on *karma* and rebirth, in which he seeks to remove several prevalent misconceptions, for example, that Buddhism is a deterministic religion.

But perhaps the most provocative chapter in the book is the seventh, which deals with *nibbāna* (nirvana). This is a subject on which countless treatises have been written recently, especially by Western savants, many of whom tend to interpret *nibbāna* as transcendental and absolute. Speculation on the nature of *nibbāna* is bound to continue endlessly. As the Buddha himself has warned us, *nibbāna* is a matter for experience, not for definition or description. The parable of the five blind men and the elephant is a very apt one. Dr. Kalupahana's statements are buttressed by quotations from the most authentic sources, the Pali Nikāyas.

The second part of the book deals with later Buddhism and contains a concise and readable account of the developments that took place after the Buddha's *parinirvāna* and the emergence of different schools of Buddhism. Here the author gives his own views regarding the Mādhyamika and the transcendentalism of the *Prajñāpāramitā* literature. These views deserve the serious attention of scholars because they are often contrary to ideas which are now generally prevalent. These remarks also apply to the author's observations regarding Zen Buddhism.

All in all, this book will be a very welcome addition to works already available for the study of a religion which has now spread throughout the world, giving spiritual solace to a very large section of humanity.

G. P. Malalasekera

Preface

Buddhism is now more than two thousand five hundred years old. Conforming to the words of its founder, Siddhârtha Gautama, that "everything in this world is impermanent," his teachings underwent transformation while catering to the needs and religious aspirations of his followers, who represent a large segment of humanity spread out over a major part of the earth's surface. In this transformation, while Buddhism contributed much to the various religious and philosophical traditions with which it came into contact, it also assimilated many of these non-Buddhist doctrines. It is for this reason that a completely satisfactory outline of Buddhist philosophy becomes an impossibility. Realizing this fact, I have devoted the present work to an examination of the original form of Buddhism and a few later schools which I consider basic to all the different varieties of Buddhist thought.

The emphasis in this book is on the philosophical outlook of early Buddhism. Although there has been a long-drawn-out controversy over the primitive core of Buddhism, and in spite of the fact that attempts to establish it are now considered by many to be hopelessly futile, I think it is worthwhile to try. Previous attempts to determine the original form of Buddhism were based on the assumption that the early discourses attributed to the Buddha contain a lot of "monkish jargon" and, therefore, the original form can be known only after leaving out such elements. This led to disastrous results, as is evident from the later works of Mrs. C. A. F. Rhys Davids, for such decisions were based more on prejudice than on scientific attitude. Avoiding this assumption, I have undertaken the task of examining the entire content of the early discourses, eliminating nothing.

Doubts have been raised regarding the authenticity of the Pali Nikāyas, especially because they were preserved by the Theravāda sect of Buddhism and hence were taken to represent the ideas of that school. But a comparative study of the Pali Nikāyas and the Chinese Āgamas shows that the Pali Nikāyas do not represent the Theravāda standpoint. In fact, there is nothing in the Nikāyas that can be called Theravāda. The Nikāyas and the Āgamas agree so well with regard to the doctrines they embody, and are so different from the *Abhidharma Piṭakas* of the various schools, that one can be very optimistic about the attempt to determine the nature of pre-Abhidharma Buddhism.

The next question to be examined is, What is the antiquity of the discourses included in the Pali Nikāyas and the Chinese Āgamas? There is no doubt that they represent the earliest sources for the study of Buddhism. One of the earliest references (other than the Buddhist texts themselves) to the existence of some of the discourses is the Bhabra Edict of King Asoka (third century B.C.) which names seven texts from the early discourses that have now been identified. The Theravāda historical records, such as the *Cullavagga* of the *Vinaya Piṭaka* and chronicles like *Dipavaṃsa* and *Mahāvaṃsa*, testify to the authenticity and antiquity of the discourses. Finally, the Mahāyānists themselves agree that the discourses (included in the Āgamas) were preached first by the Buddha because his immediate disciples could not understand anything else (see, for example, *Saddharmapuṇḍarīka-sūtra* and *Avataṃsaka-sūtra*).

It is generally agreed that the major schools of Abhidharma had taken definite form by the third century B.C. The Abhidharma is considered a systematization of the teachings of the discourses, and therefore it could be maintained that the discourses were finalized at least a century before the systematization accomplished by these Abhidharma schools. Thus the collection and arrangement of the various discourses took place during the first hundred and fifty years after the passing away of the Buddha, and it was probably the main purpose of the second Council held during the time of King Kālâśoka. It is because the *Sūtra Piṭaka* was completed so early that all the Abhidharma schools possessed the same *Sūtra Piṭaka*, but different *Abhidharma Piṭakas*.

In chapter 8 of the present work the origin and development of the Abhidharma and Mahāyāna schools have been traced back to the time of the Buddha himself. Although their origins can be traced back to such an early period, it took some time for these traditions to crystallize into major schools. In any case, the compilation of the texts of the *Abhidharma Piṭaka* and the early Mahāyāna sūtras was subsequent to the finalization of the Pali Nikāyas and the Āgamas, translated later into Chinese. Therefore, one is fully justified in depending on the Pali Nikāyas and the Chinese Āgamas for the study of early or primitive Buddhism.

The approach adopted in the present work is mainly historical. The contents of the discourses, recognized as the earliest sources by all the schools of Buddhism, are analysed in full without arbitrarily rejecting any portion as "monkish jargon." A complete picture of early Buddhism is attempted on the basis of the contents of these discourses. Having determined what constitutes early Buddhism, and keeping in mind the various circumstances that gave rise to the two major traditions, Hīnayāna and Mahāyāna, a careful attempt has been made to trace the gradual change that took place in Buddhist thought.

Analysis of the early Buddhist doctrines in their own right, without adopting a Hīnayānist or Mahāyānist perspective, has led me to some rather unpopular views regarding the nature of early Buddhism. It will be found that the doctrine of freedom (*nirvāna*) in early Buddhism is here examined in the light of the Buddha's epistemological, ontological, ethical, and other doctrines, not in isolation from them, nor in relation to what Nāgârjuna or Vasubandhu or Buddhaghosa said. The result is the rejection of either Absolutism or Transcendentalism, of the form which the Hīnayānists or Mahāyānists recognized, as part of early Buddhism.

It is rather unfortunate that the 'saintliness' (*buddhatta*, Sk. *buddhatva* or *arahatta*, Sk. *arhatva*) that is attained as a result of an understanding of the 'constitution of things' (*dhammadhātu*) and the consequent elimination of craving (*rāga*, *taṇhā*, and so on) and grasping (*upādāna*) did not satisfy the ordinary man. What he needed was an awe-inspiring breath-taking, transcendental father-figure, or a being, even though invisible, through whom he could hope to save himself. Unfortunately, the historical personality of the Buddha did not satisfy these needs.

The Buddha rejected any ultimate principle like the individual 'self' (*ātman*) or the Universal Reality (*loka* = Upaniṣadic Brahman). His rejection was based on the fact that any such Ultimate Reality, which was recognized as nonsensuous, indescribable, and transcendental, is also *metaphysical*. Metaphysics, as the Buddha saw, was a field where common sense may run riot and where there is no standard measure (*na pamāṇam atthi*) to determine whether there is any reality or not. It was because the Buddha maintained this position regarding the metaphysics of the pre-Buddhist background, that the brahmans of the Upaniṣadic tradition criticized him as a 'nihilist' (*ucchedavādī*) of the worst sort (*Vin* 1.234–5), although for the Buddha it was the Materialist teachings that were 'nihilistic' (*D* 1.34, 55). But the very same metaphysics that the Buddha rejected came to occupy an important place in Mahāyāna. Mahāyāna is dominated by speculation regarding the nature of the Buddha after death, a question which the Buddha himself considered metaphysical and left unanswered. In the *Saddharmapuṇḍarīka-sūtra*, it is held that the Enlightened Ones (*tathāgata*) remain forever (*sadā sthitāḥ*) and that their *parinirvāṇa* (passing away) is an illusion. This is to say that the *tathāgata* exists after death (*hoti tathāgato parammaraṇā*), a question the Buddha left unexplained for very important epistemological reasons (see appendix 1). Yet this is the basic theme of Mahāyāna.

Moreover, in Theravāda as well as in Mahāyāna, the Buddha was raised to the status of a transcendental being, while Mahāyāna went to the extreme of maintaining that the real body of the Buddha is the all-pervading, nondual *dharmakāya*. It was only after such a transcendentalist conception of Buddha came to dominate Buddhism that the Hindus (the successors of the Upaniṣadic sages) made the Buddha the highest incarnation (*avatār*) of Viṣṇu. Consequently, Buddhist scholars, classical as well as modern, were called upon to undertake the onerous task of distinguishing between Hindu and Buddhist forms of transcendentalism. Failing to achieve this, some scholars have declared: "The Buddha was born a Hindu. He lived a Hindu and died a Hindu."

Thus, whatever the form may be, transcendentalism, which has fascinated mankind, came to dominate Buddhist thought after the passing way of the Buddha. The emphasis on a transcendental reality led almost to a rejection of the philosophical content of Buddhism. *Sammuti* (from *saṃ* $\sqrt{mn}$ 'to think') or 'conventional' or ordinary language became *saṃvṛti* (from *saṃ* $\sqrt{vr}$, 'to cover') or that which conceals reality. Therefore, reality became indescribable (*avācya*) and indefinable (*anirvacanīya*) with consequent devaluation of philosophical discourse. (It may be noted that in the philosophy of Dinnāga, who avoided contributing to any of the transcendentalistic philosophies that went before him, there is much philosophical content.) Those who are averse to seeing Buddhism as an important philosophical movement, have tended to overemphasize its religious teachings to the utter neglect of its philosophical contributions. The main purpose of the present text is to point out the philosophical richness of early Buddhism and to redefine the religious dimensions which finally enabled it to become a world religion.

The second part of the book explains in outline the subsequent ramifications of Buddhist thought. Since the basic *philosophical* concepts were well developed before Buddhism left the shores and boundaries of India, no attempt has been made here to deal with these later schools, except for some aspects of Zen Buddhism (see appendix 2). Some space is devoted to Zen because it is generally held that Zen represents Chinese thought more than anything else, a view based on an entirely wrong conception of what the Buddha taught. There are other Chinese Buddhist schools, such as Hua Yen, which attempted to synthesize the different concepts of Buddhism. Whatever the outcome of this synthesis, the concepts dealt with here were already present in the Buddhist tradition. For these reasons, no attempt has been made here to deal with any of the schools of Ceylonese, Chinese, Japanese, or even Tibetan Buddhism.

David J. Kalupahana

Acknowledgments

The present work owes its origin to a course in Buddhist Philosophy I taught in the Department of Philosophy at the University of Hawaii during the spring semester of 1971 as a visiting faculty member. Since its completion, during the fall of the same year, many of my friends, both in Sri Lanka and in Hawaii, have read the manuscript and made excellent suggestions for improvement. To all of them I am deeply indebted.

It is with a sense of great personal loss that I record the death of my teacher and friend, Professor G. P. Malalasekera, who had been a constant source of inspiration to me since I began my undergraduate work at the University of Ceylon. He kindly consented to write a foreword to this volume which he did not live to see in print.

I extend special thanks to my colleague Professor Prithwish Neogy, chairman of the Department of Art at the University of Hawaii, for providing me with the photograph that appears on the book's cover.

I am grateful to Mrs. Floris Sakamoto for her ungrudging help in preparing the manuscript for the press.

Abbreviations

A	*Aṅguttara-nikāya*, ed. R. Morris and E. Hardy, 5 vols., London: PTS, 1885–1900; tr. F. L. Woodward and E. M. Hare, *The Book of the Gradual Sayings*, 5 vols., London: PTS, 1932–1936.
AD	*Abhidharmadīpa* with *Vibhāṣāprabhāvṛtti*, ed. P. S. Jaini, Patna: K. P. Jayaswal Research Institute, 1951.
ADV	*Vibhāṣāprabhāvṛtti*, see *AD*
D	*Digha-nikāya*, ed. T. W. Rhys Davids and J. E. Carpenter, 3 vols., London: PTS, 1890–1911; tr. T. W. Rhys Davids and C. A. F. Rhys Davids, *Dialogues of the Buddha*, 3 vols., London: PTS, 1899–1921.
DA	*Sumaṅgalavilāsinī, Digha-nikāya-aṭṭhakathā*, ed. T. W. Rhys Davids, J. E. Carpenter, and W. Stede, 3 vols., London: PTS, 1886–1932.
Dhs	*Dhammasaṅganī*, ed. E. Müller, London: PTS, 1885.
DhsA	*Atthasālini, Dhammasaṅganī-aṭṭhakathā*, ed. E. Müller, London: PTS, 1897.
GS	*The Book of the Gradual Sayings*, see *A*.
It	*Itivuttaka*, ed. E. Windish, London: PTS, 1889.
KS	*The Book of the Kindred Sayings*, see *S*.
M	*Majjhima-nikāya*, ed. V. Trenckner and R. Chalmers, 3 vols., London: PTS, 1887–1901; tr. I. B. Horner, *Middle Length Sayings*, 3 vols., London: PTS, 1954–1959.
MK	*Mūla-madhyamaka-kārikā* of Nāgârjuna, see *MKV*.

MKV *Madhyamakavṛtti* (*Madhyamakakārikās*), ed. L. de la Vallée Poussin, *Bibliotheca Buddhica* 4, St. Petersburg: The Imperial Academy of Sciences, 1903–1913.

MLS *Middle Length Sayings*, see *M*.

PTS The Pali Text Society.

S *Samyutta-nikāya*, ed. L. Feer, 6 vols., London: PTS, 1884–1904; tr. C. A. F. Rhys Davids and F. L. Woodward, *The Book of the Kindred Sayings*, 5 vols., London: PTS, 1917–1930.

Sakv *Sphuṭârthâbhidharmakośa-vyākhyā*, ed. U. Wogihara, Tokyo: The Publication Association of Abhidharmakośavyākhyā, 1932–1936.

SBB *The Sacred Books of the Buddhists*, published by the PTS.

SBE *The Sacred Books of the East*, ed. Max Müller, London: Oxford University Press.

Sdmp *Saddharmapuṇḍarīka-sūtra*, ed. H. Kern and B. Nanjio, St. Petersburg: The Imperial Academy of Sciences, 1912; romanized text, ed. U. Wogihara and C. Tsuchida, Tokyo: Seigo Kenkyu-kai, 1934–1936.

Sn *Sutta-nipāta*, ed. D. Anderson and H. Smith, London: PTS, 1913.

TD *Taishō Shinshu Daizōkyō*, ed. J. Takakusu and K. Watanabe, Tokyo: Daizō Shuppan Co., 1924–1934.

Thag *Thera-gathā*, in *Thera-therī-gāthā*, ed. H. Oldenberg and R. Pischel, London: PTS, 1883.

Ud *Udāna*, ed. P. Steinthal, London: PTS, 1948.

Vajra *Vajracchedikā-prajñāpāramitā*, ed. and tr. E. Conze, *Serie Orientale Roma* 13, Rome: Istituto italiano per il Medio ed Estremo Oriente, 1957.

VbhA *Sammohavinodanī*, *Vibhaṅga-aṭṭhakathā*, ed. A. P. Buddhadatta, London: PTS, 1923.

Vin *Vinaya Piṭaka*, ed. H. Oldenberg, 5 vols., London: PTS, 1879–1883.

VinA *Samantapāsādikā*, *Vinaya-aṭṭhakathā*, ed. J. Takakusu and M. Nagai, 7 vols., London: PTS, 1924–1947.

Vism *Visuddhimagga*, ed. C. A. F. Rhys Davids, 2 vols., London: PTS, 1920–1921.

Early Buddhism

Chapter One
Historical Background

For a long time the consensus among Indologists was that Indian culture and civilization originated with the arrival of the Aryans from central Asia (circa 1750 B.C.). The *Ṛgveda*, for the most part a collection of hymns extolling the forces of nature and believed to be the compositions of the Vedic poets, makes reference to the clash between the invading Aryans and the dark-skinned aborigines called Dasyus. The prejudices of the former against the latter, which later came to be reflected in the fourfold social stratification, were mainly responsible for the picture presented in the *Ṛgveda* of the people who occupied the Indus valley at the time of the Aryan invasion. The discovery by archaeologists of remains of a well-developed civilization in the Indus valley has changed this picture completely. The dark-skinned inhabitants conquered by the Aryans are no longer considered a race of uncultured people. They seem to have possessed a highly developed culture and an urban society, and the task of recent scholars has been to sort out the different streams of culture and civilization—the Aryan and the non-Aryan—which, as time passed, merged into the one presented in the post-Vedic literature, commencing with the Upaniṣads.

The ascetic culture which later came to dominate India is generally associated with the pre-Aryan Indus valley civilization because the celebrated Indus seal depicts a prototype of Śiva as *mahāyogin*. The Aryan culture was more mundane in its outlook, as is evident from some of the hymns extolling the *soma*-drinking, fun-loving gods. It is for this reason that the culture of the non-Aryans appeared so strange to the Aryans. This is shown in the *Keśī-sūkta* of the *Ṛgveda*[1] in which the Vedic poet expresses awe at the sight of naked, long-haired ascetics. Although the ascetic tradition of the non-Aryans was in time relegated to the background as a result of the dominance of the more mundane Aryan tradition, it could not be completely wiped out. After remaining dormant for a while, it seems to have re-emerged with fresh vigor and vitality. The history of Indian philosophy may be described as the story of the struggle for supremacy between these two traditions.

In the absence of any written records pertaining to the pre-Vedic period, research on the beginnings of Indian philosophy is generally based on study of the Vedas. Speculation concerning the nature of phenomena led the Vedic Aryans to acceptance of a conception of uniformity of nature long before systematic philosophical thinking began. Commenting on the psychological background that gave rise to the Vedic conception of gods, M. Hiriyanna says, "Unless primitive man had noticed the regularity with which natural phenomena recur and unless he were inwardly convinced that every event had a cause to account for it, he would not have resorted to the creation of such deities in explanation of them."[2] This conception of a purely physical order, which came to be known as *ṛta* (i.e., 'world order'), gradually developed into a sacrificial system and then a moral law. A brief outline of the development of the conception of gods and the sacrificial system may be helpful here.

Although the conception of gods as it appears in the *Ṛgveda* had its origin in the Indo-Iranian, if not the Indo-European, period and therefore is extremely complex, some very distinct stages of evolution have been pointed out by Indologists. The initial stage is said to be marked by an anthropomorphic view of nature. Natural forces, such as fire, wind, and rain, were thought of as having human form and human feelings, desires, and so forth. But as time passed, these beings were looked upon as divinities, mysterious, powerful, and awe-inspiring. The result was the emergence of a large pantheon of divinities on whose favors man depended for a peaceful and comfortable life. Each person, depending on the nature of his needs and desires, selected one of these gods to worship, and in the process tended to extol him as the highest among the gods. Max Müller called this stage henotheism. This conception of gods led to a twofold development: to monotheism, represented by gods like Varuṇa and later by Prajāpati and Brahmā, and monism, which culminated in the conception of Brahman-Ātman as reflected in the Upaniṣads.

Along with this development we find also the gradual evolution of sacrificial ritual. During the earliest stage, when a form of anthropomorphism was in vogue, sacrifices were simple offerings like *soma*, milk, ghee, or butter, intended to satisfy a class of beings thought of as little different from humans. These were offered as expressions of gratitude for favors bestowed. However, when the difference between man and divinity became greater and when more power was ascribed to the gods, sacrifices were performed for the purpose of appeasement and with the hope of obtaining the gods' good grace.

As sacrifice became more elaborate, there emerged a class of officiating priests (*brāhmaṇa*), who acted as intermediaries between man and god, and in fact were themselves eventually considered semidivine. The religious life of the Indians came to be dominated by extensive and elaborate rituals. Sacrifice was looked upon as an instrument by which the brahman priest could bestow health and prosperity on the worshiper or the sacrificer.

The more elaborate rituals began to utilize the simple Vedic hymns composed by the poets, as part of the sacrificial ceremonies. One of the functions of the officiating priest was to recite these hymns, and thus the priests became the custodians of the Vedas. Because the recitation of these hymns was an essential part of the sacrifice, they came to be associated with magical power. Correct recitation was a *sine qua non*, without which the desired benefits would not follow. Eventually, the human origin of the Vedas was forgotten as they came more and more to be associated with divinity. According to the earliest account of the divine origin of the Vedas, the hymns were produced by the sacrifice of the Cosmic Person (*puruṣa*).[3] When the monistic principle of explanation was current, the origin of the Vedas was attributed to it. But when monotheism was in vogue, the origin of the Vedas came to be associated with a personal divine being. Prajāpati is often credited with the task of creating them,[4] and later, as the idea of Brahmā developed, and with the identification of Brahmā with Prajāpati, we find the creation of the Vedas attributed to this great god. In one of the early Upaniṣads it is expressly stated that Vedic knowledge comes from Brahmā, who disclosed it to Prajāpati, who in turn told Manu (the first man), who in his turn passed it down to human beings.[5] The Vedas embodying this knowledge, thought to be divinely inspired, were handed down from generation to generation through a long and unbroken tradition of sages.

Thus we come to the Traditionalists who derived their knowledge wholly from the scriptural tradition and its interpretation. These were the brahmans who upheld the sacred authority of the Vedas, one of the most important features of the Aryan tradition.

Though the ascetic culture lost its vitality during the early period of Aryan domination, it could not be completely wiped out, and toward the end of the first Vedic period, represented by the Brāhmaṇa literature, it emerged into prominence again. The period represented by the Āraṇyakas saw the resurgence of this ascetic culture, and in the Upaniṣads it seems to overwhelm the so-called Brāhmaṇa culture. The emphasis now turned from sacrifice or ritual (*karma*) to knowledge or understanding (*jñāna*), from knowledge of the external world (*loka*) to an understanding of the individual (*ātman*). This emphasis on an understanding of the reality in man may have been the direct result of the practice of yogic concentration, which was the most important aspect of the ascetic tradition.

An examination of the process of yogic concentration and of the different stages of the ecstacies attained thereby, as explained by some early ascetics like Ālāra Kālāma, Uddaka Rāmaputta, and even Siddhattha Gotama, will throw light on the manner in which some of the ideas current during the Upaniṣadic period came into existence. The aim of yogic concentration is the gradual elimination of sense impressions together with the defiling impulses, such as greed, which are associated with them. The process of meditation (*jhāna*), according to the later Buddhist manuals, begins with concentration on some sense stimulus such as a circle of light red sand, or a circle of blue flowers, or even an image of the Buddha. The first stage of trance is achieved when one is able to suppress temporarily the unwholesome tendencies such as sense desire, ill-will, sloth and torpor, excitedness and perplexity. Thereupon one learns to become detached from them and to direct all one's thoughts onto the object chosen for meditation.

In the second stage one ceases to be discursive and adopts a more unified, peaceful, and confident attitude. This attitude of confidence, together with the absence of discursive thinking, leads to a sense of elation and rapturous delight. Yet this elation is itself a hindrance to peace of mind, and in its turn has to be overcome. This task is achieved in the next two stages, until in the fourth *jhāna* one ceases to be conscious of ease and dis-ease, well-fare and ill-fare, elation and dejection, promotion and hindrance. The mind is thereby made supple and receptive and can be directed either toward the development of the higher stages of meditation, the four 'formless' (*arūpa*) *jhānas*, or toward the development of extrasensory perception or knowledge (*abhiññā*). In the first of the four 'formless' (*arūpa*) or higher *jhānas*, one perceives everything as 'boundless space' (*anantâkāsa*); in the second, one perceives that 'boundless space' as mere 'consciousness' (*viññāṇa*) of space; in the third, that 'consciousness' as mere 'emptiness' (literally, 'nothing', *akiñci*); and in the fourth, one attains a state wherein one relinquishes the act that grasped the 'emptiness' and reaches the point where there is 'neither perception nor nonperception' (*nevasaññānâsaññā*).

In one of the early discourses, the Buddha himself claims that he had attained the last two stages by following the instructions given to him by Ālāra Kālāma and Uddaka Rāmaputta, respectively.[6] He goes on to maintain that he went beyond his teachers and reached a stage which he describes as 'cessation of perception and feeling' (*saññāvedayitanirodha*). The value of this meditative state will be discussed later when we analyse the Buddhist conception of *nirvāna*. What is relevant to our present discussion is that this stage of mental development is the result of yogic concentration which, as mentioned earlier, was an integral part of the ascetic culture. Describing this psychic state in Western terminology, Conze says:

> Outwardly this state appears as one of coma. Motion, speech and thought are absent. Only life and warmth remains. Even the unconscious impulses are said to be *asleep*. Inwardly, it seems to correspond to what other mystical traditions knew as the ineffable awareness of *Naked Contemplation*, a naked intent stretching into Reality, the union of nothing with nothing, or of the One with the One, a dwelling in the *Divine Abyss*, or the *Desert of the* Godhead.[7]

In other words, the individual psychic process *appears* to merge with a greater or wider reality, an Ultimate Reality.

Although the above analysis of the yogic ecstacy is based on the description of *jhāna* given by the Buddhists, there is no reason to believe that it was very much different from that developed by the pre-Buddhist, or even the pre-Upaniṣadic, ascetics. If the Āryaṇyaka literature represents a period during which the ascetic culture came to be accommodated within the Vedic tradition itself, it would be unlikely that the subsequent period represented by the

Upaniṣads would have escaped the influence of this ascetic tradition. Assuming that the ascetic tradition was thus not entirely lost, one can better understand the basic teachings of the Upaniṣadic teachers.

One of the main features of the earlier Upaniṣads, especially the *Bṛhadāraṇyaka* and the *Chāndogya*, is said to be their speculative tenor. K. N. Jayatilleke speaks of three classes of thinkers, each of which stressed a particular way of knowing—the Traditionalists, Rationalists, and Experientialists. The Rationalists, he says, "derived their knowledge from reasoning and speculation without any claims to extrasensory perception. The metaphysicians of the early Upaniṣads, the Sceptics, the Materialists and most of the Ājīvikas fell into this class."[8] He goes on to refer to another class, the Experientialists, who depended on direct personal knowledge and experience including extrasensory perception, on the basis of which their theories were founded. Jayatilleke's theory implies that the conceptions of the individual 'self' (*ātman*) and the universal 'self' (*Brahman*) found in the earliest Upaniṣads were first arrived at through speculation and rational argument and that the appeal to experience in the matter of justifying these theories or even arriving at such theories came later. But comparing the basic teachings of the early Upaniṣads—the conceptions of the individual and universal selves—with the kind of awareness that the *yogin* is said to have in the highest state of meditation (for example, the individual thought process merging with or developing into a higher form of consciousness, an Ultimate Reality), it seems very probable that the latter kind of awareness was the basis of the former kind of speculation. It seems that the early Upaniṣadic thinkers were, in a sense, directing their attention toward a rational justification of the conclusions yielded by the higher mystical contemplation, while at the same time avoiding any direct reference to extrasensory perception and yogic intuition. This was probably due to the attempt on the part of the Vedic, or rather the Brahmanical, tradition to remain aloof from the ascetic tradition which it resisted for a long time. But in the end, that is, in the middle and later Upaniṣads, we find this ascetic culture completely dominating the Aryan tradition.

But why did the Upaniṣadic teachers, if they were actually rationalizing on the findings of the mystics or contemplatives (*yogin*), differ radically from the Buddha who himself followed the method of mystic contemplation? In fact, almost all the Hindu scholars who have written about Buddhism have made persistent attempts to show that the Buddha was born a Hindu, lived a Hindu, and died a Hindu. It is true that a few centuries after the Buddha passed away and after the doctrines underwent rather drastic changes, the Buddha himself came to be looked upon as an 'incarnation' (*avatār*) of Viṣṇu. But one should not forget that in his own day the Buddha was considered a heretic of the worst kind by the orthodox religious teacher. As will be seen, a mistaken understanding and sometimes an unwarranted interpretation of the conception of *nirvāna* in early Buddhism has led many a scholar to think that as far as the conception of Ultimate Reality is concerned there is no difference whatsoever between the messages of the Buddha and those of the Upaniṣadic teachers. In the following pages we propose to show that the Buddha's teachings differ radically not only from the teachings of the Upaniṣads and later Hinduism, but also from the later absolutist forms of Buddhism.

As a kind of reaction against the metaphysical theories presented by the Upaniṣadic thinkers, who themselves depended on mystical experiences, the Materialists, some of whom claimed to be ascetics (*samaṇa*, Sk. *śramaṇa*), denied the validity of extrasensory perception and yogic intuition. The Buddha, on the other hand, followed a middle path when, without denying completely the validity of such intuitions, he emphasized their limitations and recognized the limited value of yogic trances. Thus, while extrasensory perceptions were recognized as valid means of knowing, the Buddha refused to accept the idea that such perceptions give us knowledge of certain problems, such as the beginning of the universe, or even Ultimate Reality as accepted by the Upaniṣadic thinkers. At the same time, the highest stage of trance attained by a *yogin*, a stage such as *nirodha-samāpatti* in which there is cessation of perception and feeling (*saññāvedayita-nirodha*), was considered by the Buddha to be a temporary phase of peace and quietude.

Although they adopted the mystical aspect of the ascetic culture, the Upaniṣadic teachers basically belonged to the Vedic tradition. That tradition, it was pointed out earlier, was generally opposed to the ascetic tradition. Comparatively, it was more self-assertive and egoistic, as is very clearly evident from the way in which the early Upaniṣadic teachers proceeded in their search for the true 'self' (*ātman*). The *Chāndogya Upaniṣad* includes a section that describes the progressive instruction of Indra by Prajāpati concerning the real 'self'.[9] First he was asked to look in a pan of water, and what he saw there he was to consider "the self, the immortal, fearless Brahma." This was later rejected because the 'self' too would undergo change with changes in the physical body. Then it was pointed out that "he who moves about happy in a dream—he is the Self (Ātman). . . . That is the immortal, the fearless. That is Brahma."[10] This too was found to be unsatisfactory, since in dreams there are bound to be unpleasant experiences. So it was thought, "Now when one is sound asleep, composed, serene and knows no dream—that is the Self (Ātman). . . . That is the immortal, the fearless. That is Brahma."[11] But the argument adduced in order to reject this position as being unsatisfactory actually reflects the nature of the 'self' (*ātman*) which the Upaniṣadic thinkers were looking for. Consciousness in dreamless sleep satisfied all the requirements of *ātman*, except one. The *Chāndogya Upaniṣad* says: "Then, even before reaching the gods, he (Indra) saw this danger: 'Assuredly, indeed this one does not exactly know himself (*ātmānam*) with the thought "I am he," nor indeed the things here. He becomes one who has gone to destruction. I see nothing enjoyable in this.'" No doubt what the Upaniṣadic thinkers were looking for was an immortal, eternal, but at the same time, self-conscious, 'self'.

Although the Upaniṣadic teachers, unlike the earlier Vedic thinkers, considered mundane pleasures unsatisfactory and were seeking a more exalted, supramundane happiness, yet the basic self-assertive tendency survived; hence the emphasis on belief in the immortality of the soul. The parallelism between the yogic trance and the Upaniṣadic conception of release (*vimukti*) seems very close. Just as in trance where the individual consciousness is experienced as developing into a higher form of consciousness characterized by calmness and serenity, even so, with the attainment of freedom the reality of the individual (i.e., the 'self' or *ātman*) is supposed to merge with the Ultimate Reality (Brahman). In addition to a rejection of empirical consciousness which is subject to the law of arising and passing away, and which is infested with defilements of all sorts, there is the unequivocal assertion of the true 'self' (*ātman*) residing in the individual and which came to be considered eternal and permanent, and possessing the nature of bliss.

This may be the reason why, from the time of the early Upaniṣads, newly discovered doctrines not found in the traditional Vedic learning came to be taught even in the so-called Vedic tradition. Thus, in one of the earliest Upaniṣads (*Chāndogya* 6.1.2–3), we find that a person called Śvetaketu who had learned all the Vedas (*sarvān vedān adhītya*) had to be instructed by Uddālaka with a doctrine "whereby what he has not heard [presumably in the Vedic tradition] is heard" (*yenâśrutaṃ śrutaṃ bhavati*). Thus we find that some doctrines which had not been traditionally handed down, but which were the result of higher knowledge acquired through yogic meditation, gradually became part and parcel of the early Upaniṣadic tradition. In the early Upaniṣads (*Bṛhadâraṇyaka* and *Chāndogya*) it is conceded that all Vedic learning and in general all existing knowledge is insufficient for gaining a knowledge of Ātman/Brahman. In *Chāndogya Upaniṣad* 7.1.1–3, Nārada acknowledges to Sanatkumāra that, although he is conversant with all the rational speculations, he is not conversant with the 'self' (*ātman*). The passage runs thus:

> Venerable Sir, I know the *Ṛgveda*, the *Yajurveda*, the *Sāmaveda*, *Atharvaṇa* as the fourth [Veda], the epic and the ancient lore as the fifth, the Veda of the Vedas [i.e., grammar], propitiation of the Fathers, the science of numbers [mathematics], the science of portents, the science of time [chronology], logic, ethics and politics, the science of the gods, the science of sacred knowledge, the science of elemental spirits, the science of weapons, astronomy, the science of serpents and the fine arts. This, Venerable Sir, I know. But, Venerable Sir, I am only like one knowing the words and not a knower of the self.

It is true that in the early Upaniṣads it is not explicitly stated that Brahman/Ātman is the object of extrasensory perception. But for this reason to refer to the metaphysicians of the early Upaniṣads as Rationalists (as Jayatilleke does) is to exaggerate the issue.

These, then, are the metaphysical doctrines that dominate the entire history of Indian philosophy and religion. The absolutist tendency reached its culmination as early as the period of the Upaniṣads. Reality of the individual as well as of inanimate things came to be identified with an Ultimate Reality; *ātman* became Ātman or Brahman. "That thou art" (*tat tvam asi*) summed up the teachings of the Upaniṣadic thinkers.

The first reaction to such metaphysical theories and the sources of knowledge on the basis of which they were justified came from the Materialists, variously known as the Cārvākas, the Lokāyatikas, or the Bārhaspatyas. Having rejected idealistic metaphysics, they maintained that sense perception is the only valid source of knowledge and that therefore the physical world is the only reality; consciousness is unreal because it is not an object of the five senses, hence *adṛṣṭa*. The physical world functions according to a set pattern, and this pattern they called 'inherent nature' (*svabhāva*). Human life and behavior are completely determined by this physical law. Psychic life is merely a by-product of the four great material elements (*mahābhūta*) and hence cannot exert any influence on the physical personality or the outside world. Man is nothing but an automaton. Discourse on morality and spiritual matters is meaningless and futile. With the destruction of the physical personality, man is completely cut off and annihilated. There is no afterlife. This doctrine not only denies the continuity of the human personality, but also rejects the moral law (*karma*) which affirms the continuity of the actions in the form of consequences. This is the extreme form of Naturalism in Indian thought and its emergence was to some extent a reaction to the idealistic metaphysics of the earlier period.

The Ājīvika school, which represents another form of natural determinism, combined materialism with a theory of natural evolution. The adherents of this school differed from the Materialists in that they accepted the belief in survival; but survival was thought of as analogous to the development and maturing of a plant, an evolutionary transmigration with a predetermined end. "Existence is measured as with a bushel, with its joy and sorrow, and its appointed end. It can neither be lessened nor increased, nor is there any excess or deficiency of it. Just as a ball of thread will, when thrown, unwind to its full length, so fool and wise alike will take their course and make an end of pain."[12] This, no doubt, is an extreme form of determinism or fatalism (*niyati-vāda*).

One of the most important questions facing a student of Indian philosophy is this: Why are these two schools, which deny the validity of spiritual phenomena, included in the category of the ascetic (*śramaṇa*), rather than the more mundane priestly (*brāhmaṇa*), culture? In fact, according to the *Śānti-parvan* of the *Mahābhārata*,[13] the propounder of the materialist philosophy was a great sage (*ṛṣi*) called Ajagara. Why should a *ṛṣi*, who is devoted to a life of asceticism and who probably has developed extrasensory powers, deny the validity of spiritual phenomena and advocate a materialist philosophy? If, after developing extrasensory perception, sages like Ajagara were not able to verify the existence of a transcendental reality, a Brahman or Ātman, naturally they would have been suspicious of some of the claims of the Upaniṣadic *yogins*. But, unlike the Buddha, they seem to have gone to the extreme of denying completely the validity of extrasensory powers in gaining knowledge of certain aspects of nature and also the usefulness of the ecstacies for attaining peace and tranquillity. The Buddhist texts state categorically that the Naturalists denied the validity of extrasensory perception. The denial of such forms of higher knowledge may have been prompted by a desire to eliminate the idealist metaphysics propounded on the basis of this knowledge.

The next major school of thought prior to Buddhism was Jainism, which also belonged entirely to the ascetic (*śramaṇa*) tradition. The practice of ascetic fervor (*tapas*) was carried to extremes by this school and, in fact, Buddhists refer to it as the one that emphasizes the 'fourfold restraint' (*catuyāmasaṃvara*).[14] Theirs was a deterministic theory of moral behavior (*karma*). According to them, man is responsible for his actions or behavior, but once an action is performed, it becomes something external to him because he is unable, under any circumstances, to avoid the consequences of that action. In a sense, man becomes a victim of his own actions. Perhaps it was because man is powerless to control the consequences of his actions that, as the Buddhist texts would have us believe, the Jainas attempted to expiate past actions by the practice of severe austerities, and tried to prevent the accumulation of *karma* in the future by nonaction.[15]

The Jainas are generally believed to be non-absolutists (*anekânta-vādī*) as far as their epistemological standpoint is concerned. Their philosophy represents a form of syncretism. Prompted by a desire to account for the various forms of experience, such as change, continuity, and impermanence as well as duration, they maintained that 'being' (*sat*) is multiform in that it exhibits the different characteristics of production or arising (*utpāda*), destruction or cessation (*vyaya*), and also permanence or durability (*dhrauvya*).[16] Although according to their epistemological standpoint absolute judgments are not possible at the mundane level, every judgment being relative to a certain point of view, yet they claimed 'omniscience' (*kevala-jñāna*) by which it was possible to perceive reality in its totality. Thus, while accepting impermanence (*anitya*) as a part of existence, they also believed in the existence of permanent 'souls' (*jīva*), comparable to the 'individual selves' (*ātman*) accepted by the Upaniṣadic thinkers.

A salient feature of each of these schools of philosophical thought is the dominance of various forms of absolutism. While the Upaniṣadic tradition denied change and impermanence as being illusory and upheld the reality of a permanent 'self', the materialist tradition considered matter to be ultimately real. The Jainas believed that permanence as well as impermanence are characteristics of Ultimate Reality. In the sphere of religion, the Upaniṣadic thinkers considered salvation to be the realization of the unity of the 'individual self' and the 'Universal Self'. The Materialists denied any spirituality, and the Jainas emphasized extreme forms of self-mortification in order to free the 'self' from its bondage to existence, caused by karmic particles covering the inherently pure 'self'. This, in brief, is an account of the philosophical as well as the religious atmosphere in which Buddhism arose. Buddha's contribution in these two spheres may properly be understood only against this background.

Notes

1. *Ṛgveda*, ed. Max Müller, 6 vols. (London: W. H. Allen, 1849–1874), x. 136. Cf. the *Vrātya Book* of the *Atharvaveda* (Book xv). According to some scholars, the Vrātyas were 'ecstatics' of the *Kṣatriya* class and forerunners of the *yogin*.
2. M. Hiriyanna, *Outlines of Indian Philosophy* (London: George Allen & Unwin, 1956), p. 31.
3. *Ṛgveda* x. 190.
4. *Taittirīya Brāhmaṇa* (of the Black Yajurveda with the commentary of Sāyana, ed. Rajendralal Mitra, *Bibliotheca Indica*, 3 vols., [Calcutta: Asiatic Society of Bengal, 1859]), 2.3.10.1.
5. *Chāndogya Upaniṣad* (see *The Principal Upaniṣads*, ed. and tr. S. Radhakrishnan [London: George Allen & Unwin, 1953]), 8.5.
6. *Ariyapariyesana-sutta*, *M* 1.160ff.
7. Edward Conze, *Buddhism: Its Essence and Development* (New York: Harper & Row, 1963), p. 101.
8. K. N. Jayatilleke, *Early Buddhist Theory of Knowledge* (London: George Allen & Unwin, 1963), p. 170.
9. *Chāndogya Upaniṣad* 8.7.1ff.
10. Ibid., 8.10.1.

11. Ibid., 8.11.1.
12. *D* 1.54.
13. *Mahābhārata* (Poona: Bhandarkar Oriental Research Institute, 1933), 12.179.11.
14. *D* 1.57.
15. *M* 2.214.
16. *Tattvârthâdhigama-sūtra* 5.29, quoted in S. N. Dasgupta's *History of Indian Philosophy*, vol. 1, p. 175.

Selected Readings

Barua, B. M. *A History of Pre-Buddhistic Indian Philosophy*. Calcutta: University of Calcutta Press, 1921.

Dasgupta, S. N. *History of Indian Philosophy*. Vol. 1. Cambridge: Cambridge University Press, 1922.

Deussen, Paul. *The Philosophy of the Upaniṣads*. Tr. A. S. Geden. Edinburgh: T. & T. Clark, 1906.

Hiriyanna, M. *Outlines of Indian Philosophy*. London: George Allen & Unwin, 1956.

Hume, E. R. *Thirteen Principal Upaniṣads*. London: Oxford University Press, 1934.

Radhakrishnan, S. *Indian Philosophy*. Vol. 1. London: George Allen & Unwin, 1941.

Smart, Ninian. *Doctrine and Argument in Indian Philosophy*. London: George Allen & Unwin, 1964.

Chapter Two
Epistemology

In his search for the truth about human existence motivated by a desire for release from the suffering inherent in it, Siddhattha Gotama is said to have visited teacher after teacher learning whatever he could from each. He became conversant with the various philosophies as well as the religious practices current at the time. The ascetic (*samaṇa*) culture was in its ascendency in the lower Ganges valley, and rather early in his life Gotama seems to have had some training in yogic meditation.[1] Moreover, the last two teachers under whom he had training in spiritual matters before he finally attained enlightenment are said to have instructed him in the art of yogic meditation or contemplation. By the time he accepted yogic meditation and therefore had become aware of the extrasensory powers that could be developed by such means, Gotama had already realized the limitations of sense perception as a source of knowledge. Moreover, as is evident from texts like the *Kālāma-sutta*,[2] people had already begun to suspect the validity of reasoning (*takka*) and logic (*naya*) as means of arriving at a knowledge of truth and reality. And for Gotama, even yogic contemplation and extrasensory powers were limited in scope, and he realized that these powers were misused by the ascetics who formulated metaphysical theories about the nature of reality, though such theories could not be posited on the basis of these extrasensory perceptions.[3] The situation seems therefore to have been extremely complicated, and Gotama, after his enlightenment, made an attempt to clarify the various sources of knowledge, pointing out their limitations as well as their validity, but did not fall into the extreme of agnosticism, as did one of his predecessors in the ascetic tradition—Sañjaya Bellaṭṭhiputta.

In chapter 1 it was pointed out that the pre-Buddhist thinkers fall into three classes—Traditionalists, Rationalists, and Experientialists—according to the stress laid on a particular way of knowing.[4] The Traditionalists, it was mentioned, derived their knowledge wholly from a scriptural tradition and interpretation based on it. These were the brahmans who upheld the sacred authority of the divinely revealed Vedas. Buddha's criticism of divine revelation and of several other sources of knowledge is to be found in the *Caṅkī-sutta* of the *Majjhima-nikāya.*[5] Here he is represented as saying:

> There are five things which have a twofold result in this life. What five? [Knowledge based on] faith, likes, revelation, superficial reflection, and approval of a theory thought about . . . , even if I hear something on the profoundest revelation (*svānussutaṃ*), that may be empty, hollow and false, while what I do not hear on the profoundest revelation may be factual (*bhūtaṃ*), true and not otherwise. It is not proper for an intelligent person, safeguarding the truth, to come categorically (*ekaṃsena*) to the conclusion (*niṭṭhaṃ*) in this matter that this alone is true and whatever else is false (*idam eva saccaṃ mogham aññaṃ*).

On the contrary,

> If a person has heard [from revelation, tradition or report], then in saying "this is what I have heard" [from revelation, tradition or report], he safeguards the truth, so long as he does not come categorically to the conclusion that it alone is true and whatever else is false.

The Buddha is here asserting that a theory based on tradition or report or revelation can be either true or false. In the absence of any guarantee of its truth or falseness, it is not proper to depend on the theory as a valid means of knowledge. Hence, on the basis of such knowledge one should not come to definite decisions regarding the nature of reality. Therefore, as the Buddha points out, one should suspend judgment, and that means rejection of tradition or revelation as a valid source of knowledge.

This same attitude was adopted by the Buddha with regard to the theories formulated by the Rationalists on the basis of reasoning (*takka*) or logical argument (*naya*). According to the *Sandaka-sutta* of the *Majjhima-nikāya,*[6] one of the four types of religions which are said to be unsatisfactory (*anassāsika*) but not necessarily false is that based on reason and speculation (*takka, vīmaṃsā*). It is said: "Herein...

a certain teacher is a reasoner and investigator; he teaches a doctrine which is self-evident and is the product of reasoning and speculation. But in the case of a person who reasons and speculates, his reasoning may be good or bad, true or false." Thus, according to early Buddhism, the truth or falseness of a theory with regard to its correspondence to facts cannot be judged by the consistency of its reasoning. Sometimes a well-reasoned theory may be false in the light of contingent facts and an ill-reasoned theory may be true. The soundness of reasoning should not be taken as the only criterion of truth.

The last of the three classes of pre-Buddhist philosophers were the Experientialists. We find the Buddha claiming to be one of those recluses and brahmans who had personal higher knowledge,[7] which is clear evidence in support of the view that the Buddha did not claim or consider himself to be in possession of a unique way of knowing denied to other religious teachers before and during his time. But the important point is that, as a result of this knowledge, the Buddha did not come to the same conclusions as did his predecessors. For example, the Upaniṣadic thinkers who followed this kind of experiential knowledge arrived at the theory that the 'individual self' (*ātman*) and the 'Universal Self' (*Brahman*) are one and the same and that salvation consists of realizing this fact, or, as in the later Upaniṣads, the theory that Brahmā (personal God) creates this world and that the creator and the created (the individual *ātman*) are in reality one and the same. In the *Brahmajāla-suttanta*,[8] the Buddha refers to the ascetics and brahmans who, as a result of the development of yogic concentration (*ātappam anvāya padhānam anvāya anuyogam anvāya sammā manasikāram anvāya*) attained extrasensory powers and believed either that the world (i.e., the 'Universal Self') and the 'self' (i.e., the individual self) are eternal, or that the world is created by a God (*issara*). In fact the Buddha did not consider the content of this knowledge to be identical with any Ultimate Reality. Nor did he consider such knowledge as constituting salvation. Whatever knowledge one obtains through extrasensory perception was looked upon by the Buddha as means to an end, not as an end in itself. According to the Buddha, such knowledge, when colored by one's likes and dislikes, leads to all forms of dogmatic beliefs that prevent one from seeing things as they are (*yathābhūta*) and attaining perfect freedom through nongrasping (*anupādā vimutti*).[9] But this direct intuitive knowledge, when not obstructed by likes and dislikes, provides one with insight into the nature of things so that one is able to conduct oneself accordingly and attain perfect freedom (*vimutti*). To this we shall return later (see chapter 7).

Moreover, unlike in the Upaniṣads where, in the final analysis, one's knowledge and vision is due not to one's efforts, but to the grace or intervention of Ātman or God, or even to something inexplicable and mysterious, for the Buddha it is a natural, not a supernatural, occurrence. The development of extrasensory perception (*abhiññā*) is always looked upon as a 'causal occurrence' (*dhammatā*).[10] 'Mental concentration' (*samādhi*) is always causally conditioned, and it is this mental concentration that serves as a cause (*upanisā*) for the development of extrasensory perceptions[11] by which one is able to verify the nature of existence, certain aspects of which are not completely accessible to ordinary sense perception.

This analysis makes clear the very important fact that the Buddha was aware of the limitations of all sources of knowledge. It was the realization of these limitations that prompted the Buddha to deny the kind of omniscience which was claimed by his predecessors.[12] What he claimed was a threefold knowledge (*tisso vijjā*) consisting of (1) retrocognition, (2) clairvoyance, and (3) knowledge of the destruction of defiling impulses.[13] These three are the most important of the six types of higher knowledge (*chaḷabhiññā*).

Should Buddhism be classed as skepticism because it emphasizes the limitations of all the different sources of knowledge—reason, perception, and even extrasensory perception? Apparently not. On the contrary, the emphasis on the limitations of knowledge was meant to prevent people from falling into the net of speculative theories (*diṭṭhijāla*) that posited the 'nonexistent' as the 'existent'. The knowledge of things as they are (*yathābhūtañāṇa*) therefore consists in knowing "what exists as 'existing' and what does not exist as 'not existing'" (*santaṃ vā atthîti ñassati, asantaṃ vā n'atthîti ñassati*).[14]

The Buddha also recognized the fact that subjective attitudes such as likes (*ruci*)[15] and therefore dislikes (*aruci*), as well as attachment or inclination (*chanda*), aversion (*dosa*), confusion (*moha*), and fear (*bhaya*),[16] prevent one from perceiving things as they are. The elimination of these subjective biases and of certain habits of thinking is considered conducive to the understanding of things. This question will be discussed further when we examine the Buddhist theory of nonsubstantiality (*anatta*).

The realization that subjective prejudices play a significant role in one's understanding or perception of truth made the Buddha reluctant to preach the *dhamma* after his attainment of enlightenment.[17] But once he decided to preach, he adopted the gradual method of instruction (*ānupubbīkathā*), knowing the differences in the temperaments and capabilities of people.

When questioned concerning the ways by which right understanding (*sammā diṭṭhi*) can be gained, he named two primary sources, (1) the testimony of another (*parato ghosa*), and (2) proper reflection (*yoniso manasikāra*).[18]

We have seen that the Buddha criticized the sources of knowledge such as divine revelation and testimony, but his criticism was not completely destructive. In fact, his criticism was directed mainly against those who held that these were the only valid sources of knowledge. But here we find the Buddha recognizing testimony as an initial step in arriving at knowledge or understanding. This testimony or report of another is then to be verified in the light of one's own experiences. Testimony alone could be either true or false. Proper reflection (*yoniso manasikāra*) involves both experience and reflection or reasoning. Thus the Buddha recognized *experience*, both sensory and extrasensory, and *reasoning* or *inference* based on experience as sources of knowledge.

The validity of sense perception was not denied in early Buddhism. In fact, sense data (*phassa* or *saññā*) are the primary sources of our knowledge and understanding of the world. At the same time, however, the Buddha emphasized the fact that sense perception tends to mislead man. This is not due to any defect in sense perception as such; it is due mostly to the manner in which man has been conditioned to interpret what he sees, hears, feels, and so forth.

The famous statement from the *Majjhima-nikāya* which describes the process of sense perception also shows how sense perception may mislead man:

> Depending on the visual organ and the visible objects, O brethren, arises visual consciousness; the meeting together of these three is contact; because of contact arises feeling. What one feels, one perceives; what one perceives, one reasons about; what one reasons about, one is obsessed with. What one is obsessed with, due to that, concepts characterized by such obsessed perceptions assail him in regard to visible objects cognizable by the visual organ, belonging to the past, the future and the present.[19]

This formula begins on a very impersonal note based on a statement of the general formula of causality (*paṭiccasamuppāda*), which is often read: "When this exists, that exists" (*imasmiṃ sati idaṃ hoti*, see chapter 3). This impersonal statement extends only to the point of 'feeling' (*vedanā*). Then the very character of the description, and even the grammatical structure change. The formula takes a personal approach suggestive of deliberate activity, hence the use of the third-person construction: "What one feels, one perceives", and so on. Here is to be found the intrusion of the ego consciousness which thereafter fashions the entire process of perception, culminating in the generation of obsessions, which according to the commentators are threefold, namely, craving (*taṇhā*), conceit (*māna*), and dogmatic views (*diṭṭhi*). And the final stage of this process of perception is perhaps the most interesting. "Apparently, it is no longer a mere contingent process, nor is it an activity deliberately directed, but *an inexorable subjection to an objective order of things.* At this final stage of perception, he who has hitherto been the subject now becomes the hapless object."[20] As mentioned earlier, subjective attitudes such as likes and dislikes interfere with sense perceptions and therefore distort sense impressions. The process of meditation and the development of extrasensory perception are, in a way, directed at eliminating these subjective prejudices. But, as we have seen, even after the development of extrasensory perception and the verification of the nature of things through this means, the pre-Buddhist thinkers, according to the Buddha, allowed their subjective prejudices to interfere with the interpretation of things presented to such forms of higher perception. Thus even a person who has developed extrasensory perceptions such as retrocognition may believe in a metaphysical entity such as the 'self' (*ātman*), or in the creation of the universe by an omnipotent God. However, the various forms of extrasensory perception could not be the basis of metaphysical beliefs. The extrasensory perceptions or powers recognized in early Buddhism are as follows:

1. Psychokinesis (*iddhividha*), which is not a form of knowledge but a power. It consists in the various manifestations of the 'power of will' (*adhiṭṭhāna iddhi*) in the *jhānas*.[21]

2. Clairaudience (*dibbasota*), the faculty of perceiving sounds even at a distance, far beyond the range of ordinary auditory faculties. This extension of auditory perception both in extent

and in depth enables a person to perceive directly certain correlated phenomena which are otherwise only inferred.

3. Telepathy (*cetopariyañāṇa*), which enables one to comprehend the general state as well as the functioning of another's mind.

4. Retrocognition (*pubbenivāsânussatiñāṇa*), the ability to perceive one's own past history. It is dependent on memory (*sati*), and this memory of past existences is attained through acts of intensive concentration (*samādhi*), as in the development of other faculties.

5. Clairvoyance (*dibbacakkhu* or *cut' ūpapātañāṇa*), the knowledge of the decease and survival of other beings who wander in the cycle of existences in accordance with their behavior (*karma*). This, together with retrocognition, enables one to verify the phenomenon of rebirth.

6. Knowledge of the destruction of defiling impulses (*āsavakkhayañāṇa*) which, together with the last four mentioned above, provides an insight into the four Noble Truths.

It will be noticed that there is some correspondence between these extrasensory perceptions and ordinary sense perception. The extrasensory faculties have their corresponding objects and may be related to the sensory faculties in the manner shown in Figure 1.

As the figure shows, the extrasensory perceptions have their corresponding objects, and these objects are not perceived by the normal senses. The difference between the two forms of perception seems to be a difference in the degree of penetration. Direct perception, both sensory and extrasensory, provides man with the knowledge of phenomena (*dhamme ñāṇa*), and on the basis of this direct knowledge, the Buddha made inductive inferences with regard to the *universality* of (1) causality (*paṭiccasamuppāda*), (2) impermanence (*aniccatā*), (3) unsatisfactoriness (*dukkhatā*), and (4) non-substantiality (*anattatā*). These inferences came to be known as inferential knowledge (*anvaye ñāṇa*).

Thus, after presenting a critique of the current epistemological theories, the Buddha seems to have accepted a form of empiricism (based broadly on both ordinary sense experience and extrasensory

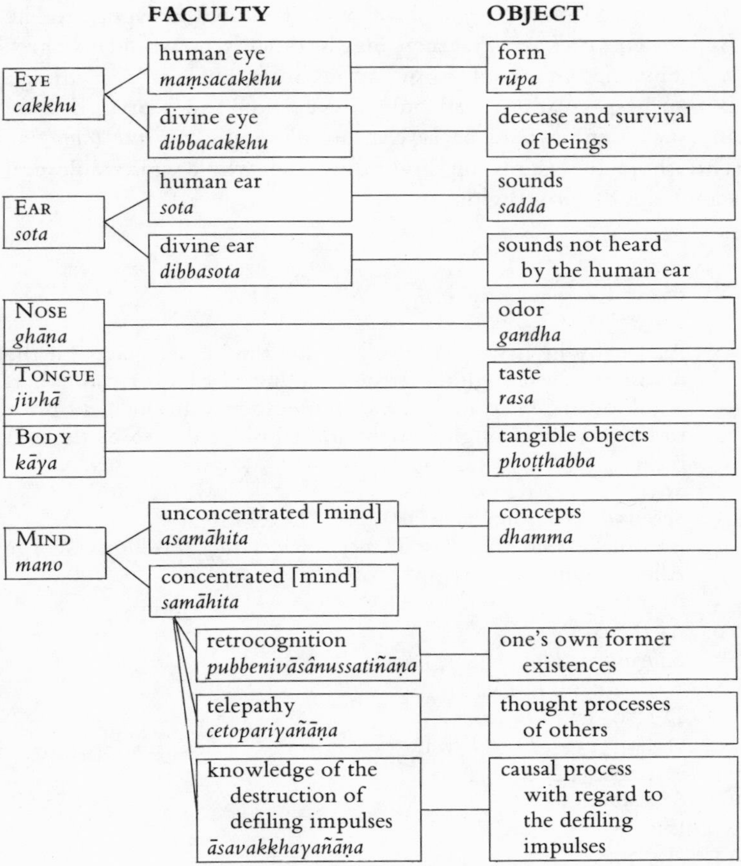

Figure 1.

perception) which is succinctly stated in a very short but extremely important discourse called *Sabba-sutta*.[22] Here, a contemporary of the Buddha, a philosopher named Jāṇussoṇī, questions him with regard to 'everything' (*sabba*), that is, the metaphysical question as to what constitutes 'everything' in this universe. The Buddha's immediate response is that 'everything' means the eye, form, ear, sound, nose, odor, tongue, taste, body, tangible objects, mind, and mental objects or concepts. In short, 'everything' consists of the six senses and the corresponding objects. And this is what is shown in Figure 1. The Buddha goes on to say that there may be others who would not agree with him and who would posit various other things as 'everything'. But such speculations lead only to vexation and worry, because any such thing would be *beyond the sphere of experience* (*avisaya*). This short text sums up beautifully the whole epistemological standpoint of early Buddhism.

Notes

1. As a baby he is said to have attained the higher *jhāna*s on the occasion of a ploughing festival conducted by his royal father, Suddhodana. He claims that he remembered this incident prior to his attaining enlightenment and considered it to be the best means.
2. *A* 1.189; *TD* 1.438.
3. See *Brahmajāla-suttanta*, *D* 1.1 ff.; *TD* 1.88b ff.
4. Jayatilleke, *Early Buddhist Theory of Knowledge* (London: George Allen & Unwin, 1963), p. 170.
5. *M* 2.170.
6. *M* 1.520.
7. *Saṅgārava-sutta*, *M* 2.211.
8. *D* 1.12 ff.; *TD* 1.90a ff.
9. *D* 1.16–17; *TD* 1.90b.
10. *A* 5.3, 313; *TD* 1.485b f.
11. *A* 3.200; *TD* 2.129a.
12. *M* 1.482.
13. Ibid.
14. *A* 5.36.
15. *Sn* 781.
16. *A* 2.18
17. *M* 1.167–168; *TD* 1.777b.
18. *M* 1.294; *TD* 1.50a.
19. *M* 1.111–112; *TD* 1.604b.
20. Bhikkhu Ñāṇananda, *Concept and Reality in Early Buddhist Thought* (Kandy: Buddhist Publication Society, 1971), p. 5.
21. *Vism* 405.
22. *S* 4.15; *TD* 2.91a–b.

Selected Readings

PRIMARY SOURCES

Brahmajāla-suttanta (*D* 1.1 ff,); 'The Perfect Net' (*SBB* 2.1 ff.); *TD* 1.88 ff.

Sāmaññaphala-suttanta (*D* 1.47 ff.); 'The Fruits of a Life of a Recluse' (*SBB* 2.65 ff.); *TD* 1.107 ff.

Tevijja-suttanta (*D* 1.235 ff.); 'On Knowledge of the Veda' (*SBB* 2.300 ff.); *TD* 1.104 ff.

Madhupiṇḍika-sutta (*M* 1.108 ff.); 'Discourse on the Honeyball' (*MLS* 1.141 ff.); *TD* 1.603 ff.

Ariyapariyesana-sutta (*M* 1.160 ff.); 'Discourse on the Aryan Quest' (*MLS* 1.203 ff.); *TD* 1.775 ff.

Mahā-taṇhāsaṅkhaya-sutta (*M* 1.256 ff.); 'Greater Discourse on the Destruction of Craving' (*MLS* 1.311 ff.); *TD* 1.766 ff.

Mahā-vedalla-sutta (*M* 1.292 ff.); 'Greater Discourse on the Miscellany' (*MLS* 1.350 ff.); *TD* 1.790 ff.

Tevijja-vacchagotta-sutta (*M* 1.481 ff.); 'Discourse to Vacchagotta on the Threefold Knowledge' (*MLS* 2.159 ff.).

Sandaka-sutta (*M* 1.513 ff.); 'Discourse to Sandaka' (*MLS* 2.192 ff.).

Cankī-sutta (*M* 2.164 ff.); 'Discourse with Cankī' (*MLS* 2.354 ff.).

Saṅgārava-sutta (*M* 2.209 ff.); 'Discourse to Saṅgārava' (*MLS* 2.398 ff.).

Sabba-sutta (*S* 4.15); 'The All' (*KS* 4.8); *TD* 2.91a.

Kālāma-sutta (*A* 1.188 ff.); 'Those of Kesaputta' (*GS* 1.170 ff.); *TD* 1.438 f.

SECONDARY SOURCES

Jayatilleke, K. N. *Early Buddhist Theory of Knowledge*. London: George Allen & Unwin, 1963.

Kalupahana, D. J. "Buddhist Tract on Empiricism." *Philosophy East and West*, 19 (1969): 65–67.

Lindquist, S. *Siddhi und Abhiññā*. Uppsala; Uppsala University, 1935.

Ñāṇananda, Bhikkhu. *Concept and Reality in Early Buddhist Thought*. Kandy: Buddhist Publication Society, 1971.

Saratchandra, E. R. *Buddhist Psychology of Perception*. Colombo: Associated Newspapers of Ceylon, 1958.

Tischner, R. *Telepathy and Clairvoyance*. London: Kegan Paul & Co., 1925.

Chapter Three
Causality

The Buddha claimed that his search for the nature of things led him to the discovery of the uniformity of the causal process (*dhammaṭ-ṭhitatā, dhammaniyāmatā*, or simply *dhammatā*). It was the knowledge of the causal pattern that enabled him to put an end to all defiling tendencies and thereby attain freedom (*vimutti*).[1] This claim of the Buddha has to be evaluated in the light of the background in which various metaphysical theories, such as that of eternal 'soul' or 'self' (*ātman*), 'inherent nature' (*svabhāva*), or creator God (*iśvara*), were posited in order to explain the functioning of phenomena. One of the most important of the discourses the Buddha addressed to the monks is the "Discourse on Causal Relations" (*Paccaya-sutta*),[2] in which he speaks of (1) causality (*paṭiccasamppāda*) and (2) causally conditioned phenomena (*paṭiccasamuppanna dhamma*).

These two concepts, according to the Buddha, explain everything in this world, the individual things and the relations existing among them. In this chapter the causal relations will be examined, leaving until later a discussion of causally conditioned phenomena, although the two are inseparably connected.

Before and during the time of the Buddha, the philosophical atmosphere in India was clouded with many metaphysical theories, and this was so even with regard to the concept of causality. There were three major theories of causality: (1) self-causation (*sayaṃ kataṃ*), (2) external causation (*paraṃ kataṃ*), and (3) a combination of self and external causation (*sayaṃ katañ ca paraṃ katañ ca*).[3]

The first was propounded by the Substantialist school, which accepted the reality of the 'self' (*ātman*) and considered causation as being due to the activity of this principle immanent in everything (*sarvaṃ*). Because the immanent 'self' is found in man as well as in the things of the outer world, it was looked upon as the agent in terms of which all the activities of man, as well as the functioning of the things of the world, should be explained. This school, by implication, denied the causal efficacy of any factor outside the 'self'.

The second theory was put forward by the Naturalists who, as a reaction against the idealist metaphysics of the Substantialist school, believed that the functioning of phenomena was due to their 'inherent nature' (*svabhāva*).

According to the Naturalist theory, 'inherent nature' (*svabhāva*) is a principle governing physical nature and man himself is determined by this physical principle, his psychic personality playing no effective part in his behavior. In contrast, the Substantialist theory held that a 'self' is recognized even in physical phenomena and is ultimately identified with the psychic principle (*cit*) considered to be the reality in man. Thus, the Naturalist conception of causation through 'inherent nature' (*svabhāva*) came to be recognized as a form of 'external causation' (*paraṃ kataṃ*) because, as far as anthropocentric philosophies are concerned, it denied man's moral responsibility.

The third theory is an attempt to combine the first two theories and was put forward by the Jainas. Although it recognizes both aspects of causation, self-causation as well as external causation, it carries with it all the metaphysical assumptions of the two.

The Buddhist theory of causality seems to have been influenced by the Naturalist theory of 'inherent nature' (*svabhāva*). Yet it differs from the Naturalist theory in two important ways. First, the Buddhist theory is not confined to physical causation alone, as is the Naturalist theory. In Buddhism, the causal pattern is recognized even in the psychic, moral, social, and spiritual realms, whereas in Naturalism everything is subordinate to physical causation. Second, unlike the Naturalists who believed that the principle of 'inherent nature' is strictly determined and that nothing can change the course of nature, Buddhists accepted a causal principle that was more or less a theory of conditionality. An examination of some features of the causal nexus as presented in the early texts will help in understanding the nature of the Buddhist theory of causality.

In the "Discourse on Causal Relations," the Buddha mentions four characteristics of causation: (1) objectivity (*tathatā*), (2) necessity (*avitathatā*), (3) invariability (*anaññathatā*), and (4) conditionality (*idappaccayatā*).

These four characteristics are said to be found in the causal relations obtaining among phenomena.

The first emphasizes the objectivity of the causal relation. It was, in fact, intended to refute the claim of some idealist philosophers who belonged to the Upaniṣadic tradition and who maintained that change, and therefore causation, are mere matters of words, nothing but names (*vācârambhanaṃ . . . nāmadheyaṃ*);[4] in other words, they are mental fabrications having no objective reality. For the Buddha, causation was as real as anything else. In fact, in one of the discourses preserved in the Chinese Āgamas,[5] the problem of the status of causation is brought up when the question is raised as to who fabricated (literally, 'made') the theory of causation. Buddha's reply is: "It is made neither by me nor by another. Whether the Tathāgatas were to arise in this world or not, this constitution of things [=*dhammadhātu*] is eternally existent. Concerning this [the constitution of things] the Tathāgata has insight, is fully enlightened." The objectivity of causation is further emphasized when its discovery is compared to the discovery of a bygone kingdom (*purāṇaṃ rājadhāniṃ*).[6]

The second and third characteristics, 'necessity' (*avitathatā*) and 'invariability' (*anaññathatā*), stress the lack of exception or the existence of regularity. The fact that a certain set of conditions gives rise to a certain effect and not to something completely different, is one of the basic assumptions of the causal principle. If this feature is not recognized, the basic pattern of events perceived in this phenomenal world cannot be explained satisfactorily. Events that appear to follow no causal pattern, events that are generally called accidental occurrences, are not really so. It is merely our ignorance of the causal pattern that prompts us to consider them accidental.[7]

The fourth characteristic of causation, 'conditionality' (*idappaccayatā*), is by far the most significant in that it steers clear of the two extremes—the unconditional necessity implied in strict determinism and the unconditional arbitrariness assumed by accidentalism. Hence it was used as a synonym for causation. It was emphasized at the time when the determinism (*niyativāda*) of Makkhali Gosāla (the leader of the Ājīvika sect) and indeterminism (*adhiccasamuppāda* or *adhiccasamuppanna-vāda*) were dominant theories.

On the basis of these characteristics of causation, the Buddha formulated the general formula that is set out in the early discourses as follows:

> When this is present, that comes to be;
> from the arising of this, that arises.
> When this is absent, that does not come to be;
> on the cessation of this, that ceases.

(*Imasmiṃ sati idaṃ hoti;*
imassa uppādā idaṃ uppajjati.
Imasmiṃ asati idaṃ na hoti;
imassa nirodhā idaṃ nirujjhati.)

This statement, found in many places in the early texts,[8] explains the conception of causality or causal uniformity which the Buddha arrived at after a perusal of the various instances of causal happening, and which came to be known as the golden mean between the two extremes, eternalism and annihilationism. It is, indeed, the truth about the world which the Buddha claimed he discovered[9] and which became the "central" doctrine of Buddhism. It was the Buddha's answer to both the eternalist theory of the Substantialists, who posited an unchanging immutable 'self' (*ātman*), and the annihilationist theory of the non-Substantialists, who denied continuity altogether. Thus the Buddha is said to have remarked: "To him who perceives through proper insight the arising of the things of the world, the belief in nonexistence [=annihilation] does not occur. To him who perceives through proper insight the ceasing of the things of the world, the belief in existence [=immutability] does not arise."[10]

One of the significant features to be noted in this conception of causality is the lack of metaphysical assumptions which are generally found in the rationalist theories of causality met with in the later schools of Indian philosophy. The metaphysical theory of the Sāṅkhya and the Sarvâstivāda schools, which emphasized the identity of cause and effect (*satkārya-vāda*), may be similar to the theory of self-causation upheld by the Upaniṣadic thinkers, and the Vaiśeṣika and Sautrāntika theories, which insisted on the difference between cause and effect (*asatkārya-vāda*), may, in a way, be related to the theory of external causation accepted by the Naturalist tradition. But because of the epistemological standpoint he adopted, the Buddha was able to formulate an empiricist theory of causality without getting involved in either of these metaphysical doctrines.

While individual instances of causal happening were verified on the basis of experience, both sensory and extrasensory, the uniformity of the causal law was reached through inductive inference based on these experiences. While causation itself is a phenomenon experienced, causal uniformity is considered an inductive inference. On the basis of the present experiences of causal happening, inductive inferences are made with regard to the past and the future.[11] While some past incidents may be brought back through reminiscences, one cannot rely on memory completely, for it tends to fade. Hence, even knowledge of the past is based on inductive inference. Because it is possible to remember past incidents through extrasensory perception, knowledge of the past may be partly experiential. But knowledge with regard to the future may be had only through inductive generalization. This may be one of the reasons why none of the extrasensory perceptions refer to the future. Thus experiential knowledge (*dhamme ñāṇa*) consists of knowledge of causally conditioned phenomena (*paṭiccasamuppanna-dhamma*) as well as the causal relations (*paṭiccasamuppāda*) of the present and partly of the past. Inferential knowledge (*anvaye ñāṇa*) is primarily of the future and partly of the past. The uniformity of the causal principle, which involves prediction into the future, is therefore an inductive generalization.

The universal applicability of the causal law is recognized in early Buddhism when it uses this causal principle to explain every phenomenon. We come across many instances in which the causal principle is applied to explain the functioning of physical, both organic and inorganic, phenomena. Among events that receive causal explanations are the evolution and dissolution of the world-process,[12] natural occurrences like drought[13] and earthquakes,[14] and also plant life.[15] A special application of the causal principle is made with reference to the human personality, a problem of prime importance to the Buddha as well as to the pre-Buddhist thinkers. This twelvefold formula of causation, which became very popular in the early Buddhist texts, will be discussed in detail below. Psychological processes are also explained in terms of the causal principle.[16] Furthermore, moral and social, as well as spiritual, behavior find causal explanations (chapters 5, 6, 7). As later scholiasts grouped them, there are five main spheres or realms in which causality predominates: (1) physical (inorganic) order (*utu-niyāma*), (2) physical (organic) order (*bīja-niyāma*), (3) psychological order (*citta-niyāma*), (4) moral order (*kamma-niyāma*), and (5) ideal spiritual order (*dhamma-niyāma*).[17]

These five groups appear to be so all-inclusive that nothing in experience is excluded. In short, everything in this universe comes within the framework of causality. Hence, to know causality is to know the truth. This explains the Buddha's statement, "He who perceives causality (*paṭiccasamuppāda*) perceives the *dhamma*."[18]

Of the various applications of the causal principle, the most prominent in the early Buddhist texts is, for obvious reasons, the formula of the twelve factors, which describes the causality of the human personality. The prominence given to the twelvefold formula seems to have led some scholars to think that this is all that Buddhism has to say about causality.[19] Even the few facts regarding the Buddhist theory of causality just presented should be sufficient to show that such a view is untenable.

The need for a rational and factual description of the life-process and how the so-called individual comes to experience happiness as well as suffering was felt by the Buddha from the very beginning of his career. In this task he was faced with insuperable difficulties created by some of the pre-Buddhist thinkers. On the one hand, when speaking of the life-process, some scholars were accustomed to thinking in terms of an immutable reality called the 'self' (*ātman*); on the other hand, there were some who denied a self and as a result denied the continuity of the life-process and along with it whatever comes under the category of morality and spirituality. In addition, there were those who believed in an omniscient being who was responsible for the creation and preservation of the world-process and hence of the life-process. The necessity of explaining the life-process without contributing to any one of these theories, with which he did not agree, led the Buddha to devise the twelvefold formula.

Since the question of the absolute beginning of the world-process was considered a metaphysical one (see appendix I), the twelvefold formula was presented in the form of a cycle or circle (*vaṭṭa*). The formula is generally stated in the following manner:

> When this is present, that comes to be; on the arising of this, that arises. When this is absent, that does not come to be; on the cessation of this, that ceases. That is to say, on ignorance depend dispositions; on dispositions depends consciousness; on consciousness depends the psychophysical personality; on the psychophysical personality depend the six "gateways" [of sense perception]; on the six "gateways" depends contact; on contact depends feeling; on feeling depends craving; on craving depends grasping; on grasping depends becoming; on becoming depends birth; on birth depend aging and death, sorrow and lamentation, suffering, dejection and vexation. In this manner there arises this mass of suffering.[20]

In this special application of the causal principle, ignorance (*avijjā*) heads the list of twelve factors. It is not the beginning of the cycle of existence, but is one of the most important factors that contribute to evil or unwholesome behavior, and that when completely eliminated lead to enlightenment and hence to the cessation of suffering. Ignorance is said to condition the dispositions (*saṅkhāra*) which play a significant role in determining the nature of man's behavior (*kamma*). The nature of one's consciousness (*viññāṇa*) also depends on the nature of the dispositions. Consciousness being the factor that determines the nature of the new psychophysical personality (*nāmarūpa*), the part played by the dispositions in determining life after death is emphasized. Dispositions therefore account for the nature of one's behavior (*kamma*) as well as one's future birth or rebirth (*punabbhava*).

The process of rebirth is explained as the combining of the two factors, consciousness (*viññāṇa*) and the psychophysical personality (*nāmarūpa*). The psychophysical personality referred to here is the foetus formed in the mother's womb (*gabbha*) and which represents the beginning of a new life span. Consciousness surviving from the past is said to become infused in this new personality, and thus a continuity is maintained between the two lives. The latent dispositions in this surviving consciousness therefore determine to a great extent the nature of the new personality.

When the individual is born, his senses, if they are not impaired, will start functioning, and through them he is fed new impressions which also will be instrumental in determining the nature of his personality. Hence the relationship between the psychophysical personality and the six "gateways" of sense perception (*saḷâyatana*). Depending on the nature of the six gateways of sense perception, there arises contact (*phassa*). Contact leads to feeling (*vedanā*), pleasurable, painful, or neutral. Depending on the nature of the feelings, there arises craving (*taṇhā*) which is generally considered to be threefold: desire for sense pleasures (*kāma*), for existence (*bhava*), and for nonexistence (*vibhava*). Craving is the cause of grasping (*upādāna*), as a result of which the process of becoming (*bhava*) is set in motion. This stage represents again the end of a life span and the beginning of a fresh one. The factors that earlier were said to be operative at the beginning of a new life process, namely, consciousness (*viññāṇa*) and the psychophysical personality (*nāmarūpa*), are also operative here, in the same way that grasping (*upādāna*) and becoming (*bhava*) are operative there. The difference is that, since the early Buddhists were interested in accounting for at least three life terms when presenting the causal process in this manner, they seem to have taken only those prominent factors which they wanted to emphasize and associated them with the beginnings of the two life processes. Thus birth (*jāti*) in the third phase is given as the result of becoming (*bhava*). Birth, then, is considered the cause of the entire mass of suffering that one is faced with in this life.

Since rebirth is the cause of suffering and is invariably associated with decay and death (*jarā-maraṇa*), avoiding future birth or becoming (*punabbhava*) is the goal of the religious life. How is one able to put an end to future rebirth? According to the causal process it would seem that development of right understanding (*sammā diṭṭhi*), which would replace ignorance (*avijjā*), and the elimination of craving (*taṇhā*), which results in nongrasping (*anupādāna*), would put a halt to this process of becoming. Deathlessness or immortality (*amata*, Sk. *amṛta*) is therefore nothing more than rebirthlessness or 'becoming-less-ness' (*apunabbhava*). But in later Mahāyāna, deathlessness seems to have been interpreted as the absence of death even at the end of the present life span, and hence the Buddha's *parinibbāna* is looked upon as being unreal or as a fiction. (This will be discussed in Chapter 10.)

Deathlessness is the ultimate consequence of the attainment of enlightenment and the elimination of craving. But the immediate result of enlightenment is the attainment of perfect happiness (*parama sukha*) arising from the absence of craving or attachment (*virāga*). Viewed in this light, we can understand the paeans of joy expressed by the monks and nuns, as recorded in the *Thera-gāthās* and *Therī-gāthās*.

Notes

1. *Ud* 1 ff.
2. *S* 2.25 ff.; *TD* 2.85 b.
3. *S* 2.18; *TD* 2.81 a.
4. *Chāndogya Upaniṣad* 6.1.4–6.
5. *TD* 2.85 b.
6. *S* 2.105–106.

7. H. Van Rensselar Wilson, "On Causation," in *Determinism and Freedom in the Age of Modern Science*, ed. Sidney Hook (New York: New York University Press, 1965), pp. 225 ff.
8. *M* 1.262 ff.; *TD* 1.562c; *S* 2.28; *TD* 2.85b.
9. *Ud* 1 ff.
10. *S* 2.17; *TD* 2.85c.
11. *S* 2.58; *TD* 2.99c.
12. *D* 3.80 ff.; *TD* 1.36b ff.; *A* 4.100–103; *TD* 2.736b–c.
13. *A* 3.243.
14. *A* 4.312; *TD* 2.753c.
15. *A* 1.223–224; *S* 3.45; *TD* 2.8c; *S* 4.315; *TD* 2.231a.
16. *M* 1.111–112, 190; *TD* 1.604b, 467b.
17. *DA* 2.432; *DhsA* 272.
18. *M* 1.190–191; *TD* 1.467a.
19. A. B. Keith, *Buddhist Philosophy in India and Ceylon* (Oxford: The Clarendon Press, 1925), p. 264.
20. *S* 2.28; *TD* 2.98a.

Selected Readings

PRIMARY SOURCES

Mahā-nidāna-suttanta (*D* 2.55 ff.); 'The Great Discourse on Causation' (*SBB* 3.50 ff.); TD 1.60 ff.

Nidāna-samyutta (*S* 2.1–133) including 93 discourses; 'The Kindred Sayings on Cause' (*KS* 2.1–94); roughly corresponding to TD 2.79–86.

Ārya-śālistamba-sūtra, restored from quotations and Tibetan and Chinese translations by L. de la Vallée Poussin, *Théorie des Douze Causes*, Ghent: University of Ghent, 1913; by N. A. Sastri, Adyar Library Series 76, Adyar: Adyar Library, 1950, together with restorations of *Pratītyasamutpādavibhaṅganirdeśa* and *Ārya-pratītyasamutpāda-sūtra*.

SECONDARY SOURCES

Conze, Edward. *Buddhist Thought in India*. London: George Allen & Unwin, 1962. Pp. 144–158.

de la Vallée Poussin, L. *Théorie des Douze Causes*. Ghent: University of Ghent, 1913.

Grimm, George. *The Doctrine of the Buddha: The Religion of Reason and Meditation*. Leipzig: W. Drugulin, 1926. Pp. 165–226.

Jayatilleke, K. N. *Early Buddhist Theory of Knowledge*. Pp. 443–457.

Kalupahana, David J. *Causality: The Central Philosophy of Buddhism.* Honolulu: The University Press of Hawaii, 1975.

Rhys Davids, C. A. F. *Buddhism: A Study of the Buddhist Norm.* Home University Library. London: Williams and Norgate, 1914. Pp. 78–106.

Smart, Ninian. *Doctrine and Argument in Indian Philosophy.*

Tatia, N. "Paticcasamuppāda." *Nava-Nālandā Mahāvihāra Research Publication*, 1 (1957):177–239.

Thomas, E. J. *History of Buddhist Thought.* London: Kegan Paul, Trench, Trübner & Co., 1953. Pp. 58–70.

Chapter Four
The Three Characteristics of Existence

In chapter 3 it was pointed out that the Buddha's discourse pertained to two aspects of reality, namely, causality and the causally conditioned phenomena. According to his teaching, there is nothing in this world that does not come within the realm of the causal law. Causality explains the arising and passing away of things. Hence, the direct corollaries of the theory of causality are that all things in this world are (1) impermanent (*anicca*, Sk. *anitya*), (2) unsatisfactory (*dukkha*, Sk. *duḥkha*), and (3) nonsubstantial (*anatta*, Sk. *anātman*). These three characteristics were emphasized because the Eternalist theory, which dominated the philosophical atmosphere during the time of the Buddha, held that the reality in phenomena was the immutable 'self' or 'substance' (*ātman*).

The theory of impermanence in Buddhism has been generally misunderstood because it came to be confused with a later theory known as the 'doctrine of moments' (*kṣaṇavāda*), which was formulated from a *logical* analysis of the process of change (*pariṇāma*) by the later Buddhist scholars belonging to the scholastic (*Abhidharma*) tradition. But such a theory is conspicuous by its absence in the early discourses. Therefore, although there were statements in the early discourses that could be interpreted as a theory of momentariness, statements such as "There is no moment, no inkling, no particle of time that the river stops flowing,"[1] the most important view was the one which recognized that a finite segment of time constitutes our immediate experience. The theory of impermanence as stated in the early texts could be correctly described as an empiricist theory. A passage found in many of the discourses runs thus: "Impermanent indeed are the compounded [i.e., conditioned] things; they are of the nature of arising and passing away. Having come into being, they cease to exist. Hence their pacification is tranquillity." (*Aniccā vata saṅkhārā uppādavayadhammino, uppajjitvā nirujjhanti tesaṃ vūpa-*

samo sukho.)[2] According to this statement, things are impermanent not because they are momentary, but because they are characterized by arising (*uppāda*) and passing away (*vaya*). An extended definition is sometimes met with in the early texts which analyses the process of change into three stages: arising (*uppāda*), passing away (*vaya*), and decay or change of what exists (*ṭhitassa aññathatta*).[3] The theory of moments may be derived from a logical analysis of this decay or change (*ṭhitassa aññathatta*), which literally means change of what exists. But even here the change is not commuted in terms of moments. Whatever is born is considered to be impermanent since it is sure to perish. In short, impermanence is a synonym for 'arising and passing away', or 'birth and destruction'. The *Assutavā-sutta* of the *Saṃyutta-nikāya* presents this empiricist account of change in the statement: "This physical body made up of the four great elements is seen to exist for one, two, three, four, five, ten, twenty, thirty, forty, fifty, one hundred or more years."[4] This certainly is an empiricist account of change. It is not a result of metaphysical inquiry or of any mystical intuition, but a straightforward judgment arrived at by investigation and analysis. It is founded on unbiased thought and has a purely empirical basis.

From the fact of the impermanence of the world, it follows that all things are unsatisfactory (*dukkha*). The word *dukkha* is rendered variously as 'ill', 'suffering', 'pain', and so on, which may be correct in certain contexts. But in other contexts, for example, where it is said that the five aggregates of grasping (*pañc' upādānakkhandha*) are *dukkha*,[5] the term is used in the wider sense of 'unsatisfactory'. That this fact has been overlooked seems to be one of the main reasons why some Western interpreters considered Buddhism to be pessimistic. Early Buddhism never denied the satisfaction (*assāda*, Sk. *āsvāda*, from *ā* + $\sqrt{}$*svad* 'to taste') that man can derive from worldly things. While not denying satisfaction, it emphasized the fact that this satisfaction is generally followed by evil or harmful consequences (*ādīnava*). This is true for several reasons. The nature of man is such that he craves for eternal or permenent happiness. But the things from which he hopes to derive such happiness are themselves impermanent. Happiness or satisfaction derived from impermanent or ephemeral things would surely be temporary and therefore fall short of his expectation, that is, permanent happiness. Hence his *suffering*. The things from which he tries to derive satisfaction may therefore, in the ultimate analysis, be *unsatisfactory*. Thus it seems that human suffering is due to attachment to things that are themselves unsatisfactory.

The Upaniṣadic theory of an eternal and immortal 'self' seems, therefore, to have been intended to satisfy this deep-seated craving of man for permanent happiness. But for the Buddha, who realized that everything in this world is impermanent, such a solution was not in the least satisfactory. While realizing that there is no permanent or immutable entity called the 'self', he also found that belief in such an entity led to further suffering. Belief in a permanent entity such as the *ātman* often led to selfishness and egoism (*ahamkāra*, *mamaṃkāra*). This, for him, was the root cause of craving and its attendant suffering. Inculcation of the virtue of selflessness on the basis of a belief in 'self' (*ātman*), as was the practice of the Upaniṣadic teachers,[6] was, according to the Buddha, neither satisfactory nor correct.

This led to the statement of the third characteristic, namely, 'nonsubstantiality' or 'no-self' (*anatta*, Sk. *anātman*). There is no doctrine more misunderstood and misinterpreted than this doctrine of nonsubstantiality. Many seem to think that acceptance of the doctrines of rebirth and moral responsibility on the one hand, and denial of a permanent self on the other, lead to a paradoxical situation which early Buddhism cannot avoid. This belief stems from a misunderstanding of the theory of nonsubstantiality. A careful look at the background in which it was presented should be helpful in clearing up some of these misunderstandings.

It has been pointed out that the Upaniṣadic conception of a permanent 'self' (*ātman*) was the result of a rational interpretation of the content of mystical experience, especially on the part of those belonging to a mundane, self-assertive tradition like that of the Āryans. According to the Buddha (and centuries later, according to Freud also), man's behavior as well as his outlook on life are determined by several instincts such as 'desire to live' (*jīvitukāma*), 'desire to avoid death' (*amaritukāma*), 'hankering for happiness' (*sukhakāma*), and 'aversion to pain' (*dukkhapaṭikkūla*).[7] The Upaniṣadic theory of 'self' is intended, no doubt, to satisfy this deep-seated craving on the part of man for self-preservation. The acceptance of this eternal and immutable 'self' enabled the Upaniṣadic thinkers to explain without much difficulty many problems such as rebirth, continuity, and moral responsibility. But for the Buddha a theory that simply accords with one's own inclinations (*diṭṭhinijjhānakkhanti*) or one that is merely consistent or plausible (*bhabbarūpa*) is not true in itself. These are not the criteria of truth. Truth for him was what accords with facts (*yathābhūta*), not that which caters to one's likes. Hence he did not want to contribute to a theory which merely caters to the instincts of the individual.

On the other hand, rejection of this belief in an immutable 'self' did not lead the Buddha to the opposite extreme of denying rebirth, continuity, moral responsibility, and the like, as was the case with the Materialists. Therefore, he undertook the task of redefining the concept of man. According to him, this was merely a "bundle of perceptions" (*saṅkhārapuñja*) or a group of aggregates (*khandha*), not discrete and discontinuous,[8] but connected and continuous by way of causality, a 'bundle' (*kāya*) which, for the sake of convenience, is designated by such names as Sāriputta and Moggallāna. Hence the declaration of one of his disciples named Selā:

> For, just as when the parts are rightly set,
> The word 'chariot' ariseth [in our minds],
> So doth our usage covenant to say:
> 'A being' when the aggregates are there.
>
> (*Yathā hi aṅgasambhārā hoti saddo ratho iti,*
> *evaṃ khandhesu santesu hoti satto ti sammuti.*)[9]

Moreover, the Buddha was not prepared to posit an agent or a mental substance behind the psychological process represented by such things as feeling (*vedanā*), perception (*saññā*), dispositions (*saṅkhārā*), and consciousness (*viññāṇa*). "I think, therefore I am" (*mantā asmi*;[10] cf. the Cartesian *cogito ergo sum*) is a conclusion to be repudiated. The heretical view put forward by a monk called Sāti and the Buddha's analysis and repudiation of this heresy throw much light on the question. It is said in the *Mahātaṇhāsaṅkhaya-sutta* that a monk named Sāti held the view that according to the Buddha's doctrine 'it is this consciousness which transmigrates and not another'.[11] (Sāti held this view probably because the Buddha spoke many times of consciousness as the factor that survives death or that connects two lives. See chapter 5). What is important to note is that the Buddha did not repudiate immediately Sāti's view. He proceeded to clarify what Sāti meant by this consciousness and therefore raised the question: "What, now, Sāti, is this consciousness?" (*katamaṃ Sāti taṃ viññāṇaṃ*). Sāti's answer was that it is "he who speaks, feels, and he who experiences the effects of good and bad deeds here and there." It is quite evident from this answer that what Sāti had in mind was the agent behind the acts of speaking, feeling, experiencing—a sort of 'inner controller' (*antaryāmin*). This certainly was the Substantialist theory, and immediately the Buddha rebuked Sāti for misrepresenting his doctrine. The Buddha insisted that this consciousness is itself causally conditioned (*paṭiccasamuppanna*).

The other aspect of the theory of 'self' which was rejected by the Buddha was the idea of permanence associated with it. There are passages in the Pali Nikāyas and the Chinese Āgamas in which the Buddha refers to the belief in a 'permanent, immutable, eternal and nonchanging self' (*attā nicco dhuvo sassato avipariṇāmadhammo.*[12] Taking up each of the factors that constitute the human personality—material form (*rūpa*), feeling (*vedanā*), perception (*saññā*), dispositions (*saṅkhārā*), and consciousness (*viññāṇa*)—the Buddha points out that none of them can be identified with the kind of 'self' described above.

Thus two aspects of the Upaniṣadic theory of 'self' were criticized by the Buddha. One is the permanence or eternality of the 'self' and the other is the agency attributed to it. At this stage it might be said that what the Buddha denied was that the five aggregates (*khandhā*) are the permanent and eternal 'self' (*ātman*) and that the Buddha did not actually deny a 'self' that is over and above, or not identical with, the aggregates. In fact, as a result of the Buddha's criticism of the Upaniṣadic teaching, the later Hindu schools emphasized the transcendental nature of the 'self' (although this transcendentalism may be implied in the Upaniṣads where the sages refuse to identify the 'self' with anything empirical or phenomenal). Did the Buddha say anything regarding a transcendental 'self'? This brings us to the problem of the ten undeclared (*avyākata*, Sk. *avyākṛta*) questions.

Of the ten (and sometimes fourteen) undeclared questions, two pertain to the problem of 'self': (1) Is the 'self' (or soul, *jīva*) identical with the body (*sarīra*)? (2) Is the 'self' different from the body? The first refers to the theory put forward by a school of Materialists and the second, to the Upaniṣadic theory.

As a reaction against the Idealist theory of self presented by the Upaniṣadic thinkers, the school of Materialists insisted that, if one wants to believe in a 'self', it is better to consider the physical body, which maintains some identity from birth to death, as the 'self', rather than looking out for it in the psychic personality. This, the Materialists generally believed, is because the physical personality is more real than the psychic personality. This particular school of Materialists, who identified the 'self' with the material body (*śarīra*), came to be known as the *Tajjīvataccharīra-vāda* (cf. *taṃ jīvaṃ taṃ sarīraṃ*). But to the Buddha, the 'self', whether it is identical with the body or different from the body, is a metaphysical entity. It is a metaphysical entity solely because it is unverifiable, either through sense perception or through extrasensory perception. In short, it is not given in experience (*avisaya*), and therefore the Buddha left these questions undeclared. His silence on these questions was interpreted as implying that there *is* a reality, a transcendental 'self', but that it does not come within the sphere of logical reasoning (*atakkāvacara*). According to the Buddha, even what came to be considered mystical experience does not give us a knowledge of a transcendental 'self'. Hence, it is an unverifiable metaphysical entity.

The theory of an immortal soul was not even considered useful as a regulative theory. In fact, as pointed out earlier, it was a theory harmful to the religious life in that it tends to generate selfishness and egoism. It is significant that some popular beliefs such as heaven (*sagga*, Sk. *svarga*) and hell (*apāya*), which for the Buddha were nothing but pleasurable and painful feelings (*vedanā*) one experiences in this life,[13] were considered useful in that they regulate the moral and religious behavior of man, but belief in an immortal soul was looked upon as pernicious. The wide prevalence of the theory of 'self' was not taken as an indication of its truth and validity. Although a later Buddhist school, the Personalists (Puggalavāda, Sammitīya, or Vātsīputriya), put forward a theory of 'self' comparable to that of the Hindu schools, all the other Buddhist schools at least claimed to be non-Substantialist (*anātmavādin*), in spite of the fact that some of them presented theories of reality that came dangerously close to the theory of 'self' (*ātman*).

The theory of nonsubstantiality is also considered to be the 'middle path' between the two extremes of eternalism (*sassata-vāda*) and annihilationism (*uccheda-vāda*). While denying a permanent 'self', the Buddha did not go to the other extreme of denying continuity as the Materialists did. On the contrary, the causal law was formulated to account for continuity. Thus, nonsubstantiality becomes a synonym for causality, and for those who, either in the East or in the West, are conditioned to think in terms of an immortal soul or are engrossed (*papañcita*) with the belief in a 'self', it is a difficult theory to understand.

Notes

1. *A* 4.137; cf. *TD* 1.682b.
2. *D* 2.157; *S* 1.191, 3.146; *TD* 2.153c.
3. *S* 3.38; *A* 1.152; *TD* 2.607c.
4. *S* 2.94, 96; *TD* 2.81c, 82a.
5. *S* 5.421.
6. *Bṛhadāraṇyaka Upaniṣad* 2.4.5.
7. *S* 4.172ff.; *TD* 2.313b. Cf. Freudian "life instinct" or the drive for self-preservation and the "pleasure principle."
8. Cf. David Hume, *A Treatise of Human Nature* (Oxford: The Clarendon Press, 1889), p. 31.
9. *S* 1.135; *TD* 2.327b.
10. *Sn* 916.
11. *M* 1.256ff.; *TD* 1.766c.
12. *M* 1.136; *TD* 1.764c.
13. *S* 4.206.

Selected Readings

PRIMARY SOURCES

Alagaddūpama-sutta (*M* 1.130ff.); 'Discourse on the Parable of the Water-snake' (*MLS* 1.167ff.); *TD* 1.763 ff.

Mahātaṇhāsaṅkhaya-sutta (*M* 1.256ff.); 'Greater Discourse on the Destruction of Craving' (*MLS* 1.311ff.); *TD* 1.766ff.

Assutavā-sutta (*S* 2.94f.); 'The Untaught' (*KS* 2.65f.); *TD* 2.81f.

Khandha-saṃyutta (*S* 3.1–188 consisting of 158 discourses); 'Kindred Sayings of Elements' (*KS* 3.1–154); roughly corresponding to *TD* 2.1–22.

SECONDARY SOURCES

Conze, Edward. *Buddhist Thought in India*. Pp. 34–46.

Grimm, George. *The Doctrine of the Buddha*. Pp. 61–161.

Kalupahana, David J. *Causality: The Central Philosophy of Buddhism*. Pp. 67–88.

Malalasekera, G. P. "Anattā." *Encyclopaedia of Buddhism*. Colombo: Government of Ceylon. Vol. 1, pp. 567–576.
Nyanaponika Thera. *Anattā and Nibbāna*. Kandy: Buddhist Publication Society, 1959.
Rahula, Walpola. *What the Buddha Taught*. New York: Grove Press, 1962.
Rhys Davids, C. A. F. *Buddhism*. Pp. 48–77.
Thomas, E. J. *History of Buddhist Thought*. Pp. 92–106.
Wijesekera, O. H. de A. *The Three Signata. Anicca, Dukkha, Anatta*. Kandy: Buddhist Publication Society, 1960.

Chapter Five
Karma and Rebirth

Karma and rebirth are two aspects of life personally verified by the Buddha through extrasensory perception. Of one who has developed such powers, it is said: "With his clear paranormal clairvoyant vision he sees beings dying and being reborn, the low and the high, the fair and the ugly, the good and the evil each according to his karma."[1] These claims on the part of the Buddha and his disciples are generally ignored by many scholars who have written on the Buddhist theories of *karma* and rebirth. Hindu scholars writing on Buddhism made such statements as this: "Early Buddhism is not an absolutely original doctrine. It is no freak in the evolution of Indian thought."[2] But even a more sober scholar from the West felt that "Buddhism started from special Indian beliefs, which it took for granted. The chief of these were the belief in transmigration and the doctrine of retribution of action. . . . They were already taken for granted as a commonly accepted view of life by most Indian religions."[3]

Such interpretations of the Buddhist doctrines of *karma* and rebirth appear to be based on two assumptions: first, that they were accepted by the Buddha mainly because they were present in the mainstream of the Brahmanic and ascetic traditions and not because they were personally verified and found to be true, and second, that they are in no way different from the pre-Buddhist theories and that Buddhism had nothing to contribute since the pre-Buddhist theories had attained finality even as far as the statement of these theories was concerned.

Concerning the first assumption, the best refutation so far is that of Jayatilleke who says:

> With all deference to scholarship, we wish to submit that this conclusion arises from both an unhistorical as well as an uncritical survey of the material. In fact, that a belief is found in a stratum A and in a chronologically successive stratum B,

> provides no conclusive evidence that the thinkers of the stratum B uncritically and dogmatically accept it from the stratum A. If we say so, it would follow that even a good scientist uncritically and dogmatically accepts the theories of his predecessors with whom he happens to agree, merely on the grounds of this agreement![4]

A college student may take certain scientific theories to be true because he finds them in a textbook on science. But a competent scientist does not do this. In the same way, a lay disciple of the Buddha who has not developed extrasensory perception may be expected to depend on the Buddha-word, but one is not justified in saying the same of a person like the Buddha who had mastered all the techniques of *yoga* and who had developed all the extrasensory powers to such an extent that his own teachers, the ascetics Ālāra Kālāma and Uddaka Rāmaputta, considered him to be on a par with them.

With regard to the second assumption, it may be pointed out that only a superficial study of the pre-Buddhist and Buddhist theories of *karma* and rebirth would yield the conclusion that they are identical. If they are identical, why did some of the Buddha's contemporaries accuse him of propounding a theory of annihilation of the sentient being (i.e., denying rebirth and moral responsibility by denying a permanent and immutable 'self')? Or, what made some of the monks who lived during the Buddha's own day raise the question: "Since body, feelings, perceptions, dispositions, and consciousness are without self, what self can deeds done by the self, affect?"[5] That is, how can *karma* be explained when the Buddha has rejected the immutable self? The Materialists, who denied a permanent 'self', denied both rebirth and moral responsibility. But the Buddha, while denying such a 'self', retained the doctrines of *karma* and rebirth. The problem of reconciling the doctrines of *karma* and rebirth with the doctrine of nonsubstantiality (*anatta*) is, therefore, not a problem faced only by Western students of Buddhism, for it created difficulties also for contemporaries of the Buddha, as well as for many of his later disciples. This fact alone should be sufficient to show that the Buddhist theories of *karma* and rebirth are very different from the pre-Buddhist theories. In fact, one of the most significant contributions of the Buddha to Indian philosophical and religious thought lies in the explanation of the phenomena of *karma* and rebirth without positing an unverifiable metaphysical entity such as the 'self' (*ātman*).

Of these two doctrines let us consider first the doctrine of *karma*, though, as will be seen later, the two are inseparably connected. The Buddhist doctrine of *karma* may be understood better in the background of the pre-Buddhist theories. They are as follows:

1. The Upaniṣadic theory of *karma* or moral responsibility according to which the 'self' (*ātman*) is the 'doer' (*kartṛ*) as well as the 'enjoyer' (*bhoktṛ*) of the consequences. *Karma* thus becomes an activity and the experiences of the eternal 'self' in man. The result is emphasis on self-causation of suffering and happiness. All factors other than the 'self' come to be almost excluded.

2. The materialist as well was the Ājīvika theories which denied an eternal 'self' and as a consequence rejected the efficacy of *karma*. They denied any form of moral responsibility and upheld the view that suffering and happiness experienced by man is due entirely to the 'natural law' which they called 'inherent nature' (*svabhāva*) of physical phenomena. Thus everything is determined by causes other than the 'self'. This is the theory of external causation referred to in chapter 3.

3. The Jaina theory according to which *karma* is an inexorable law. According to the Jainas, *karma* is, the individual's responsibility. But once a *karma* is performed, it becomes something beyond his power to control. That is to say, it becomes an external force that man cannot alter.

A careful study of these theories will reveal the fact that *karma* is either emphasized to the neglect of other things or completely denied. While he recognized that *karma* is a causally efficient phenomenon, the Buddha realized that it is not the only determining factor in the life of man. Thus the doctrine of *karma*, as stated by the pre-Buddhist thinkers, was found to be unsatisfactory.

After rejecting all these views as being unsatisfactory, Buddha gave a causal account of *karma* (which later came to be known as *kamma-niyāma*). Before explaining how *karma* determines the life of man, he examined the causality of *karma* itself, and found that behavior (*karma*) of man is determined by one of three factors: (1) external stimuli, (2) conscious motives, or (3) unconscious motives.

At one point, when the problem of the causality of behavior was raised, the Buddha pointed out that "contact (*phassa*) is the cause of behavior (*kamma*)."[6] Taking 'contact' in a more physical sense, this statement may be understood as an explanation of behavior in terms of a stimulus-response sort of model, where reflex movement or behavior follows sensory excitation. Examples are given occasionally, as at *M* 1.324, where it is said that "an innocent little baby lying on its back quickly draws back its hand or foot if it happens to touch a live ember." Of course, such behavior is unmotivated (*asañcetanika*, *acetanika*) and is caused by purely physical stimulation. Hence, responsibility for it is not laid on man himself.

Apart from such physical causes of *karma*, there are certain motives that determine the behavior of man. Conscious motives are those such as greed or attachment (*rāga*), hate or aversion (*dosa*), and confusion (*moha*).[7] Generally it is evil behavior that is produced by these motives, while morally good behavor is motivated by the absence of greed, hate, and confusion (*alobha*, *adosa*, and *amoha*). In these cases, of course, the responsibility of the individual is undeniable. This is the reason why the Buddha emphasized the psychological aspect of behavior and equated *karma* with volition (*cetanā*).

Unconscious motives also influence behavior. Among the unconscious motives are the desire to perpetuate life (*jīvitukāma*) and the desire to avoid death (*amaritukāma*),[8] both of which relate to what Freud called the "life instinct"; and the desire for pleasure (*sukhakāma*) and aversion to pain (*dukkhapaṭikkūla*), both of which compare with the Freudian "pleasure principle." These motives, though unconscious, result from mistaken understanding of the nature of human existence. Hence an individual may be held responsible for behavior determined by them.

Having examined the Buddhist theory of the causality of human behavior, it is now possible to understand the Buddha's view of the causal efficiency of behavior itself. While human behavior is itself conditioned by causes, it is followed by correlated consequences. This correlation between action (*kamma*) and consequence (*vipāka* or *phala*) constitutes the doctrine of *karma* in Buddhism. This is yet another doctrine that has been misunderstood and misinterpreted by scholars. The misunderstanding is due primarily to the fact that emphasis is laid on the *correlation*, to the complete neglect of the *correlated*. This has given rise to a strictly deterministic interpretation of *karma*, which the Buddha himself was rejecting. A deterministic theory was actually advocated by the Jainas.

What the Buddha emphasized was the fact that, depending on

the nature of *karma* and the circumstances in which it is committed, there would be appropriate consequences. This position is made extremely clear by a discourse included in the *Aṅguttara-nikāya*.[9] Here the Buddha says that if a person were to maintain that "just as this man does a deed, so does he experience its consequences," then the living of the holy life would be rendered meaningless, for there would be no opportunity for the complete destruction of suffering. But if one accepts the theory that "just as this man does a deed whose consequences would be determined in a certain way [literally, 'a deed whose consequences would be experienced in a certain way'], so does he experience its consequences," then the religious life will be meaningful and there will be an opportunity for the complete destruction of suffering. The distinction drawn here is clear: In the first case, there is complete *determinism* between *karma* and consequence; in the second, recognition of the circumstances in which the action is committed, and so on, makes the effect *conditional* upon such circumstances.

This situation is illustrated by an apt simile. If a man throws a grain of salt into a small cup filled with water, the water in the cup becomes salty and undrinkable because of that grain of salt. If a man were to throw a similar grain of salt into the river Ganges, because of the great mass of water therein the water would not become salty and undrinkable. Similarly, some trifling evil deed of one person may lead him to hell. But a similar trifling evil deed committed by another person may bring consequences experienced in this very life, consequences, indeed, that may be barely noticeable. Here we find two people committing similar, if not identical, evil deeds but reaping different consequences in different ways. The reason is that the circumstances or factors surrounding the actions are very different. Thus, the same discourse states:

> A certain person has not properly cultivated his body, behavior, thought, and intelligence; [he] is inferior and insignificant and his life is short and miserable; of such a person . . . even a trifling evil deed done leads him to hell. In the case of a person who has proper culture of the body, behavior, thought, and intelligence, who is superior and not insignificant, and who is endowed with long life, the consequences of a similar evil deed are to be experienced in this very life, and sometimes may not appear at all.

This discourse should help to clear the misconceptions of those who tend to see strict determinism in the Buddhist theory of *karma*. The emphasis is on the very significant fact that the effect (*vipāka*, *phala*) of a deed (*kamma*) is not determined solely by the deed itself, but also by many other factors, such as the nature of the person who commits the deed and the circumstances in which it is committed. This is in conformity with the principle of causality as formulated by the Buddha (see chapter 3).

The same discourse also brings to light other interesting features of the early Buddhist theory of *karma*. It makes the points that the effects (*phala*) of certain actions may sometimes be so insignificant that they are not even perceived; sometimes the consequences may be experienced in this very life, and sometimes in a future existence. This is the point at which the doctrine of *karma* becomes closely associated with the doctrine of rebirth or survival. This association of *karma* with survival is found in many of the early Buddhist texts, of which the *Culla-* and *Mahā-kammavibhaṅga-suttas* of the *Majjhima-nikāya* are the most important.

The *Culla-kammavibhaṅga-sutta*[10] maintains that a person who kills living creatures and has no compassion for them would, on account of that behavior, be reborn in an evil state after death. If he were reborn in an evil state and as a human, he would be short-lived. This theory is not the outcome of mere speculation but is verified by extrasensory perception. Yet it is possible even for those who have personally verified the facts of *karma* and rebirth through such means to come to wrong conclusions regarding these facts. This is one of the points mooted in the *Mahā-kammavibhaṅga-sutta*.[11] Here the Buddha refers to some recluses and brahmans who, by thorough application and concentration of mind, were able to see beings who led immoral lives and were reborn in an evil state. As a result of this telepathic insight, they came to the conclusion: "He who takes life, steals, . . . who holds wrong views, would be reborn in an evil state after death. They who know this have right knowledge. Others are mistaken." According to the Buddha, to consider this to be "the only truth and that everything else is false" (*idam eva saccaṃ mogham aññaṃ*) is a grave error. For, on the other hand, there were other ascetics and brahmans, who, through extrasensory perception, saw people who were reborn in happy states after having led immoral lives during previous existences. These ascetics and brahmans reached conclusions diametrically opposed to the one mentioned above. They held that no deeds, whether good or bad, affect one's future existences (cf. the materialist theory).

Both of these opposing theories, one representing a deterministic view of *karma* and the other a form of indeterminism, derive from inductive inferences based on data acquired through extrasensory perception. Therefore, *either* what is given in extrasensory perception is contradictory, *or* the conclusions arrived at on the basis of reason are wrong. From the description in the *Mahā-kammavibhaṅga-sutta* it appears that some of the contemporaries of the Buddha, who had developed extrasensory powers by which they could verify the decease and survival of beings, ignored certain important aspects of the causal process when drawing their inferences. Thus it may be possible for a person who has done evil at a certain time to be reborn in a happy state of existence. If so, absolute determinism in the sphere of moral responsibility may not be true. But the Buddha points out that this should not lead one to the opposite theory of absolute indeterminism. On the contrary, it is possible that the evildoer underwent a change of heart at the moment of death (i.e., evil dispositions may have been replaced by good dispositions) or that he had done some good at some stage in his life. Those who upheld an absolutist theory of *karma*, according to the Buddha, ignored such factors. This is a good example of interpretation by some religious teachers of the content of extrasensory perceptions according to their own likes and dislikes (i.e., taking into consideration only those factors that support one theory to the neglect of others). To this we shall return (see appendix 1).

As we have seen, the Buddha's conception of causality is more conditional than deterministic. *Karma*, or behavior, being one of the causal processes, is no exception. Thus, as mentioned in the *Mahā-maṅgala-sutta*,[12] there are three factors that could be considered auspicious (*maṅgala*) in the life of man: (1) merit acquired in the past, (2) life in appropriate surroundings, and (3) proper resolve or application. Here, past *karma* as well as present resolve (i.e., *karma*) are only two factors. Other important factors such as good surroundings have to be taken seriously in determining consequences. Moreover, according to the *Mahā-kammavibhaṅga-sutta* quoted above, it is possible for an evildoer to be reborn in a happy existence provided he attempts to change his personality right now. (Recognition of this fact led to the adoption of certain religious practices later on, for example, the reading of the "Book of Merits" [*puñña-potthaka*,

Sinhalese *pin-pota*] at the moment of one's death.) It is this possibility of changing one's personality that gives meaning to moral or religious life. Instead of the deterministic theory of *karma* according to which everything experienced in this life is due to one's past *karma*, the Buddha emphasized that *karma* is *one* of the contributory factors in the evolution of the human personality. Hence his statement, "Action is the field, consciousness the seed, and craving the moisture which lead to the rebirth of a being."[13]

The problem generally associated with this theory of human behavior and moral responsibility, as pointed out early in this chapter, is one of reconciling it with the theory of nonsubstantiality (*anatta*). It is certainly a problem for those who are in the habit of mistaking identity for continuity, for those, that is, who believe in an immutable and immortal 'soul' when there is only a constantly changing process which, for the sake of convenience, is designated by a name. But once this belief in an unverifiable entity called the 'soul' or 'self' is given up, and once the process of life is understood as it really is, without bias or prejudice or preconceived notions, then the two sets of doctrines, *karma* and rebirth on the one hand, and nonsubstantiality on the other, will appear perfectly consistent.

How is rebirth or survival explained in the early Buddhist texts? Here, the human personality is analysed in two ways: first, in terms of six elements—earth, water, fire, air, space, and consciousness[14]—probably with a view to refuting the belief in a material 'self' (see chapter 1); and second, in terms of the five aggregates—material form, feeling, perception, dispositions, and consciousness—mainly for the purpose of rejecting the belief in a psychic 'self'. Generally, the human personality is denoted by the term *nāmarūpa* (psychophysical personality).

Explaining the causation of the human personality, it is said that there are three factors necessary for the birth of a being: (1) coitus of the parents, (2) the mother being in the proper season to conceive, and (3) the presence of a *gandhabba*.[15] The first two factors go to produce what is called *gabbha*, or foetus that is formed in the mother's womb. This living organism is called *nāmarūpa* or the psychophysical personality. It becomes complete only when influenced by a surviving consciousness (*viññāṇa*) which, in the above context, is represented by *gandhabba*. A rather gross description of this process is found in the *Mahā-nidāna-suttanta*,[16] where it is said that if consciousness (*viññāṇa*) did not enter the mother's womb, the psychophysical personality (*nāmarūpa*) would not be constituted therein; or if it were to leave the womb (after some time) the psychophysical personality would not grow to maturity. A foetus formed in the mother's womb, therefore, has to be influenced by a surviving consciousness. This connection between a surviving consciousness and the psychophysical personality is emphasized in the twelvefold formula of causation (see chapter 3). It is also stated that in the case of a person who has attained enlightenment and has therefore eliminated craving for existence (*bhavataṇhā*), consciousness finds no support (*patiṭṭhā*) in a new psychophysical personality, and as a result he is not reborn.[17]

All this is evidence that it is consciousness that serves as a connecting link between two lives, and this, of course, is unequivocally stated in the early Buddhist texts. Several times it is mentioned that a person who has developed extrasensory perception is able "to perceive a man's unbroken flux of consciousness established both in this world and in the next."[18] This stream of consciousness (*viññāṇasota*) is the same as the stream of becoming (*bhavasota*) mentioned often in the early discourses.

It is important to note that in the early texts there is no mention of this consciousness surviving even for a moment without the support of a psychophysical personality. In other words, early Buddhism does not contribute to a theory of disembodied existence. But some of the later schools of Buddhism came to believe in some form of intermediate existence (*antarābhava*). But according to early Buddhism consciousness survives only if established in a new psychophysical personality. In this manner, a continuity is maintained on the basis of the psychic personality, and, as the Buddha himself claimed, knowledge of one's past (i.e., *pubbenivāsânussati*, retrocognition) follows in the wake of memory.[19]

A. J. Ayer, the chief exponent of Logical Positivism today, once made the remark:

> . . . even if someone could remember the experiences of a person who is long since dead, and even if this were backed by an apparent continuity of character, I think that we should prefer to say that he had somehow picked up the dead man's memories and dispositions rather than that he was the same person in another body. The idea of a person's leading a discontinuous existence in time as well as in space

> is just that much more fantastic. Nevertheless, I think that it would be open to us to admit the logical possibility of reincarnation merely by laying down the rule that if a person who is physically identified as living at a later time does have ostensible memories and character of a person who is physically identified at an earlier time, they are to be counted as one person and not two.[20]

Ayer's comment is quoted here in order to show that the theory of rebirth as presented in the early Buddhist texts could be considered a *logical* possibility.

The main problem a student of Buddhism faces in his study of the doctrines of *karma* and rebirth is the denial of identity which is implied by the doctrine of nonsubstantiality (*anatta*). As mentioned earlier, the denial of identity does not imply denial of continuity. According to Buddhism, impermanence, causality, and continuity are perfectly consistent and harmonious doctrines. The philosophical importance of the Buddhist theory of rebirth seems to have support even from philosophers like Ayer. Doubts are generally raised regarding this doctrine mainly because it is not verified in the normal way. Aside from the possibility of verification through extrasensory perception, there are innumerable instances of people, especially children, who remember their past lives; these are being carefully studied and recorded. In addition, valuable evidence is supplied by people under hypnosis. It is for these reasons that C. D. Broad believes that the question of the possibility of human survival after bodily death is partly empirical and partly philosophical. He says:

> It is empirical in the sense that if it can be clearly formulated and shown to be an intelligible question, the only relevant way to attempt to answer it is by appeal to specific observable facts. . . . The relevant observable facts are some of those investigated by psychical researches and in particular, certain phenomena of trance-mediumship.[21]

Notes

1. *D* 1.82.
2. S. Radhakrishnan, *Indian Philosophy* (London: George Allen

and Unwin, 1962), vol. 1, p. 360.

3. E. J. Thomas, "Buddhism in Modern Times," *University of Ceylon Review* (Colombo), 9 (1951):216.
4. Jayatilleke, *Early Buddhist Theory of Knowledge*, pp. 371–372.
5. *M* 3.19.
6. *A* 3.415; *TD* 1.600a.
7. *A* 1.134; *TD* 1.438c.
8. *S* 4.172; *TD* 2.313b.
9. *A* 1.249; *TD* 2.433.
10. *M* 3.202ff.; *TD* 1.705a ff.
11. *M* 3.207ff.; *TD* 1.707b ff.
12. *Sn* 260.
13. *A* 1.223f.
14. *M* 3.239; *TD* 1.690b.
15. *M* 1.266; *TD* 1.769b.
16. *D* 2.62f.; *TD* 1.61b.
17. *S* 1.122; *TD* 2.347b.
18. *D* 3.105; *TD* 1.77b.
19. *D* 3.134.
20. *Concept of a Person and Other Essays* (London: Macmillan, 1963), p. 127.
21. *Human Personality and the Possibility of its Survival* (Berkeley and Los Angeles: University of California Press, 1955), p. 1.

Selected Readings

PRIMARY SOURCES

Cūla-kammavibhaṅga-sutta (*M* 3.202ff.); 'Discourse on the Lesser Analysis of Deeds' (*MLS* 3.248ff.); *TD* 1.703ff.

Mahā-kammavibhaṅga-sutta (*M* 3.207ff.); 'Discourse on the Greater Analysis of Deeds' (*MLS* 3.254ff.); *TD* 1.706ff.

Āsivisa-sutta (*S* 4.172ff.); 'The Snake' (*KS* 4.107ff.); *TD* 2.303f.

Nidānāni (*A* 1.134ff.); 'Causes' (*GS* 1.177ff.).

Loṇaphala (*A* 1.249ff.); 'A Grain of Salt' (*GS* 1.227ff.); *TD* 1.433f.

Nibbedika (*A* 3.410ff.); 'A Penetrative Discourse' (GS 3.291ff.); *TD* 1.599f.

SECONDARY SOURCES

Jayatilleke, K. N. *Survival and Karma in Buddhist Perspective*. Kandy: Buddhist Publication Society, 1969.

Nyānatiloka Mahāthera. *Karma and Rebirth*. Kandy: Buddhist Publication Society, 1959.

Rhys Davids, C. A. F. *Buddhism*. Pp. 107–149.
Thomas, E. J. *History of Buddhist Thought*. Pp. 107–118.

Chapter Six
Morality and Ethics

Buddhism, like any other Indian religion, does not divorce knowledge from conduct, theory from practice. Philosophy is meaningful only as it provides an understanding of reality on which to regulate one's life. Understanding man and nature is not an end in itself; it is only a means to an end. The ultimate goal of knowledge or insight (*paññā*) is freedom (*vimutti*). Why is man searching for freedom? The American philosopher John Dewey began his work *The Quest for Certainty* with the remark:

> Man who lives in a world of hazards is compelled to seek for security. He has sought to attain it in two ways. One of them began with an attempt to propitiate the powers which environ him and determine his destiny. It expressed itself in supplication, sacrifice, ceremonial rite and magical cult. In time these crude methods were largely displaced. The sacrifice of a contrite heart was esteemed more pleasing than that of bulls and oxen; the inner attitude of reverence and devotion more desirable than external ceremonies. If man could not conquer destiny he could willingly ally himself with it; putting his will, even in sore affliction, on the side of the powers which dispense fortune, he could escape defeat and might triumph in the midst of destruction.[1]

These remarks seem to be a good starting point for a discussion of ethics and morality in early Buddhism. In his *Discourse on The Noble Quest* (*Ariyapariyesana-sutta*),[2] the Buddha points out that his quest or search, as was the case with the Upaniṣadic sages, was for a way to overcome what Dewey calls the "world of hazards." The world of hazards for the Buddha as well as the Upaniṣadic sages was that world tormented by birth, decay, and death. As pointed out in chapter 3, according to the natural causal law, that which arises conditioned by causes is sure to pass away when the causes disintegrate. There is nothing that is seen to be permanent and eternal. Hence, for a being who is born, death is a certainty. The goal of the religious life is therefore the attainment of freedom from birth (*jāti*), and thus avoidance of decay and death. The paean of joy uttered by the Buddha after his attainment of enlightenment expresses this in very vivid terms:

> For countless births did I wander in this existence looking for the house-builder [i.e., the cause of rebirth] but without success; for unsatisfactory are repeated births. O house-builder! You have now been discovered. You shall never build this house again. All your rafters are broken and the ridge-pole shattered. The mind has reached the state of freedom from dispositions and has seen the end of craving.
>
> (*Anekajātisaṃsāraṃ sandhāvissaṃ anibbisaṃ,*
> *gahakārakaṃ gavesanto dukkhā jāti punappunaṃ.*
> *Gahakāraka diṭṭho' si puna gehaṃ na kahasi,*
> *sabbā te phāsukā bhaggā gahakūṭaṃ visaṅkhitaṃ*
> *visaṅkhāragataṃ cittaṃ taṇhānaṃ khayam ajjhagā.*)[3]

The two ways of overcoming the world of hazards and attaining security referred to by Dewey closely resemble the two ways adopted in Brahmanism and Buddhism. Giving up the practice of propitiation of the powers that environ man, using various forms of worship such as supplication, sacrifice, ceremonial rite, and magical cult as accepted in the Brahmanical religion, Buddhism emphasized the need for self-culture or moral rectitude to gain freedom from the trammels of existence. The Buddha states it thus:

> I lay no wood, brahman, for fires on altars,
> only within burneth the fire I kindle.
> With this fire incessantly burning,
> and with the self ever restrained,
> I live the noble and higher life.[4]

These remarks show the kind of change brought about by Buddhism in the religious life of the Indians. It does not mean that such morality was not known to the pre-Buddhist religions of India. It only emphasizes the extent to which the Brahmanical religion had deteriorated during the Buddha's day. In fact, the Buddha speaks of the moral standing of the brahman priests who lived before the sacrificial ritual was elaborated.[5]

A disciple of the Buddha who has attained freedom from suffering is called "one who has done what has to be done" (*katakaraṇīyo*). But to reach this goal the disciple has to do all that is to be done by gradual and ordered stages. Early Buddhism emphasizes the fact that a beginner is not in a position to reach the final state of freedom all at once, but only by a gradual process of training (*anupubbasikkhā*), gradual working out (*anupubbakiriyā*), and gradual practice (*anupubbapaṭipadā*).

One of the most important features of the early Buddhist theory of the 'path to perfection' is this gradualness of approach; it is emphasized in the two discourses included in the *Majjhima-nikāya*—*Mahā-assapura-sutta*[6] and *Gaṇakamoggallāna-sutta*.[7] This aspect was emphasized because it was recognized that even an immoral person is able to reach the state of moral perfection culminating in the attainment of freedom. Human beings, in different stages of moral and spiritual development, are generally compared to lotuses growing in a pond. Those that attain the highest stage of moral perfection are like the lotuses that grow in the muddy water but rise above and remain unsmeared (*anupalitta*) by the water.[8]

Virtuous or moral behavior consists of two aspects, the negative aspect of avoiding evil (*pāpassa akaraṇa*) and the positive one of cultivating good (*kusalassa upasampadā*). In fact, they complement each other. For example, restraint from killing or hurting living creatures, oneself included, is presented as the negative aspect, and the positive aspect is given as showing compassion for all beings, oneself as well as other.

The moral virtues are grouped into various categories. The most elementary are those comprising the group of five virtues (*pañca sīla*). They are restraint (1) from taking life, both of oneself and of others, (2) from taking what is not given, (3) from wrong indulgence in sense pleasures, (4) from falsehood, and (5) from indolence consequent on the use of intoxicants.[9] Then there are the ten moral virtues (*dasa sīla*)—the first four just mentioned together with restraint (5) from slander, (6) from harsh or rough speech, (7) from frivolous chatter, (8) from covetousness, (9) from malevolence, and (10) from false or heretical views.[10]

A detailed analysis of moral virtues is found in the *Brahmajāla-suttanta*,[11] where they are categorized under three groups: the shorter section (*cūla*), the middle-length section (*majjhima*), and the longer section (*mahā*). The moral virtues discussed there are too numerous to be mentioned here, and they pertain to a wide range of topics, such as bribery and corruption, gambling, sacrifices and oblations, auguries and prognostications, use of spells and incantations, and so on, besides, of course, restraint from the great offences of killing, stealing, lying, and unchastity. Although these moral precepts are worded negatively, the positive side of ethics is not ignored. Of the many discourses in which positive descriptions of morals are given, the *Mahā-maṅgala-sutta* and *Dhammika-sutta* of the *Sutta-nipāta*, as well as the *Siṅgālovāda-sutta* of the *Dīgha-nikāya*, are of great importance.

One of the main criticisms leveled against the early Buddhist ideal of 'perfect man' or 'worthy one' (*arahant*) is that it is a selfish, rather than altruistic, ideal. But it should be remembered that a 'perfect man' is the final product of the cultivation of moral virtues starting from the very elementary ones discussed in the discourses mentioned above. These elementary moral virtues in one way or another are intended to bring about not only the moral development of the individual, but also social uplift, harmony, and concord. Only those who have gone through such moral training are able to attempt the cultivation of the higher moral virtues (*adhisīla*) and the mental concentration (*adhicitta*) which is necessary for the development of higher knowledge (*adhipaññā*), and are able thereby to attain freedom (*vimutti*).

The Noble Eightfold Path (*ariyo aṭṭhangiko maggo*) represents a digest of these moral virtues together with the processes of concentration and the development of insight. The eight factors are generally presented thus:

1. right view (*sammā diṭṭhi*)
2. right thought (*sammā saṅkappa*)
3. right speech (*sammā vācā*)
4. right action (*sammā kammanta*)
5. right living (*sammā ājīva*)
6. right effort (*sammā vāyāma*)
7. right mindfulness (*sammā sati*)
8. right concentration (*sammā samādhi*)

What did the Buddhists intend to achieve by following this path of moral perfection? At the beginning of this chapter it was pointed out that the Buddha was seeking a solution to the hazards of existence. The hazards involved were considered to be birth, decay and death, and uncertainty with regard to the things of the world. We have seen (chapter 5) that the cycle of becoming is caused by craving (*taṇhā*) and grasping or clinging (*upādāna*). While craving and grasping are the causes of major hazards like birth, decay, and death, they also lead to the unhappiness and suffering that man experiences once he is born. Thus, craving leads not only to suffering here and now, but also to further suffering in the future in the form of rebirth and consequent decay and death. Therefore, the attainment of happiness in this present existence and the elimination of future suffering by putting an end to the vicious cycle of existence (*saṃsāra-vaṭṭa, bhava-cakka*) can be attained by the elimination of craving.

The most effective way of eliminating craving is renunciation (*nekkhamma*). The ideal of renunciation is therefore emphasized throughout in the Buddhist texts. Renunciation, both physical and mental, can be achieved only through a gradual process of training. Hence, as pointed out earlier, the gradualness of the path came to be emphasized. The suppression of craving is not what is intended, for that can be lead to all sorts of complications. Repressed desires can be harmful to the development of one's personality since they remain latent in the unconscious and influence one's behavior. What is expected is the pacification (*vūpasama*) of craving and desires, to be achieved through a process of *understanding* and gradual renunciation. It may not be far from the truth to say that this attitude of renunciation is behind every moral virtue. Not only those who leave everyday life and embrace the life of a monk, but everyone, is expected to practice renunciation to the extent to which he is able. Without such sacrifices, there cannot be perfect harmony in society. Thus, even the simplest of virtues, such as generosity, liberality, caring for one's parents, family, fellow beings, and others, cannot be practiced without an element of renunciation or sacrifice. This is the 'sacrifice' the Buddha emphasized.

Now it will be possible to examine the basis of ethical judgment according to Buddhism. One way of deciding whether an action is right or wrong, good or bad is by finding out whether it leads to detachment (*virāga*) or attachment (*rāga*). Very often the Buddha remarked that such and such an action ought not to have been done (*akaraṇīyaṃ*), the *reason* being that that action does not lead to detachment (*virāga*) and pacification (*vūpasama*) of desires. Yet this is not the final criterion of good and bad.

Why are those things or actions that lead to nonattachment (*virāga*) considered good and those that lead to attachment (*rāga*) considered bad? The reason is that the former lead to happiness (*sukhudrayaṃ*, *sukhavipākaṃ*) and freedom, while the latter are conducive to suffering (*dukkhudrayaṃ*, *dukkhavipākaṃ*) and bondage. The emphasis on happiness as the goal of ethical conduct seems to give the Buddhist theory a utilitarian character. But a major difference between the early Buddhist and the utilitarian analyses of happiness is that according to the latter, happiness includes pleasures derived from the senses, while according to the Buddhists, sense pleasures lead finally to suffering rather than to happiness. Of course the Utilitarians, though they included pleasures under happiness, still distinguished between animal pleasures and the more exalted forms of human pleasure.

The noblest happiness, according to early Buddhism, is to be achieved through the control of all hankering for the world (of sense pleasures), all coveting of its false values, together with the dejection to which their impermanence and lack of enduring satisfaction give rise. This is achieved through right, complete, or perfect mindfulness. It is said: "A monk lives contemplating body in the body, ardent, circumspect, mindful, having controlled the hankering and dejection of the world. He so dwells contemplating the feeling in the feelings, and consciousness in the consciousness. And finally he dwells contemplating mental objects in mental objects, ardent, circumspect, mindful, having controlled the hankering and dejection of the world."[12] As I. B. Horner has pointed out, "The control of hankering, which here results from right mindfulness, certainly brings great results, ideally culminating as it does in the attainment of *nibbāna*."[13] Complete elimination of hankering is achieved only with the attainment of *nibbāna*. But this control may be achieved in differing degrees, and this is all that is expected of a person living in society. The quality of happiness that one achieves through renunciation is certainly superior to that achieved through attachment or craving.

It is now possible to determine what early Buddhism meant by "good" and "bad." The terms used to denote these two concepts are *kusala* and *akusala* respectively. *Kusala* conveys the idea of 'wholesome' or 'healthy' and *akusala*, 'unwholesome' or 'unhealthy'; so it is possible to say that 'good' is what is conducive to 'health', physical as well as mental, and 'bad' is what leads to 'ill health', again physical as well as mental. This is clearly stated in the *Ambalaṭṭhikā-Rāhulovāda-sutta* of the *Majjhima-nikāya*,[14] which can be considered the *locus classicus* for the study of the concepts of good and bad in early Buddhism. Here good and bad are defined in the following manner:

> Whatever action, bodily, verbal, or mental, leads to suffering [*byābādha*, literally, illness] for oneself, for others or for both, that action is bad (*a-kusalaṃ*). Whatever action, bodily, verbal or mental, does not lead to suffering for oneself, for others or for both, that action is good (*kusalaṃ*).

Thus, in determining whether an action is good or bad, the criterion is whether or not that action leads to happy or pleasant consequences. If an action involves oneself only, then it is one's own happiness that becomes the criterion; if it involves others only, it is the happiness of others; if it involves both, it is the happiness of both. Hence, according to the Buddha's analysis, there are four types of people in the world:

1. One who torments himself (*attantapa*), like the ascetic who practices self-mortification.
2. One who torments others (*parantapa*), like the hunter who deprives others of life.
3. One who torments himself as well as others (*attantapo ca parantapo ca*), like the monarch who undertakes large-scale sacrifices, for which the monarch as well as the subjects undergo endless suffering while making arrangements for such sacrifices; the animals that are sacrificed also suffer.
4. One who torments neither himself nor others (*neva attantapo na parantapo*), like the *arahant*.

This definition of good and bad presented in the *Ambalaṭṭhikā-Rāhulovāda-sutta* is generally described as the 'Mirror of the Dhamma' (*dhammâdāsa*)—looking into it one is able to determine for oneself whether an action is good or bad.

This brings us to another interesting problem with regard to the definition of good and bad. If it is the mirror of the *dhamma* that helps us to find out what is good and bad, it may be said that the criterion is the *dhamma* itself. The concept of *dhamma* is also used in the sense of truth (*sacca*, Sk. *satya*). It is, in fact, identified with the truth about the world which the Buddha discovered, that is, causality (*paṭiccasamuppāda*).[15] From this, then, we get the equations:

Good (*kusala*) = truth (*dhamma*, *sacca*).
Bad (*akusala*) = untruth (*a-dhamma*, *musā*).

This involves us in one of the most crucial problems of ethics in modern Western philosophy, namely, the truth value of ethical statements. Ludwig Wittgenstein, whose ideas have influenced the modern positivistic approach to this problem, on the basis of his picture theory of language drew the conclusion that there can be no propositions of ethics. His arguments may be presented thus: According to the picture theory of language, a proposition as well as its negation are both possible. Which of these is true, the assertion or the negation, is accidental. If everything in the world is accidental, there can be no "value" in the world, because anything that has value cannot be accidental. Here, a distinction is made between the world and value, and the denial pertains not to value but to value in the world. Thus, propositions can state only what is in the world, what is true or false, not what is good or bad. What is good and bad exist only in relation to a subject. Hence the positivist definition of ethics as a matter of emotion.

The Buddha was very clearly conscious of the relativity of ethical judgments. But, unlike Wittgenstein, he refused to recognize a distinction between reality or truth and value. In the famous *Aṭṭhaka-vagga* of the *Sutta-nipāta*, the Buddha maintained that statements about good and bad are notoriously subjective.[16] But in the same way he considered claims about what is true (*sacca*) and false (*musā*) as being equally relative. These are relative to one's likes (*ruci*) and dislikes (*aruci*), for what is true for one is false for another. (This might also be the reason why Wittgenstein considered truth and falsehood to be accidental!) Thus, for the Buddha, truth values are not distinguishable from moral values or ethical values; both are values that participate in nature. For the Buddha, what is called the world (*loka*) is not a set of mere objects found in space and time, related or unrelated. It includes also feelings and dispositions, likes and dislikes. The world consists not only of mountains and rivers, trees and stones, but also of men and animals with behavioral patterns. Causality (*paṭiccasamuppāda*) as explained earlier, describes the pattern according to which all these things function. Human dispositions, likes and dislikes, constitute an important causal factor in the world. Thus, if man's dispositions make every judgment about truth and falsehood or good and bad relative rather than absolute, the pacification of all such dispositions (*sabbasaṅkhārasamatha*) reached along with the attainment of freedom (*nibbāna*) should enable one to understand truth and falsehood, good and bad, as they are. For this reason, the *Sutta-nipāta* emphatically states that conflicts regarding what is true and false, good and bad, do not reach the sage (*muni*).[17]

Does this mean that truth (*sacca*) and good (*kusala*) become undifferentiated when a person attains freedom? If so, can such a situation be explained philosophically, that is, in terms of the basic teaching of the Buddha, which is causation (*paṭiccasamuppāda*)? It was pointed out in chapter 3 that, according to the Buddha's perception, causation (*paṭiccasamuppāda*) is the truth (*sacca*) about the world. In fact, he maintained that "a person who sees causation, sees the *dhamma*."[18] The Buddha was probably the first Indian philosopher to explain the processes of both bondage (*saṁkilesa*) and freedom (*vodāna*) or purity (*visuddhi*), in terms of causation. The process of bondage is a natural causal happening (*dhammatā*), in the same way as is the process of freedom. The causal process determined by dispositions (*saṅkhāra*), both good and bad, and therefore called the 'conditioned' (*saṅkhata*), leads to bondage (*bandhana*) and unhappiness or suffering (*dukkha*). The causal process undetermined by dispositions, hence called the 'unconditioned' (*asaṅkhata*), leads to freedom (*vimutti*) and happiness (*sukha*). It is therefore not surprising to see the early Buddhists identifying truth (*sacca*) as well as good (*kusala*) with the second of the causal processes. This is the spiritual process that came to be denoted by the term *dhamma-niyāma*.

Thus, *dhamma* (plural *dhammā*) or factor of experience which can be analyzed in terms of the categories of reality or unreality, truth or falsehood, can also be a *dhamma* signifying what is good (and also an *a-dhamma*, what is bad). All this seems to indicate that attachment (*sarāga*) or detachment (*virāga*), representing the presence or absence of dispositions (*saṅkhāra*), provide the basis for moral judgments in early Buddhism.

This in brief is the treatment of morality and ethics in the early Buddhist texts. Considering the practical value of the path of moral perfection as well as its gradualness, which was emphasized in early Buddhism, it would be relevant to discuss a set of concepts which came to be accommodated within the fold of Buddhism and which were meant for the religious edification of the uninitiated. These are the concepts of heaven and hell, gods and departed beings.

The pre-Buddhistic concepts of gods and evil spirits became much modified in early Buddhism in conformity with its theory and practice. During the pre-Buddhist period, the gods were thought to be extremely powerful beings who bestowed favors on their worshipers. Sacrifice to the gods (or God) was looked upon as an effective means of obtaining what one desired. On the other hand, evil spirits were supposed to bring calamity to the people, and various charms were devised for avoiding such evil influences. Buddhism, with its emphasis on the value of human exertion and on the ability of man to work out his own salvation without depending on outside powers, began to devalue the concepts of heaven and hell, gods and evil spirits, without discarding them altogether.

Realizing that man's fundamental nature is to hanker after happiness (*sukhakāma*) and detest pain (*dukkha-paṭikkūla*), the Buddha seems to have utilized the beliefs in gods and spirits as *regulative* concepts. Having brought down the gods from the high and exalted positions they occupied during the earlier period, the Buddha described them as a class of beings who, as a result of their past moral behavior, enjoyed all the forms of sense pleasures imaginable. Heaven (*sagga*) is the abode of these gods. Sakka (Indra of the earlier pantheon) is said to have attained preeminence as the chief among gods because he had practiced the sevenfold virtuous conduct, consisting of such virtues as caring for one's parents, respecting elders, and looking after one's family.[19] In the eyes of ordinary lay followers, Sakka's position became an enviable one. With the possibility left open of attaining such a position after death, the ordinary uninitiated person would, it was hoped, make an attempt to reach it by following a path of moral rectitude. But compared with the Buddha and the *arahant*s, the gods are inferior beings, for, while occupying a position in which they become engrossed with sense pleasures, they are unable to attain freedom from suffering.

On the other hand, the evil spirits (*bhūta*, *pisāca*) or the spirits of the departed (*peta*), who, during the earlier period, were believed to be a class of powerful beings, came to be looked upon in Buddhism as beings reduced to a woeful state as a result of past immoral behavior. They are the denizens of the various hells. They are made to depend on the charity and munificence of human beings even for food and clothing. But since such material gifts cannot reach these beings, human beings who are compassionate are expected to bestow on these unfortunate creatures the merits they have acquired by virtuous conduct, such as liberality (*dāna*). This again is a means of inculcating moral virtues and the idea of renunciation. The threat of hell, presented as a horrible place where evildoers undergo extreme forms of suffering as a result of their past immoral behavior, serves as a deterrent to immorality.

A careful study of these concepts of heaven and hell, gods and evil spirits, reveals that they were accepted in Buddhism as *regulative ideas* or *concepts* only. The fact that they are merely theories based on speculation is well brought out in certain statements of the Buddha. To a brahman who questioned the Buddha as to whether there are gods, the Buddha replied, "It is not so." When he asked whether there are no gods, the Buddha's reply was the same, "It is not so." And finally to the brahman who was baffled by these replies, the Buddha said, "The world, O brahman, is loud in agreement that there are gods" (*ucce sammataṃ kho etaṃ brāhmaṇa lokasmiṃ yadidaṃ atthi devâti*).[20] The same is the attitude of the Buddha with regard to the concept of hell. In *Samyutta-nikāya*[21] he is represented as saying that it is only the uneducated ordinary man (*assutavā puthujjano*) who believes that there is a hell beneath the great ocean. According to the Buddha's view, hell is another name for unpleasant feelings (*dukkhā vedanā*).

Notes

1. John Dewey, *The Quest for Certainty* (Gifford Lectures 1929), Fourth Impression (New York: Putnam, Capricorn Books, (1960), p. 3.
2. *M* 1.160ff.; *TD* 1.775ff.
3. *Dhammapada*, ed. Suryagoda Sumangala (London: PTS, 1914), pp. 153–154.
4. *S* 1.169; *TD* 2.320f.
5. *Sn* 50ff.
6. *M* 1.271ff.; *TD* 1.724ff.

7. *M* 3.1 ff.; *TD* 1.652 ff.
8. *A* 2.39.
9. *S* 2.69.
10. *S* 4.342.
11. *D* 1.1 ff.
12. *S* 5.9.
13. I. B. Horner, *The Basic Position of Sīla* (Colombo: The Bauddha Sāhitya Sabhā, 1950), p. 18.
14. *M* 1.414 ff.; *TD* 1.436 ff.
15. *M* 1.190–191; *TD* 1.467a.
16. *Sn* 878–894.
17. *Sn* 780, 843, etc.
18. *M* 1.190–191; *TD* 1.467a.
19. *S* 2.228–232; *TD* 2.290b–c.
20. *M* 2.213.
21. *S* 4.206; *TD* 2.119c.

Selected Readings

PRIMARY SOURCES

Sigālovāda-suttanta (*D* 3.180 ff.); 'The Sigāla Homily' (*SBB* 4.173); *TD* 1.70 ff.

Ariyapariyesana-sutta (*M* 1.160 ff.); 'Discourse on the Aryan Quest' (*MLS* 1.203 ff.); *TD* 1.775 ff.

Mahā-Assapura-sutta (*M* 1.271 ff.); 'The Greater Discourse at Assapura' (*MLS* 1.325 ff.); *TD* 1.724 f.

Ambalaṭṭhikā-Rāhulovāda-sutta (*M* 1.414 ff.); 'Discourse on Exhortation to Rāhula at Ambalaṭṭhikā' (*MLS* 2.87 ff.); *TD* 1.436 f.

Kīṭāgiri-sutta (*M* 1.473 ff.); 'Discourse at Kītāgiri' (*MLS* 2.146 ff.); *TD* 1.749 ff.

Gaṇakamoggallāna-sutta (*M* 3.1 ff.); 'Discourse to Gaṇaka-Moggallāna' (*MLS* 3.52 ff.); *TD* 1.652 f.

Sundarīka-Bhāradvāja-sutta (*S* 1.167 ff.); 'The Sundarikāyan' (*KS* 1.209 ff.); *TD* 2.320 f.

Mahā-maṅgala-sutta (*Sn* 258 ff.); 'The Boon of Boons' (Harvard Oriental Series, vol. 37 [1932], p. 65 ff.).

Dhammika-sutta (*Sn* 376 ff.); 'Dhammika's Enquiry' (Harvard Oriental Series, vol. 37, p. 91 ff.).

SECONDARY SOURCES

Hopkins, E. W. *Ethics of India*. New Haven: Yale University Press, 1924.

Saddhatissa, H. *Buddhist Ethics*. London: George Allen & Unwin, 1970.

Tachibana, S. *Ethics of Buddhism*. London: Oxford University Press, 1926.

Wijesekera, O. H. de A. "Buddhist Ethics." In *Knowledge and Conduct. Buddhist Contribution to Philosophy and Ethics*. Kandy: Buddhist Publication Society, 1963.

Chapter Seven
Nirvana

We are now in a position to examine the goal or *summum bonum* of early Buddhism. Innumerable treatises have been written by scholars on the subject; one feels that the last word has been said. The latest addition to this vast storehouse of interpretative literature is Rune E. A. Johansson's *Psychology of Nirvana.*[1]

Introducing his work, Johansson says: "It is a well known fact that nibbāna is the summum bonum of Buddhism and that a person who has attained this ultimate goal is called *arahant.* But here the agreement ends." The reason for this, according to him, is that "different scholars have started from different strata of the extensive literature and then often generalized their findings and supposed them to be valid for other strata as well. Buddhism has often been considered much more homogeneous than it really is.... Invalid generalizations seem to be one of the cardinal sins of scholarly works." Hence, he sets himself to the task of "collecting and describing all the evidence in the Pali Nikāyas as objectively as possible and if possible let it explain itself and not force any extraneous explanations upon it."[2]

Johansson made a determined attempt to remain faithful to this undertaking, but unfortunately the age-old interpretation of nirvana weighed too heavily on him, especially with regard to the very same problems that created divergence among earlier scholars. The misinterpretations, we feel, are due mainly to the fact that the conception of nirvana in early Buddhism is not examined in the light of other doctrines like causality, *karma,* and rebirth, but independently of them. When nirvana is not studied in its proper context, such misinterpretations cannot be avoided. For this reason, we propose to examine the conception of nirvana in the light of the various doctrines that we have discussed so far and especially in relation to the empiricism of early Buddhism. To avoid confusion, we shall discuss the conception of nirvana in its two main aspects, namely, nirvana attained by the *arahant* in this life and the nirvana of the *arahant* after death.

The description of nirvana in the *Itivuttaka*[3] is one of the most valuable in any attempt to understand this conception. Here the two forms are referred to as (1) nirvana with the substrate left (*saupādisesa*, that is, nirvana attained in this life) and (2) nirvana without substrate (*anupādisesa*, that is, nirvana of the dead *arahant*).

Let us consider first the nature of the attainments of the *arahant* in this life. The description runs thus:

> Herein, monks, a monk is a worthy one who has destroyed the defiling impulses, lived [the higher] life, done what has to be done, laid aside the burden, achieved the noble goal, destroyed the fetters of existence, and is freed through insight. He retains his five senses, through which, as they are not yet destroyed, he experiences pleasant and unpleasant sensations and feels pleasure and pain [or happiness and suffering]. This cessation of craving, hate, and confusion is called the *nibbāna* with the substrate left.

In chapter 1 we referred to the Upaniṣadic conception of freedom or nirvana which, according to our analysis, represented the experience of a *yogi* in the highest state of meditation. This experience came to be interpreted as the merging of the individual 'self' (*ātman*) with the universal 'self' or the cosmic reality (*Brahman*, *Ātman*). The highest form of meditation attained by the Buddha was the state of 'cessation of perception and feeling' (*saññāvedayitanirodha*) which is sometimes called the 'state of cessation' (*nirodhasamāpatti*). The attainment of this state of undifferentiated consciousness is the result of intensive mind control. When the mind is trained to reach, not this highest state, but merely the fourth *jhāna*, it becomes supple and pliant, and the *yogi* is able to turn or direct his mind to perceiving things that are generally beyond the range of the normal senses. The development of extrasensory perception and verification of doctrines like rebirth and moral responsibility are achieved in this manner.

But when the *yogi* attains to the highest stage of meditation, characterized by the cessation of perception and feeling, it cannot be said that he perceives anything; he merely remains in that state enjoying a spell of peace and tranquillity, for he is not troubled by impressions flowing into him through the senses. This spell of peace and tranquillity is temporary. After remaining in this state for some time, the *yogi* reverts to the normal state. Very often we find references to the Buddha as well as the other *arahant*s enjoying this form of quietude. In fact, according to the *Mahā-parinibbāna-suttanta*, the Buddha attained to this state just before he died. Probably it was an attempt to overcome the pangs of death. This is the impression one gets from the famous utterance of Anuruddha: "His mind was firm, without exhalation and inhalation. When the sage passed away, free from desire, having found peace, he *endured pain* with active mind; the liberation of the mind was like the extinction of a lamp."[4]

It is also reported that when the Buddha attained the state of cessation (*nirodhasamāpatti*) just before passing away, Ānanda, his favorite disciple, informed venerable Anuruddha that the Buddha had died. And Anuruddha had to correct him saying: "Friend Ānanda, the Blessed One has not yet passed away; he has attained to the state of cessation of perception and feeling."[5] In fact, the Buddha emerged from that state before he finally passed away. Thus, it would not be proper to identify the state of consciousness in the highest state of yogic meditation either with *nibbāna* or with *parinibbāna* (i.e., *nibbāna* attained with death).

What then is the nature of *nibbāna* with substrate left (*saupādisesa*), in other words, the nature of the living *arahant*? In our explanation of the causal principle it was pointed out that according to the Buddha the human personality and human experience are causally conditioned (chapter 3). It was held that when the individual is born, his sense faculties start functioning and through these he is fed new impressions. These sense impressions or sense data (*phassa*) produce in him feelings (*vedanā*), pleasurable, painful, or neutral. From here on, it is stated simply that from feeling arises craving, and craving gives rise to grasping. A more detailed analysis of this part of the process is found in the *Madhupiṇḍika-sutta* which has already been discussed (chapter 2).

Explaining this causal process, we pointed out that, in the process of perception immediately after feeling, the ego-consciousness intrudes and thereafter fashions the entire process, culminating in the generation of obsessions. The individual then becomes the hapless object of these obsessions. This is the normal order of things—*dhammatā*. Attachment (*rāga*) and aversion or revulsion (*paṭigha*) that one develops toward things of the world are, therefore, due to ignorance of the nature of existence. The intrusion of the ego-consciousness culminating in the generation of obsessions is a result of this ignorance. This is the way in which ordinary human beings behave when they come into contact with the outside world. Such a person is called the 'one who follows the stream' (*anusotagāmī*), that is, one who gives in to one's inclinations, following one's will. Thus it is said:

> Those who give rein to passions, in this world
> Not passion-freed, in sense desires delighting,
> These oft and oft subject to birth and eld;
> Bondsmen to craving, down the current go.[6]

To be contrasted with him are three types of persons. The first type attempts generally to follow a good life avoiding evil actions. In this attempt he may suffer but is not discouraged by that suffering. He can be compared with the 'stream entrant' (*sotāpanna*), but in the present context is called 'one who goes against the stream' (*paṭisotagāmi*). The second type of person is one who has advanced further in the path of spiritual progress and has reached the stage of 'non-returner' (*anāgāmi*) (to this world) because he has destroyed the five kinds of fetters (*samyojana*). The last type of person is the one who is fully enlightened and is completely freed and therefore remains unsmeared by the world, like a person who has 'crossed over' (*pārangata*) and remains in safety when everything outside him is in turmoil.[7] Such a person has trained his mind through meditation and is able to control it as he wishes. When an external object impinges on his senses he can prevent the intrusion of ego-consciousness because he understands the nature of the process of perception. Once the intrusion of the ego-consciousness is prevented, it is possible to arrest the influx of such unhealthy elements (*akusalā dhammā*) as coveting (*abhijjhā*) and dejection (*domanassa*). When he is confronted with the outside world, he does not generate attachment (*rāga*); instead he generates detachment (*virāga*).

Perceiving the aggregates that constitute the psychophysical personality as being nonsubstantial (*anatta*) and preventing the ego-consciousness from assailing himself when the process of perception takes place, "a learned Āryan disciple has revulsion for (*nibbandati*) the physical form (*rūpa*), feeling (*vedanā*), perception (*saññā*), dispositions (*saṅkhārā*), and consciousness (*viññāṇa*). Having revulsion, he is not attached; being nonattached he is freed, and in him who is thus freed there arises the knowledge of freedom: 'Destroyed is birth; lived is the higher life; done is what ought to be done; there is no future existence.'"[8]

This means that with the elimination of the ego-consciousness by the development of insight, the normal process of perception is changed. With the attainment of mental concentration or restraint (*saṃvara*), one is able to prevent the influx of impurities (*kilesa*) such as attachment (*rāga*) and aversion (*paṭigha*). According to the description in the text, this is going against (*paṭisota*) the normal causal pattern. Yet it represents a causal pattern with different causal factors. This causal pattern may be stated as follows: The elimination of ego-consciousness produces revulsion (*nibbidā*) with regard to things which earlier were grasped as being substantial. Revulsion produces detachment (*virāga*). Detachment produces freedom (*vimutti*), and therefore one attains stability (*ṭhitatā*) of mind so that one does not tremble or is not agitated as a result of gain (*lābha*) or loss (*alābha*), good repute (*yasa*) or disrepute (*ayasa*), praise (*pasaṃsā*) or blame (*nindā*), happiness (*sukha*) or suffering (*dukkha*). These are the eight worldly phenomena (*aṭṭhalokadhamma*) by which one is constantly assailed in this life.[9] Hence, the highest point of 'blessedness' (*maṅgala*) is achieved, according to the *Mahā-maṅgala-sutta*, by a person "whose mind is not overwhelmed when in contact with worldly phenomena (*lokadhamma*), is freed from sorrow, taintless and secure."[10] Such a person feels secure and at peace in the midst of all the destruction and confusion prevailing in the world.

But what about 'death' (*maraṇa*) which, as pointed out earlier, is the greatest hazard man has to face in this world? Just as impermanence (*aniccatā*), unsatisfactoriness (*dukkhatā*) and nonsubstantiality (*anattatā*) of the things of the world cannot cause consternation or agitation in a person who has overcome craving (*vītarāga*), even so death does not overwhelm him. Sāriputta is reported as saying:

> Not fain am I to die nor yet to live.
> I shall lay down this mortal frame anon
> With mind alert, with consciousness controlled.
>
> With thought of death I dally not, nor yet
> Delight in living. I wait the hour
> Like any hireling who hath done his task.[11]

Such is the *arahant*'s attitude toward death. What, then, is the nature of immortality (*amata*, Sk. *amṛta*) spoken of so often? According to what has been said so far, immortality or deathlessness would mean rebirthlessness (*apunabbhava*)[12] only. With the elimination of craving and the consequent realization that one is freed, a person will not be in any way interested in the afterlife. As Sāriputta asks, how can a person be interested in the afterlife, if he is not in any way attached to the present life?

In chapter 6 it was mentioned that the Buddha recognized two causal processes, one 'determined by dispositions' (*saṅkhata*) and the other 'undetermined by dispositions' (*asaṅkhata*). The first four causal patterns discussed in chapter 3 may be classed under the former and the last, the *dhamma-niyāma*, under the latter. Human beings whose lives are determined by dispositions are those described as 'following the stream' (*anusotagāmi*). Those whose lives are not determined by dispositions, those who have attained 'the pacification of all dispositions' (*sabbasaṅkhārasamatha*) either go against the stream or remain steadfast or have crossed over the flood of existence (*samsār'ogha*). This going against the stream or remaining steadfast or crossing over is possible because of the understanding of the world and the absence of craving for it. It is this and only this that makes the life of one who has attained nirvana 'transcendent' (*lokuttara*), like the lotus (*puṇḍarīka*) that remains unsmeared by the surrounding pollution. In this way, ordinary human existence (*samsāra*) is contrasted with the freedom of nirvana.

In the *Udāna* is found a very important description of the state of the saint freed from suffering. This passage, quoted below in full, has been utilized by almost all Buddhist scholars to prove the existence of an ineffable transcendental reality in Buddhism. In the *Udāna* there are four discourses placed in a particular order, all of them pertaining to nirvana (*nibbāna-paṭisaññutta*).

[1]

> There is, monks, that sphere wherein there is neither earth nor water nor fire nor air; there is neither the sphere of infinite space nor of infinite consciousness nor of nothingness nor of the sphere of neither-perception-nor-nonperception; where there is neither this world nor the world beyond nor both together, nor moon nor sun; this I say is free from coming and going, from duration and decay; there is no beginning nor establishment, no result, no cause; this indeed is the end of suffering.

[2]

Nonsubstantiality is indeed difficult to see. Truth certainly is not easily perceived. Craving is mastered [literally, penetrated] by him who knows, and for him who sees, there is nothing [grasped].

[3]

Monks, there is a not-born, not-become, not-made, not-compounded. Monks, if that not-born, not-become, not-made, not-compounded were not, no escape from the born, become, made, compounded would be known here. But, monks, since there is a not-born, not-become, not-made, not-compounded, therefore an escape from the born, become, made, compounded is known.

[4]

For him who is attached, there is vacillation; for him who is not attached, there is no vacillation. When there is no vacillation, there is calm; when there is calm, there is no delight; when there is no delight, there is no coming-and-going [i.e., continuous birth and death]; when there is no coming-and-going, there is no disappearance-and-appearance; when there is no disappearance-and-appearance, there is nothing here nor there or between them; this indeed is the end of suffering.[13]

A careful examination of these passages shows that they are merely descriptions of nirvana as a state to be contrasted with *saṃsāra*. The last two passages, especially, are very clear on this point. Compared with the person caught up in the vacillating world of human existence, one who has eliminated craving or attachment remains steadfast. But this steadfastness does not imply an "undifferentiated consciousness" but only the ability to remain unmoved when in contact with the external world or when experiencing happiness and suffering. The contrast between an ordinary person and one who has attained nirvana may be understood in the following manner: A physically weak person is seen to tremble at the slightest electric shock administered on his body, whereas a physically strong person experiencing such a shock will remain unmoved. So too will a weak and untrained mind become agitated, while a healthy and well-controlled mind will remain steadfast in the face of things, such as gain or loss, happiness or suffering, which normally cause agitation.

If this is what is meant by freedom or nirvana, then there is no doubt that even the first two passages quoted above describe the individual who is not established on (*appatiṭṭhita*) or not leaning against (*anissita*) anything in this world. For such a person it is *as if* there is neither the physical world (*rūpaloka*) consisting of earth, water, fire, and air, nor the formless world (*arūpaloka*) represented by the four higher *jhānas*. As a result of his elimination of craving, nothing in this world worries him or causes him suffering, neither day nor night, neither birth nor decay and death, neither coming nor going.

The omission of *saññāvedayitanirodha* or the state of cessation of perception and feeling in the first passage in the *Udāna*, while the four stages of contemplation preceding it are found, is significant in that it points to a common denominator between *nibbāna* and *saññāvedayitanirodha*. As in *nibbāna*, there is no craving in the state of cessation of perception and feeling (*saññāvedayitanirodha*), for in the absence of any perception or feeling there can be no craving (cf. the statement of the twelvefold formula of causation: *vedanā paccayā taṇhā*, "depending on feeling arises craving"). Nibbāna signifies the absolute end of craving (*anto dukkhassa*), not because a person in this state does not experience pleasant (*manāpa*) or unpleasant (*amanāpa*), happy (*sukha*) or unhappy (*dukkha*) feelings, but because he is unmoved by them (see *Itivuttaka* 38, already quoted). On the other hand, the person who has attained the state of cessation of perception and feeling need not even make an effort to remain unmoved because, while in that state, he does not come into contact with, and thus is not aware of, the outside world. In the former state a person has knowledge of the nature of contact (*phassa*) and therefore he remains unmoved. In the latter, he does not have such knowledge nor any feeling of it. In fact, even if the entire earth were to tremble, he who has reached this state of contemplation will remain unmoved.

The story is related in the *Mahā-parinibbāna-suttanta* that, when the Buddha was living in a place called Ātumā, two people were killed, being struck by lightning, but the Buddha, who was seated under a tree close by, did not hear a sound.[14] This ability to remain unmoved, although in different ways, is a common factor in *nibbāna* and *saññāvedayitanirodha*. For this reason, in the description in the *Udāna*, when this ability on the part of the *arahant* is explained, reference to *saññāvedayitanirodha* was avoided.

While there is this similarity between the two states, there is the significant difference that an *arahant* in his waking consciousness is fully aware of what goes on before him, while one who has attained the state of cessation of perception and feeling will not be aware of anything, since the activities of his senses are temporarily suspended. He is like a dead person except that, "in the case of a dead person (*mato kālakato*), his dispositions, bodily, verbal, and mental, cease to exist and are pacified; life has come to an end; breath is calmed and the senses are destroyed. But in the case of a person [who has] reached the state of cessation of perception and feeling, even though his dispositions have ceased to exist or are pacified, his life has not come to an end, breath is not calmed, and the senses are not destroyed."[15]

To return to the description in the *Itivuttaka*. It is very important to distinguish between nirvana and the cessation of perception and feeling. It is for this reason that the passage from the *Itivuttaka* quoted at the beginning of this chapter is significant. The description of nirvana with substrate (*saupādisesa*) does not imply that a saint develops "a level of consciousness . . . experienced as empty, impersonal, undifferentiated, peaceful, stable, and immovable" (as he would to attain the state of cessation of perception and feeling). What is stated unequivocally is that the saint, although he has experienced all of the impressions coming through the senses, is able to prevent the generation of attachment (*rāga*) or aversion (*paṭigha*), because these impressions are properly understood through insight (*paññā*) and because he has mastery of the psychic process. Although these impressions produce their respective feelings, pleasurable or painful, the saint is unmoved by them. It is as if he were able to jam the brakes without much effort.

The very fact that the *arahant* experiences pleasurable as well as painful feelings shows that his consciousness is not undifferentiated—if "undifferentiated" is taken to mean the kind of consciousness in the highest state of *jhāna*, which is not disturbed by the different impressions coming through the senses. The view that the *arahant* has undifferentiated consciousness seems to stem from an erroneous interpretation of the concept of *papañca* (Sk. *prapañca*). The literal meaning of *papañca* is 'diffusion' or 'proliferation'. Since sense perception is said to culminate in *papañca*, it is generally believed that *papañca* means 'conceptual proliferation', and that, with the elimination of *papañca*, consciousness becomes an undifferentiated awareness that gives us an understanding of the *ultimate ground* of all differentiation. Hence also the belief that Ultimate Reality is indescribable and not conceptually grasped.[16] But, as pointed out in chapter 2, the interpretation of the term as 'obsession' seems to be more appropriate, for in the process of perception conceptualization starts immediately after feeling (*vedanā*) and is essential for the next stage, which is *saññā*, 'perception' or 'recognition', and is certainly prior to 'reasoning' (*vitakka*).

The most important aspect of *nibbāna* is that of the *arahant* who has passed away. It is also the most misunderstood aspect of *nibbāna* and is often misinterpreted. Referring to the state of the dead *arahant*, the *Itivuttaka* says:

> Herein, monks, a monk is a worthy one, who has destroyed the defiling impulses, . . . is freed through insight. Monks, all his experiences [literally, things he has felt], none of which he relished, will be cooled here itself. This is called the *nibbāna* without substrate.[17]

Here, of course, there is no reference to any kind of survival whatsoever. Unlike the case of one who has attained a temporary cessation of perception and feeling (*saññāvedayitanirodha*), here the experiences or feelings (*vedayitāni*) which even as a living person he did not delight in (*anabhinanditāni*) are completely cooled (*sītibhūtāni*). This leads us to a very important problem which led to the development of Mahāyāna (see appendix 1). The problem pertains to the state of the saint after death.

The question whether or not the *arahant* exists after death is invariably dependent on epistemological facts. In chapter 2 it was pointed out that predictions into the future can be made on the basis of present or past experiences. This is called inferential knowledge (*anvaye ñāṇa*). On the basis of this epistemological standpoint, what can we say about the state of the dead *arahant*? A being is born, according to the doctrines of *karma* and rebirth (see chapter 5), as a result of ignorance (*avijjā*), craving (*taṇhā*), and the resultant grasping (*upādāna*). Freedom (*vimutti*) or the attainment of *nibbāna* consists in eliminating these three causes by the development of insight or knowledge (*vijjā*) and elimination of craving (*taṇhakkhaya*) and non-grasping (*anupādāna*). Therefore, the only thing that we can know with any certainty on the basis of inference into the future is that there will be no more rebirth, and this, of course, is the knowledge that dawns on the *arahant* at the moment of enlightenment. Hence the paean of joy (*udāna*) expressed by the Buddha as well as many an *arahant*: "Destroyed is birth; lived is the higher life; done is what has to be done; there is no more tendency for future birth or existence" (*Khīṇā jāti vusitaṃ brahmacariyaṃ kataṃ karaṇīyaṃ nâparaṃ itthattāyā ti*).

But this answer did not satisfy the soul yearning for immortality, and we find a brahman student named Vacchagotta raising the same question: What happens to the *arahant* after death? Buddha's discourse to Vacchagotta[18] has been quoted by many a scholar[19] to show that the Buddha accepted an Ultimate Reality that is neither logically explanable nor conceptually describable. When the Buddha maintained that a monk with a freed mind (*vimuttacitta*) can be described neither as "will be reborn" nor as "will not be reborn," and so on, Vacchagotta was confused. And the Buddha pointed out that his confusion was justified, for "the dharma is profound, difficult to see, difficult to understand, peaceful, excellent, *beyond the sphere of logic*, subtle, and to be understood by the wise" (*gambhīro h'ayam . . . dhammo duddaso duranubodho santo paṇīto atakkâvacaro nipuṇo paṇḍitavedaṇīyo*). The reason for this is that it is not readily comprehended by one who holds a different view and has different leanings and inclinations, different involvement and instruction (*so . . . dujjāno aññadiṭṭhikena aññakhantikena aññarucikena aññatrayogena aññathâcariyakena*). It is clear from this statement that the conception of *nibbāna* is beyond logical reasoning (*atakkâvacara*), not because it is an Ultimate Reality transcending logic, but because logic or reason, being the 'slave of passions', makes it difficult for one who has a passion for an alien tradition to understand the conception of *nibbāna*. Vacchagotta was from the Brāhmaṇa tradition, hence deeply imbued with the belief in an immortal soul or 'self'. Such a person possibly could not accept any idea that would lead to a denial of this immortal 'self', and no *logic* could convince him of the truth of anything leading to such a denial.

From here it is easy to go on to understand the implications of the next passage in the *Aggi-Vacchagotta-sutta*:

> But if somebody should ask you, Vaccha: "This fire in front of you that is extinguished, in what direction has that fire gone from here, east, west, north, or south?" What would your answer to such a question be?

> That does not apply, O Gotama. For that fire that burned because of fuel consisting of straw and wood has consumed this, and not being given anything else is extinguished and therefore called 'extinguished' (*nibbuto*) through lack of fuel.
>
> Just so, the form (*rūpa*) by which one would like to designate the *tathāgata*, that form of the *tathāgata* is given up, its root is broken, uprooted like a palm, free from further growth and renewed existence in the future. The *tathāgata* is free from everything called form (*rūpa*), is deep, immeasurable, unfathomable, like the deep ocean. [The same is said with regard to the other aggregates—feeling, perception, disposition, and consciousness.][20]

The theory of the five aggregates (*pañcakkhandha*) in early Buddhism was intended to replace the belief in a permanent 'self' (*ātman*). Therefore, a person who upheld the belief in a 'self' would naturally be inclined to understand the dead *arahant* in terms of the five aggregates. The Buddha tries to prevent this by saying that the 'saint' (*tathāgata*) (who is dead) is free from everything called form (*rūpa*).

The statement that the *tathāgata* gives up the five aggregates after death and that these aggregates are completely destroyed does not mean that he exists in a different form, nor that he is completely annihilated. Just as it is impossible to know whether the *tathāgata* or the *arahant* survives death, even so it is not possible to know whether he is annihilated after death. If, after denying that the *tathāgata* survives death, the Buddha had maintained that he is annihilated, he would have been guilty of saying something that is not based or dependent on any source of knowledge. Hence, the most reasonable way to interpret the Buddha's statements on this problem and not misrepresent him would be to say that the state of the *arahant* after death cannot be known by the available means of knowing (*pamāṇa*, Sk. *pramāṇa*). This explains the Buddha's decision to leave these questions undeclared (*avyākata*). It is in this light only that we should interpret the Buddha's answer to the question raised in the *Suttanipāta*: "Is the one who has achieved the goal annihilated or is he eternally free from illness?" (*Atthaṅgato so uda vā so n'atthi udāhu ve sassatiyā arogo*).[21] And the Buddha's answer was:

> There is no measure of [or means of knowing] him who has achieved the goal. That by which one could define him [i.e., words or description], that is not for him. When all phenomena (*dhammā*) are removed, then all means of description are also removed.[22]

In the phrase "when all phenomena are removed," the word "phenomena" (*dhammā*) is sometimes interpreted as "mental processes." From this it is concluded:

> This would give an easily understandable psychological meaning. For one of the effects of meditation is to make the mind (*citta* or *viññāṇa*) stable and empty of mental contents (*dhammā*). As we know that *citta* was thought to survive, it can easily be understood that an empty *citta* is more difficult to read and recognize than the more complicated and desire-ridden normal *citta*: it is the more impersonal. In order to "read" a person's mind, there must be a mind to read and this mind must be as differentiated and rich in content as possible. *Sabbesu dhammesu samūhatesu* [when all phenomena are removed] may well imply the same psychological process as *viññāṇassa nirodhena* [with the cessation of consciousness] in *A* I 236.[23]

A careful examination of the contexts in which the word 'phenomenon' (*dhamma*) occurs in the early Buddhist texts shows without doubt that it conveys two distinct meanings: (1) phenomena or things in general, and (2) mental processes. It is possible to say that the phrase "when all phenomena are removed" (*sabbesu dhammesu samūhatesu*), when used to describe the living *arahant* (or for that matter, any person) who attains to the higher *jhānas*, may mean "when all mental processes are removed." Yet in the case of a dead *arahant* it would certainly mean "when all phenomena (his physical personality included) are removed," as is evident from the *Itivuttaka* passage describing the state of nirvana without substrate.

On the basis of this discussion we maintain that nirvana is the elimination of craving (*taṇhakkhaya*), hence a state of detachment (*virāga*). Because of this state of detachment, the *arahant* is free from suffering. Hence nirvana comes to be characterized as the end of suffering (*dukkhass' anta*) and a state of perfect happiness (*parama sukha*). This interpretation of nirvana will contradict the views expressed later in both Theravāda and Mahāyāna, according to which nirvana is something more than mere cessation of craving (*taṇhakkhaya*) or elimination of defilements (*kilesa pahāṇa*). The idea that nirvana represents a transcendental reality beyond any form of conceptualization or logical thinking has dominated Buddhist thought since the death of the Buddha.

Modern scholars too have made persistent attempts to see transcendentalism in early Buddhism. A careful analysis of their arguments reveals their futility and untenability. The most widely accepted view is the one according to which a person who attains nirvana reaches a form of transcendental consciousness "uncognizable by logical thought"[24] or "a level of consciousness . . . experienced as empty, impersonal, *undifferentiated*, peaceful, stable and immovable."[25]

The passages from the early texts often quoted in support of this view are found in the *Udāna*.[26] (My interpretation of these passages appears earlier in this chapter.) Before discussing these *Udāna* passages, Johansson examined the negative descriptions of nirvana in the early discourses and classified them into five groups. According to him, there is one group of negations that refer to the social world; another referring to conditions of life, such as birth, becoming, old age, and death; another, to the ethical state; still another, to a group of entirely psychological attributes negating the normal psychic processes; and finally, the epithets that represent nirvana as a complete contrast to the physical world.[27] Johansson then presents the theory that the third passage from the *Udāna* refers to "*personal conditions* before and after the attainment of *nibbāna*."[28] Scholars who commented on this passage earlier believed that it refers to nirvana as a metaphysical reality, something absolute, eternal, and uncompounded, and hence a sort of noumenal behind the phenomenal.[29] According to my understanding, both these views are untenable. Johansson seems to be interested in showing that the personal condition of the *arahant* before and after death is such that he is endowed with a "level of consciousness . . . experienced as empty, impersonal, undifferentiated, peaceful, stable and immovable." On the other hand, Dutt seems to present the age-old interpretation that nirvana, being the Ultimate Reality, is metaphysically similar to the Hindu Ātman/Brahman.

Having implied the existence of an undifferentiated consciousness in the living saint, Johansson makes an attempt to show that it is this higher form of consciousness that survives bodily death.[30] This, of course, is a view held by many scholars who have written on the subject. One of the arguments adduced in favor of this thesis is the fact that it is not only the *arahant* who has passed away who is considered to be deep, immeasurable, and as unfathomable as a deep ocean (*gambhiro appameyyo duppariyogāho seyyathā'pi mahāsamuddo*,[31] but even the living *arahant* is described as difficult to comprehend (*ananuvejjo*).[32] To quote Johansson: "In this life the *arahant* of course exists in the conventional meaning and although he still has his body and even his *citta*—a *citta* in purified and 'liberated' form—he cannot be known or recognized. As a physical recognition could not be any problem, I take it to mean that his *citta* or *viññāṇa* cannot be studied or even identified by means of mind reading (except by other arahants)." This fact is used by him to prove that "there is no essential difference between a living Tathāgata and a dead Tathāgata."[33]

I feel strongly that this is a very superficial comparison. The reason that the living *arahant* is said to be difficult to comprehend is quite different from the reason that the dead *arahant* is said to be immeasurable and unfathomable. A living *arahant* cannot be known easily by an ordinary person, nor even by gods (Indra, Brahmā, or Prajāpati),[34] because his ways are very different from their own. From their standpoint or according to their values, the *arahant* may even look like an abnormal person. But an *arahant* can be known by another *arahant*. On the other hand, the nature of the dead *arahant* cannot be known even by an *arahant*. Just as the origin of the universe is not known to an *arahant* because of the limitations of experience (see chapter 2 and appendix 1), even so, no one can have direct experience of the state of the dead *arahant* (except, of course, the dead *arahant* himself who unfortunately cannot come back to tell others of his experiences). When a dead *arahant* was compared to a great ocean, deep, immeasurable, and unfathomable, it meant only that there is *no way of knowing* what he is like. (It should be remembered that at the time the simile was used the ocean was considered unfathomable; hence, it was appropriate at the time to use that simile to illustrate the unknowability of the nature of the dead *arahant*.) Moreover, it would not be proper to conclude that "the quotation proves that the Tathāgata was thought to continue existing in some form after death, as the ocean certainly exists."[35] It cannot be denied that this is stretching the simile too far.

There certainly is a passage in the *Samyutta-nikāya* in which the question regarding the status of the dead *arahant* is discussed.[36] A monk named Yamaka is reported to have misrepresented the Buddha by maintaining that according to the Buddha "a brother who has destroyed the *āsavas* [i.e., cankers] is broken up and perishes when the body breaks up: he becomes not after death." Sāriputta, who confronts Yamaka on this issue, questions him with regard to the nature of the aggregates (*khandha*). Yamaka admits that all the aggregates are impermanent, whereupon Sāriputta points out that a person who realizes this fact puts an end to rebirth, and so on. Having stated this, Sāriputta raises the following questions:

1. Is the *tathāgata* (i.e., the person who has destroyed the *āsavas*) identical with the body (*rūpa*)? (The same with regard to the other aggregates.)
2. Is the *tathāgata* different from the body? (The same with regard to the other aggregates.)
3. Is the *tathāgata* in the body? (The same with regard to the other aggregates.)

It is significant that identical questions are raised regarding the nature of the soul or 'self' (*ātman*). In fact, the two questions—"Is the soul (*jiva*) identical with the body (*sarīra*)?" and "Is the soul different from the body?"—were considered to be metaphysical and left unanswered (*avyākata*) (see appendix 1). For this reason, the search for the ultimately real *tathāgata* is not different from the search for the 'self' (*ātman*). Finally, Sāriputta asks: "Since in this very life a *tathāgata* is not to be regarded as existing in truth, in reality, is it proper for you to assert: 'As I understand the doctrine taught by the Exalted One, in so far as a brother has destroyed the *āsavas*, he is broken up and perishes when the body is broken up: he becomes not after death'?" From this question of Sāriputta too, it becomes evident that the two types of questions—Does the *tathāgata* exist in truth and reality? and, Is the *tathāgata* annihilated after death?—are very similar. Both are metaphysical, and no empirical answers can be given. But it would be utterly improper and illogical to infer from this that there is no difference between the living *tathāgata* and the dead *tathāgata*.

Discussing the passage from the *Aggi-Vacchagotta-sutta*,[37] Johansson says:

> From these quotations we can see that the difference between the two stages of nibbāna is not very essential. In this life the fire can flare up again as there is fuel left: this is impossible after death, when there is no more fuel.[38] It is not possible to obtain a direct answer to the question what happens to the arahant in death, as the Buddha has always refused to give an answer (D III 135, D II 168). But some indications can be gleaned. We know from the last quotation that he is like a fire that is extinguished. So what was the early Buddhist position about the extinct fire? Evidently, it was not thought to be annihilated, as the Buddha here changes over to another analogy: the deep, immeasurable ocean."[39]

Here too we find that, while recognizing the fact that the Buddha refused to answer the question as to what happens to the *arahant* after death, Johansson was trying to find some indications. Hence, he raises the question; "So what was the early Buddhist position about the extinct fire?" And the Buddha or the early Buddhists would certainly have replied, *n'eso kallo pañho*, "It is not a proper question." Even Vacchagotta himself admitted this with the words, *na upeti bho Gotama*, "Gotama, that does not apply." The change of analogy from fire to the deep, immeasurable ocean seems to have been done deliberately by the Buddha who anticipated questions like the ones raised with regard to the fire, questions such as "Where did the extinct fire go?" And it may be observed here that the attempt to give answers to questions that the Buddha himself, for a variety of reasons, refused to answer has been the bane of Buddhist scholarship, classical as well as modern.

Finally, in order to show that *citta* (mind) survives in *nibbāna*, Johansson has made a persistent attempt to show a difference between *citta* and *viññāṇa* (consciousness). He says:

> It remains to be said about *viññāṇa*, that it is probably one aspect of *citta* or a name for some of the processes of *citta*. Both are said to be involved in rebirth: the instrumental processes are the *viññāṇa* processes of *citta*. The basis of rebirth (*ārammaṇa*, *upādāna*) is the intense wish (*upādāna*) to go on living. When *viññāṇa* has stopped, there are practically

no *viññāṇa*-processes left in *citta* and there is no base for rebirth.[40]

This dichotomy of *citta* and *viññāṇa*-processes proposed by Johansson goes against the nonsubstantialist position of early Buddhism and is not warranted according to the early Buddhist texts. In fact, there are specific statements in the early texts to the effect that the terms *citta*, *mano*, and *viññāṇa* are synonyms.[41] Common sense suggests parts and wholes, substances and attributes. But on closer examination it would seem that there are no wholes apart from parts, no substances apart from attributes. The concept of 'self' (*ātman*) was, in a way, intended to unify the different experiences. But is there any 'self', the Buddhist may ask, when these experiences are removed? If we suppose there is, how do we know? (see appendix 1). From individual experience we infer only that there must be a whole of which the parts are parts.[42] The conception of *citta* as presented by Johansson is, therefore, not much different from the conception of 'self' (*ātman*), which, as pointed out in chapter 1, was rejected by the Buddha as a metaphysical principle. It is true that the word *citta* never occurs in the early Buddhist texts in the description of rebirth (except in the later commentarial literature where the words *cuticitta*, 'thought at the moment of death', *paṭisandhicitta*, 'thought at the moment of rebirth' and *carimakacitta*, 'last thought moment [of the *arahant*]' occur in connection with death and rebirth). It is almost always the word *viññāṇa* that occurs in this connection. This is because the term *viññāṇa*, while being used as a synonym of *citta* and *mano* to mean consciousness in general, has two other uses, the cognitive and the eschatological. For instance, in examples like 'visual consciousness' (*cakkhuviññāṇa*), it is used to refer to a cognitive process, and in examples like 'stream of consciousness' (*viññāṇa-sota*), it is used in an eschatological sense. The term *citta* came to be used as a generic term. But nowhere do we find a reference to the view that *citta* is manifest without the mental coefficients. And this fact is emphasized even in the Abhidharma where we come across a distinction between *citta* (mind) and *cetasika* (mental coefficients).

Another statement in the Pali Nikāyas, already quoted, that may be taken to support the view that there is another form of existence to which the *arahant* attains after death is the one occurring everywhere in connection with the declaration of gnosis (*aññā*) on the part of the enlightened ones. It runs thus: "Rebirth has been destroyed; the higher life has been lived; what has to be done has been done; and there is no further tendency toward 'this-ness' (i.e., rebirth)." The phrase "there is no tendency toward this-ness," (*nâparaṃ itthattāya*) could be interpreted as implying that there is a different form of existence, a form of transcendental existence. But this would be to read one's own thought into it. In fact, the Chinese translation of this passage always reads: "There is no future existence" (*pu yu hou yu*), without any qualification as to whether it is transcendental or worldly.

Although Johansson feels that "it is fairly well documented that *citta* was thought to survive death,"[43] the passage he quotes need not necessarily be interpreted as implying the idea of survival of the saint. He refers to a passage at *S* 5.370, where it is said: "[Even if the body is devoured by crows and vultures] yet his *citta*, if for a long time practiced with faith, virtue, learning, and renunciation, soars aloft and wins the excellent." "Soars aloft" should not be interpreted too literally to mean that the *citta* rises above the body and survives in death. "The excellent" won might as well be the nirvana with substrate. If *citta* was thought to survive the death of the *arahant*, there is no reason why the Buddha should not have openly declared it to be so. In fact, he would have had no difficulty in explaining immortality (*amata*) if he had maintained that *citta* survives death. But to insist on saying that something survives, when the Buddha himself refused to answer either in the positive or in the negative, would be to misrepresent (*abbhācikkhana*) his teachings.

As has been pointed out repeatedly, what he maintained was that prediction with regard to things about which we know nothing, because of the limitations of empiricism, would be futile and would constitute mere speculation leading to all kinds of conflicting views. Jayatilleke, in his *Early Buddhist Theory of Knowledge*, made a great effort to show that early Buddhism was empiricist and did not accept any metaphysical principle or any empirically unverifiable entity. But the interpretations of Buddhism by Western, Hindu, and Far Eastern scholars were so overwhelming that in the end he admitted the existence of a "transempirical which cannot be empirically described and understood but which can be realized and attained [after death],"[44] thereby undermining the whole basis of Buddhist empiricism which he was endeavouring to establish. If, after the Buddha has said that the *arahant* after death cannot be described as existing (*atthi*) or as not existing (*n'atthi*), without any qualifications as to whether that existence is empirical or transempirical, and we continue to say that the *arahant* survives and is not annihilated, we are merely trying to understand this question according to our own likes (*ruci*) and dislikes (*aruci*), or according to our inclinations (*chanda*). Here, no doubt, the human inclination to survive (*jīvitukāma*, *amaritukāma*; see chapter 5) intervenes in attempts to interpret the question regarding the dead saint. This is one of the reasons why the Buddha considered these questions to be 'not within the sphere of logic' (*atakkâvacara*) (see appendix 1).

If early Buddhism accepted a transempirical reality, there was no reason why the Hindus should have considered the Buddha a heretic. It should be remembered that the Buddha was made an *avatār*, an 'incarnation', of Viṣṇu, not during his own lifetime, but centuries later when Mahāyāna with its transcendentalism reached the highest point of its development. If it is maintained that early Buddhism recognized a transempirical reality, it should not be considered different from any other form of transcendentalism or absolutism.

Notes

1. Rune E. A. Johansson, *Psychology of Nirvana* (London: George Allen & Unwin, 1969).
2. Ibid., pp. 9–10.
3. *It* 38f.; *TD* 2.579a.
4. *D* 2.157. Emphasis mine.
5. *D* 2.156.
6. *A* 2.5f.; *GS* 2.6.
7. Ibid.
8. *S* 3.83 ff.
9. *D* 3.260; *TD* 1.52b.
10. *Sn* 268.
11. *Thag* 1002–1003.
12. *S* 1.174; *TD* 2.407c.
13. *Ud* 80–81.
14. *D* 2.130.
15. *S* 4.294; *TD* 2.150.
16. This seems to be the conclusion reached by Bhikkhu Ñāṇananda in his book, *Concept and Reality in Early Buddhist Thought*, p. 18.

17. *It* 38.
18. *M* 1.483 ff.
19. T. R. V. Murti, *The Central Philosophy of Buddhism* (London: George Allen & Unwin, 1955), pp. 44 ff.
20. *M* 1.487.
21. *Sn* 1075.
22. *Sn* 1076.
23. Johansson, *Psychology of Nirvana*, p. 64.
24. Conze, *Buddhist Thought in India*, pp. 76 f.
25. Johansson, *Psychology of Nirvana*, p. 56. Emphasis mine.
26. *Ud* 80 f.
27. *Psychology of Nirvana*, pp. 45 ff.
28. Ibid., p. 54. See also p. 46.
29. Nalinaksa Dutt, *Early Monastic Buddhism* (Calcutta: Calcutta Oriental Book Agency, 1960), p. 288.
30. *Psychology of Nirvana*, p. 60.
31. *M* 1.486; *TD* 2.245.
32. *M* 1.140.
33. *Psychology of Nirvana*, p. 61.
34. *M* 1.140.
35. Johansson, *Psychology of Nirvana*, p. 61.
36. *S* 3.110; *TD* 2.31a–b.
37. *M* 1.486.
38. It is not possible to understand what Johansson means by fuel here, whether it is attachment (*rāga*), hate (*dosa*), or confusion (*moha*), or whether it is the physical personality. If it is maintained that the fire can flare up again, it is tantamount to saying that the *arahant* can fall from his *arahat*ship—a theory advocated by the later school of Sarvâstivādins.
39. *Psychology of Nirvana*, pp. 60 f.
40. Ibid., pp. 76 f. See also p. 61.
41. *S* 2.95.
42. Cf. the commonsense notion of a thing and its parts or states, as explained by L. S. Stebbing, *A Modern Introduction to Logic* (London: Methuen, 1961), pp. 265 ff.
43. Johansson, *Psychology of Nirvana*, p. 62.
44. *Early Buddhist Theory of Knowledge*, pp. 475 f.

Selected Readings

PRIMARY SOURCES

Mahā-parinibbāna-suttanta (*D* 2.72 ff.); 'The Book of Great Decease' (*SBB* 3.78 ff.); *TD* 1.11 ff.

Alagaddūpama-sutta (*M* 1.130ff.); 'Discourse on the Parable of the Water-snake' (*MLS* 1.167ff.); *TD* 1.763ff.
Tevijja-Vacchagotta-sutta (*M* 1.481ff.); 'Discourse to Vacchagotta on the Three-fold Knowledge' (*MLS* 2.159ff.)
Aggi-Vacchagotta-sutta (*M* 1.483ff.); 'Discourse to Vacchagotta on Fire' (*MLS* 2.162ff.); *TD* 2.245ff.
Udāna, *Pāṭaligāmiya-vagga* (*Ud* 80ff.); 'Verses of Uplift' (*Minor Anthologies of the Pali Canon*, tr. F. L. Woodward, London; PTS, 1955, 2.97ff.)
Itivuttaka, *Duka-nipāta* (*It* 31ff.); 'As It Was Said' (*Minor Anthologies of the Pali Canon*, 2.132ff.); *TD* 2.579.

SECONDARY SOURCES

de la Vallée Poussin, L. *Nirvana*. Paris: G. Beauchesne, 1925.
Grimm, George. *The Doctrine of the Buddha*. Pp. 229–267.
Horner, I. B. *The Early Buddhist Theory of Man Perfected. A Study of the Arahan*. London; Williams & Norgate, 1936.
Jayatilleke, K. N. *Early Buddhist Theory of Knowledge*. Pp. 464–476.
Johansson, Rune E. A. *The Psychology of Nirvana*. London; George Allen & Unwin, 1969.
Nyanaponika Thera. *Anattā and Nibbāna*.
Rahula, Walpola. *What the Buddha Taught*. Pp. 35–44.
Stcherbatsky, T. I. *The Conception of Buddhist Nirvana*. Leningrad: The Academy of Sciences of the USSR, 1927.
Thomas, E. J. *History of Buddhist Thought*. Pp. 119–132.

Later Buddhism

Chapter Eight
Beginnings of Scholasticism and Mahāyāna

The "Discourse on the Great Decease" (*Mahāparinibbāna-suttanta*),[1] which relates the incidents connected with the last days of the Buddha, recounts two episodes which are of great significance for an understanding of the major developments that took place in the history of Buddhist thought during the two subsequent centuries.

The first is the occasion when the Buddha, shortly before he passed away, advised Ānanda regarding the future of the Order. The Buddha is represented as saying:

> If, Ānanda, it occurs to you: "The doctrine is such that it is rendered teacherless; we are without a teacher," you should not consider it so. Ānanda, whatever doctrine I have taught and discipline I have instituted, that will be your teacher after my death.[2]

The reluctance on the part of the Buddha to appoint one of his disciples to lead the Order of monks and his request, instead, that the monks consider the doctrine (*dhamma*) and the discipline (*vinaya*) their guide, led his disciples to concentrate their attention more on the problem of determining the nature of the doctrine and the discipline than they would otherwise have done.

Moreover, even during the Buddha's lifetime, there were instances when his teachings were misinterpreted. Two of the more prominent of these instances are recorded in the *Majjhima-nikāya*. The first was the statement by a monk named Ariṭṭha that the pleasures of sense, according to the Buddha, are not 'stumbling blocks' (*antarāyikā dhammā*).[3] The other was the case of the monk Sāti who insisted that in the Buddha's teaching, it is the 'consciousness' (*viññāṇa*) that transmigrates and not something else.[4] While the Buddha was alive he was kept informed of such misconceptions and immediately took steps to eradicate them.

Furthermore, a set of three important discourses—*Pāsādika-suttanta*,[5] *Saṅgīti-suttanta*,[6] and *Sāmagāma-sutta*—refer to the death of the Jaina leader Nigaṇṭha Nātaputta and the conflicts that arose in the Jaina Order after his death. When the Buddha was informed of this, he declared:

> Wherefore, Cunda, do you, to whom I have made known the truths that I have perceived, come together in company and rehearse all of you together those doctrines and quarrel not over them, but compare the meaning with meaning, phrase with phrase, in order that this true doctrine may last long and be perpetuated, in order that it may continue to be for the good and happiness of the great multitude, out of love for the world, to the good and gain and weal of gods and men.[8]

This certainly would have induced the monks to collect all the discourses preached by the Buddha even during his lifetime. But the necessity for doing this was felt even more strongly after the Buddha's death, and for this reason the task of collecting the discourses delivered by him to various people at different times at different places was carried out with unabated enthusiasm. This seems to have been the major undertaking of those who took part in the first Council held three months after the passing away of the Buddha.

This Council, no doubt, marks the beginning of scholasticism. The first hundred years following the Buddha's death saw the collection and classification of the whole mass of discourses into five groups (*nikāya*), as also the greater part of the disciplinary rules (*vinaya*) in a separate collection. Scholastic activity did not stop there. The study of this whole collection of discourses, whose style was characterized by the use of similes, anecdotes, illustrations, and, above all, the unending repetitions, must certainly have appeared cumbersome, especially at a time when it was feared that the teachings would be misinterpreted. Just as the collection of discourses was necessary for the perpetuation of the Buddha's teachings, the listing and classification of the basic doctrines, scattered all through the discourses, was considered indispensable for preventing any misinterpretation. Thus, in the three discourses mentioned above—*Pāsādika, Saṅgīti and Sāmagāma*—we find listed the most important doctrines. While the complete discourses were handed down by word of mouth, an attempt was also made to list and classify the main 'topics' (*mātikā*, Sk. *mātṛkā*), such as 'aggregates' (*khandha*), 'elements' (*dhātu*), and 'gateways' (of sense perception) (*āyatana*), on which the Buddha had discoursed. These became the nucleus of the third collection of canonical texts, the *Abhidharma Piṭaka*, dealing mostly with philosophical analysis and synthesis. Two distinct versions of the *Abhidharma Piṭaka* are found, one written in Pali and preserved by the Theravāda tradition in Ceylon, and the other written in Sanskrit and belonging to the Sarvâstivāda school. These two groups of texts, together with their ancillary literature, represent the scholastic tradition in Buddhist thought.

The second event of significance mentioned in the "Discourse on the Great Decease" is the lamentation of gods and men (including Ānanda who had not then attained *arahant*-ship) on hearing of the imminent death of the Buddha. Following are the words of the lamenting gods:

> The Blessed One passes away too soon; the Well-gone One passes away to soon; the eye of the world disappears too soon.[9]

On the other hand, Ānanda laments a different loss:

> Lord, in the past, the monks who had observed the rainy season came from different directions too see the Tathāgata. This gave us the opportunity of seeing and associating with these noble-minded monks. But, Lord, after the passing away of the Blessed One, we will miss this opportunity of seeing and associating with such noble-minded monks.[10]

In both laments is an expression of the feeling of a certain vacuum created in the lives of the ordinary followers with the passing away of the Buddha. The Buddha's advice to all of them was this:

> There are four places which should be seen by, and which create emotion in the clansmen with faith. Which four? "Here the Tathāgata was born"; this, Ānanda, is a place which should be seen and which creates emotion in the clansmen with faith. "Here the Tathāgata attained supreme and perfect enlightenment." . . . "Here the Tathāgata set the

incomparable wheel of *dhamma* rolling." . . . "Here the Tathāgata passed away in the element of *nibbāna* without substrate left"; this, Ānanda, is a place which is seen by and which creates emotion in the clansmen with faith.[11]

Ordinary people are generally led by their emotions (*saṃvega*). Even though emotions tend to obscure the perception of truth and, therefore, ought to be controlled on reaching the higher levels of spiritual development, yet religious emotions add color to the lives of ordinary people and enable them to improve their lot spiritually. The Buddha pointed out that faithful devotees—monks and nuns, male and female lay followers—will visit these four places which are apt to arouse emotion.[12]

This second incident reveals the manner in which the Buddha's disciples (excluding the *arahants*) felt the need for the perpetuation of the memory of their great teacher. This led to an insatiable thirst for knowledge regarding the life as well as the nature of the Buddha. The result was the compilation of texts like the *Buddhavaṃsa* and the *Jātaka-nidāna-kathā* in Pali and the *Mahāvastu*, the *Avadānas*, and the *Lalitavistara* in Sanskrit. These works, although they embody some historical kernels regarding the life of the Buddha, are mainly devoted to speculation on the nature of the Buddha. This aspect was emphasized by the Mahāsāṅghikas who took up the cause of the ordinary followers needing religious edification. The Mahāyāna is the culmination of this trend.

Notes

1. *D* 2.72ff.
2. *D* 2.154.
3. *M* 1.130ff.; *TD* 1.763.
4. *M* 1.256ff.; *TD* 1.766.
5. *D* 3.117ff.; *TD* 1.72ff.
6. *D* 3.272ff.; *TD* 1.49ff.
7. *M* 2.243ff.; *TD* 1.752ff.
8. *D* 3.127; cf. *TD* 1.73.
9. *D* 2.140.
10. Ibid.
11. Ibid.
12. *D* 2.141.

Chapter Nine
Scholasticism—Theravāda, Sarvâstivāda, and Sautrāntika

The doctrines elaborated in the Abhidharma literature belonging to both Theravāda[1] and Sarvâstivāda are too numerous to be treated in a short chapter. Hence, I shall attempt to pick out the most important philosophical trends in the Abhidharma literature and show their relationships to the teachings of early Buddhism, and also to examine the way in which they contribute to the development of Mahāyāna philosophy. All three schools examined in this chapter accept the basic teachings of the Buddha; the differences among them have arisen as a result of the differing interpretations given to these doctrines. No attempt will be made here to sort out the teachings of the three schools and present them separately. Instead, each philosophical problem will be considered separately and the interpretation given by each school will be explained.

Scholasticism in Buddhism arose, as pointed out in chapter 8, because of the need to perpetuate the teachings of the Buddha without allowing dissentions to mar its unity.[2] One of the methods adopted for this purpose was to collect and classify the basic teachings of the Buddha, as in the *Saṅgīti-suttanta*, so that there would be no disagreement, at least with regard to them. In the process of selecting and enumerating these basic doctrines, the usual method of exposition adopted by the Buddha was modified. The use of similes, anecdotes, illustrations, and the like, which played an important role in the discourses, was abandoned. This difference was noted by the classical scholars themselves,[3] who observed that the discourses were originally taught in the discursive style (*sappariyāya desanā*), which makes free use of the simile, the metaphor, and the anecdote, while the nondiscursive style (*nippariyāya desanā*), which employs a very select, precise, and impersonal terminology, is characteristic of the Abhidharma.

Although this was the original distinction between the discourses (*suttanta*) and the scholastic treatises (*abhidhamma*), as time passed, various other distinctions came to be recognized. For example, the discourses were looked upon as popular teachings (*vohāra desanā*) and the Abhidharma as discourses on Ultimate Reality (*paramattha desanā*).[4] The earlier distinction refers to style only, but the latter implies a difference regarding the very subject matter. This led to emphasis on the difference between *dhamma* and *abhidhamma*, the latter being defined as "special *dhamma*" (*abhivisiṭṭho dhammo*). While the discourses were looked upon as dealing with *dhamma*, the Abhidharma treated of the special *dhamma* or Ultimate Reality (*paramattha*).

A later Theravāda scholiast takes *abhidhamma* to mean "the analysis (of *dhamma*) into mind and matter" (*nāmarūpapariccheda*).[5] According to him, the preachings in the discourses (*sutta* or *suttanta*) that pertain to *dhamma* consist of *dhamma* in terms of morality (*sīla*) and mental culture (*samādhi*); the teachings in the 'discipline' (*vinaya*) pertain to transgression (*āpatti*) and nontransgression (*anāpatti*); but the sphere of the Abhidharma is the analysis of reality into mind (*nāma*) and matter (*rūpa*). The Sarvâstivādins too defined *abhidharma* as "analysis of *dharma*" (*dharma pravicaya*) and claimed it to be pure wisdom (*amalā prajñā*). In both traditions, the enlightenment (*bodhi*) of the Buddha is said to consist of this *dharma-pravicaya* or *nāmarūpapariccheda*. The belief that the Buddha preached the Abhidharma to the gods, and not to human beings, seems to symbolize the exalted position accorded it.

This exalted status of the *abhidharma* signaled the beginning of the absolutist tendency in Buddhism. Mind and matter came to be recognized as Ultimate Reality (*paramattha*). In fact, according to a later Abhidharma manual, even *nibbāna* is to be included under the category of mind.[6] I do not propose to examine the different lists of ultimate categories presented in the two main Abhidharma traditions.[7]

When phenomena were analysed into two distinct groups of reality as mind and matter, the Ābhidharmikas had to provide a definition of each of them. Thus mind (*citta*) or mental coefficients (*cetasika*) came to be defined as nonmaterial (*a-rūpa*) and matter (*rūpa*), as nonmental (*a-cetasika*, *cittavippayutta*). Thus was created a sharp dichotomy between these two elements, leaving the Ābhidharmikas with several philosophical problems that are generally associated with dualism.

One of these major problems is the difficulty of explaining the process of perception. The question was, How is it that the mind, which is of a completely different nature, comes to be sensitive to matter? This problem, though implicit in the Pali Abhidhamma, was really made explicit by Buddhaghosa when he said, "Where there is difference of kind, there is no stimulus. The Ancients (*porāṇā*) say that sensory stimulus is of similar kinds, not of different kinds."[8] To explain this problem, the Ābhidharmikas made use of the analysis of matter (*rūpa*) as it was found in early Buddhism. According to the discourses, matter (*rūpa*) consists of the four great or primary elements or existents (*cattāro mahābhūtā*) and derived elements (*upādāya rūpa*).[9] But in the discourses we do not find any attempt to speculate on the nature of the primary elements by going beyond experience. When the question was raised regarding the primary elements—earth, water, fire, and air—the only definition given was in terms of experience, that is, the manner in which the individual is affected by them. For example, earth is defined as that which is hard (*kakkhala*) and rigid (*kharigata*), and so on.[10] But the question whether there is anything beyond hardness and rigidness was neither raised nor answered, for that would be contrary to the empiricist standpoint.

However, according to the Abhidharma, a distinction between a thing (*dhamma*) and its characteristic (*lakkhaṇa*), though not really existing, is necessary for the sake of definition or determination (*kappanā*).[11] (This, of course, is to forget the fact that *abhidhamma* is discourse on Ultimate Reality, *paramattha*, rather than on 'conventional truth', *vohāra*!) It is this kind of analysis that paved the way for the emergence of the theory of 'substance' (*sabhāva*, Sk. *svabhāva*) in the post-Buddhaghosan Theravāda as well as in Sarvâstivāda. It seems to have been arrived at in the same way in which John Locke, the British empiricist, presenting a similar form of dualism, arrived at the idea of substance. He says:

> The idea then we have, to which we give the general name substance, being nothing but the supposed, but unknown support of those qualities we find existing, which we imagine cannot subsist, *sine re substante*, without something to support them, we call that support *substantia*; which according to the true import of the word, is in plain English, standing under or upholding.[12]

Although for Locke substance was a mere idea, for the Ābhidharmikas (as for Descartes who also presented a dualistic theory), it was something more than that. It was the very basis of derived matter (*upādāya rūpa*); hence it was itself not derived (*no upādā*) or is irreducible.[13] It was the *material substance*. This theory of a 'substance' or 'substratum' (*svabhāva*) was, therefore, the inevitable consequence of the rigid dichotomy between mind (*nāma*) and matter (*rūpa*).

In the same way, the Ābhidharmika analysis of psychic phenomena (*nāma*) into two types, mind (*citta*) and mental coefficients (*cetasika*), leads ultimately to a theory of *mental substance*. As in the case of the analysis of matter, the Ābhidharmikas were hard put to it to explain mental phenomena without positing a kind of substrate that gives a certain unity to the different mental elements (*sabbasaṅgāhaka*).[14] The mental coefficients (*cetasika*) are here defined as "those which are associated with the mind (*citta-sampayuttā*) and arising in the mind (*citte bhavā*)."[15] The very recognition of the mind (*citta*) as an entity distinct from the mental coefficients (*cetasika*) would finally lead to a substantialist view of mental phenomena.

This is the dualism that is characteristic of the entire Abhidharma philosophy. Although the 'self' (*ātman*) or, to use an expression from Gilbert Ryle, 'the ghost in the machine' was eliminated, the machine itself became a substance, an Ultimate Reality, a status it did not have in early Buddhism.

These ideas constitute the common stock of the two Abhidharma traditions, Theravāda and Sarvâstivāda, and are generally opposed by the Sautrāntikas, who made a persistent effort to remain faithful to the original discourses—hence their name, Sautrāntika (*sūtrānta-ika*). They considered the discourses as primary sources (*sūtrapramāṇika*), while the Sarvâstivādins claimed that the Abhidharma was the primary source (*śāstrapramāṇika*). But in spite of their dependence on the discourses, the Sautrāntikas have accepted certain doctrines that are not found there, but which may be considered later developments. These are the doctrines of moments (*khaṇavāda*, Sk. *kṣaṇavāda*) and atomism (*paramâṇuvāda*), which are found in all the scholastic schools of Buddhism—post-Buddhaghosa Theravāda, Sarvâstivāda, and Sautrāntika. Significantly, they are not found in the pre-Buddhaghosa Theravāda tradition.[16]

Instead of the early Buddhist definition of impermanence (*anicca*, Sk. *anitya*) as arising (*uppāda*), passing away (*vaya*), and the change of what exists (*ṭhitassa aññathatta*) (see chapter 4), the Sarvâstivādins, as a result of the logical analysis of the process of change, commuted impermanence in terms of nascent (*jāti*), static (*sthiti*), decaying (*jarā*), and cessant (*nāśa*) moments,[17] taking "change of what exists" (*ṭhitassa aññathatta*, Sk. *sthityânya-thātva*) as signifying two moments, static (*sthiti*) and decaying (*anyathātva-jarā*). Post-Buddhaghosa Theravāda refers to three moments, nascent (*uppāda*), static (*ṭhiti*), and cessant (*bhaṅga*).[18] The Sautrāntikas, on the other hand, accepted two moments only, the nascent (*utpāda*) and the cessant (*vyaya*), and rejected the static moment (*sthitikṣaṇa*) in the hope of being more faithful to the theory of impermanence in early Buddhism.[19]

As a result of the acceptance of the theory of moments in one or the other of these forms, the scholiasts were faced with several philosophical problems, the solutions to which created substantial doctrinal differences. Two of the major spheres in which the scholiasts had to face problems resulting from this theory of moments are perception and causality.

Let us consider first the problem of perception. The two schools that recognized a static moment put forward a theory of direct perception. Since the object of perception was believed to exist for at least one moment, the object is said to come into focus at this static moment and thus would be directly perceived. Here one could raise the issue that, although the external object comes into focus at the static moment, a complete perception is not had as a result of this contact because perception is a rather complicated process involving memory, recognition, understanding, or assimilation, and so on. Hence the object should remain for more than one moment if the whole process of perception is to be completed. Not only the continued existence of the object, but also continuity of the mental process should be available.

In the process of explaining these problems, Buddhaghosa presented an ingenious theory, based on the general remark made by the Buddha that thought changes faster than the physical body.[20] In his commentary on the *Vibhaṅga*, Buddhaghosa maintains that sixteen thought moments arise and cease to exist during the lifetime of a single moment of matter. The moment or point-instant of matter that arises at the same time as a moment of thought dies simultaneously with the seventeenth moment of the existence of thought.[21] He refers to the various moments in the process of perception, such as those of attending to, receiving, examining, determining, and registering the external object. Anuruddha's *Compendium of Philosophy* (*Abhidhammatthasaṅgaha*) gives an elaborately worked out theory which follows the general pattern set out by Buddhaghosa.

The process of perception, according to Anuruddha, begins with the vibration of the unconscious process (*bhavaṅga*) for two moments, and in the second moment the unconscious mind is cut off. The succeeding moments are those of attention (i.e., attention at the five doors of sense, *pañcadvārâvajjana*), sensation (*cakkhuviññāna*), assimilation (*sampaṭicchana*), seven moments of cognition (*javana*), and two of registration (*tadārammaṇa*). By adding one moment of thought at the beginning of the process of perception, a thought moment which occurs before the material object comes into contact with the sense organ, the number of thought moments totals seventeen.[22]

It is important to note that, as a result of the analysis of the process of perception into discrete moments, the Ābhidharmikas had to posit the existence of a mental base or substance on which the different objects leave their impressions and which maintains continuity of the discrete moments. The formulation of the theory of the unconscious mental process (*bhavaṅga*) was the direct result. It was a kind of repository of all the impressions, and it was this same theory of the unconscious that later developed into the theory of the 'store consciousness' (*ālayavijñāna*) of the Yogācāra school (see chapter 12) and which was looked upon by the other schools of Buddhism as a 'substantialist theory', an *ātmavāda* in disguise. It is in a sense a mental substance.

The Sarvâstivādins, too, by accepting the conception of a static moment, contributed to a theory of direct perception. According to the *Abhidharmadīpa*,

> The substance called eye is of the nature of that which sees [a "seer"]. In it is produced an action of seeing, when its power is awakened on account of the emergence of the totality of its causes and conditions. The eye does not apprehend independently of consciousness (*vijñāna*), nor does the eye-consciousness know the object unsupported by the active eye. The eye as well as eye-consciousness, with the help of such accessories as light, cooperate simultaneously toward bringing the perception of a given object. The object, the eye, the eye-consciousness, and the light, all manifest

> their power, i.e., become active and flash forth simultaneously. The object appears, the eye sees, and the eye-consciousness knows it. This is called the direct knowledge of an object.[23]

Thus the Sarvâstivādins as well as the later Theravādins have attempted to justify direct perception as well as the real existence of the object. For this reason, they may be designated realists.

The Sautrāntikas, who denied the conception of a static moment (*sthitikṣaṇa*) were, on the other hand, compelled to accept a theory of indirect perception. Going on the premise that an object must endure if it is to be available for cognition, the Sautrāntikas maintained that, since both the object and consciousness are without duration, there cannot be direct perception of the external object. The commentary on the *Abhidharmadīpa* refers to the argument put forward by the Dārṣṭāntikas (another name for the Sautrāntikas) as follows:

> The organs and the objects of the five sense-consciousnesses, being causes of the latter, belong to a past moment. When the object (*rūpa*) and the eye exist, the visual consciousness is nonexistent. When visual consciousness exists, the eye and the object are not existing. In the absence of their duration (*sthiti*) there is no possibility of the cognition of the object.[24]

This led them to conclude that "all [sense] perceptions are indirect" (*apratyakṣa*).[25] The Sautrāntikas held that the subject is capable of receiving an impression of the likeness of the object. What is directly cognized is this impression or representation of the object and not the object itself which, by the time of cognition, is a thing of the past. The object is merely inferred on the basis of the sense impression. This is the representative theory of perception, or the theory of the inferability of the external object (*bāhyârthânumeya-vāda*).[26] These then are some of the divergent theories of perception developed from the theory of moments.

The acceptance of the theory of atoms (*paramâṇu*) also created innumerable logical problems for the scholiasts, with the result that their adversaries, the Mādhyamikas, took advantage of the weakness of their solutions to justify the Mahāyāna transcendentalism.

The Sarvâstivādins upheld the theory that the object of perception is an aggregate of atoms (*paramâṇusaṅghāta*). They believed that the atoms exist individually, and that when they are in aggregate form (*saṅghātarūpa*) they become perceptible. But this aggregate is not a unity (*eka*); it is a multiplicity only (*aneka*). The neo-Sarvâstivādins, led by Saṅghabhadra, tried to avoid this paradox by insisting that "the individual atoms, when they do not depend on others or are not related to others (*anyanirapekṣa*) are imperceptible (*atîndriya*), but that they are grasped by the senses when they are in a multitude (*bahavaḥ*) and when they depend on each other (*parasparâpekṣa*) for their existence."[27] The Sautrāntikas, although claiming that the external object is not directly perceived, spoke of the atoms that go to form the object. They maintained that the atoms are indivisible units which can coalesce or mingle together to form an object. Thus, while the Sarvâstivādins believed in the aggregation (*saṅghāta*) of atoms, the Sautrāntikas advocated the coalescence (*saṃyoga*) of atoms.[28] A criticism of these different theories is found in Dinnāga's *Ālambanaparīkṣā*, and it is interesting to note that he adduced empirical arguments to refute these atomic theories.[29]

The most noticeable differences between early Buddhism and these later schools are those having to do with the interpretation of causality (*paṭiccasamuppāda*). Here too, the differences arose as a result of the acceptance of the theory of moments (*kṣaṇa*), which made it difficult for the scholiasts to explain causal continuity.

The emergence of the conception of substance (*svabhāva*) in the Abhidharma traditions was referred to earlier. The Sarvâstivādins made full use of this concept to explain the problem of continuity of phenomena, which they analyzed into momentary existences. Four different theories were suggested by the four famous Sarvâstivāda teachers—Dharmatrāta, Ghoṣaka, Vasumitra, and Buddhadeva.[30]

Dharmatrāta upheld a theory of change of existences (*bhāvânyathātva*). He maintained that when a *dharma* passes through the three periods of time, there is a change of existence or state (*bhāva*), but not of substance (*dravya* = *svabhāva*). This is illustrated with the example of gold, which may be seen in various shapes or forms, while the gold itself remains unchanged.

Ghoṣaka propounded a theory of change of characteristics or aspects (*lakṣaṇânyathātva*). A past *dharma*, according to him, is possessed of the characteristic of pastness, but dispossessed of the characteristics of presentness and futurity, like a man who is attached to one woman, but is at the same time not unattached to other women.

Vasumitra's was a theory of change of condition (*avasthânyathātva*); he held that a *dharma* passing through the three periods of time, having come to each state or condition, is called past or present or future. The state or condition is determined by the causal efficiency or causal activity (*arthakriyā-kāritva* or *kāritra*). If the causal efficiency is present, it is called the present; if the causal efficiency is no more, it is called the past; and if the efficiency is not yet manifest, it is called the future. In like manner, a coin placed in a group of one hundred coins is said to be one of a hundred; if placed in a pile of a thousand, it is one of a thousand.

Finally, Buddhadeva proposed a theory of change of relations (*anyonyathātva*). A *dharma* is said to be past in relation to the present and future, present in relation to the past and future, and future in relation to the past and present. It is like a woman who is a mother in relation to her daughter and a daughter in relation to her own mother.

According to all four theories, there is one aspect of a *dharma* that changes, while another remains unchanged. That which remains unchanged is the basis or the substance (*dravya*) of a thing. It is this doctrine, which maintains that the 'existence' (*astitva*) of the substance of 'everything' (*sarva*) remains unchanged during the three periods of time, past, present, and future, that gave the Sarvâstivādins their name.

The theory that 'substance' (*svabhāva*) remains unchanged was used to explain the connection between cause and effect. For example, the argument goes, a mango seed gives rise to a mango tree and not to any other tree. The 'mango-ness' of the mango tree exists because that 'mango-ness' was found in the mango seed. 'Mango-ness' is the substance or 'own nature' which connects the seed and the tree. Identity was therefore maintained on the basis of 'own nature', and it is this theory that came to be known as the identity theory of causality (*satkāryavāda*). It was almost identical with the Sāṅkhya theory of causation, which too was based on a conception of a primordial substance (*prakṛti* = *svabhāva*) considered to be the underlying substratum of everything.

The Sautrāntikas rejected the theory of 'substance' or 'own nature' (*svabhāva*), calling it a theory of 'self' (*ātman*) in disguise. To say that a thing arises because of its own nature is to say that it arises from the 'self' (*svabhāvata ity ātmataḥ*).[31] By denying substance and at the same time accepting a theory of moments, the Sautrāntikas were left with the task of explaining causal continuity. They held that existence is merely a series of moments, one moment following another without pause or gap. A seed is nothing but a series of point-instances, arising and passing away, creating the appearance of a seed. But then they had to explain the origin of the series—how a seed-series gives rise to a tree-series. Thus questioned, the Sautrāntikas maintained that the seed-series, being nonexistent (*abhūtvā*), comes into existence (*bhavati*). The *Abhidharmakośa-vyākhyā* of Vasubandhu refers to a statement in the *Paramārthaśūnyatā-sūtra* (quoted by the Sautrāntikas, who denied that a *dharma* can exist during the past and the future). It runs thus:

> When the organ of vision [eye] is produced, it does not come from some other place; when it disappears it is not going to be stored up in another place. [Consequently] a thing becomes, having not been before; having become, it ceases to be.[32]

Moreover, according to the *Śikṣāsamuccaya* of Śāntideva, "A thing becomes having not been before and having become ceases to be, because it has no substance" (*svabhāvarahitatvāt*).[33] This means that by denying substance (*svabhāva*) the Sautrāntikas were compelled to admit the production or arising of an effect that did not exist earlier (*abhūtvābhāvautpāda*), and this certainly was the same as the non-identity theory of causality (*asatkāryavāda*) presented by the Vaiśeṣika school. The only valid form of causality for the Sautrāntikas would therefore be contiguity or immediate succession (*samanantara-pratyaya*). It resembles the theory of causality upheld by the British philosopher David Hume, who also analyzed existence in terms of momentary impressions.

The Theravādins, too, appear to have contributed to a similar theory, as is evident from Buddhaghosa's statement:

> He understands thus: "There is no heap or store of unrisen mind and matter [existing] prior to its arising. When it arises, it does not come from any heap or store, and when it ceases, it does not go in any direction. There is nowhere any depository in the way of a heap or store or hoard of what has ceased. But just as there is no store, prior to its arising, of the sound that arises when a lute is played, nor does it come from any store when it arises, nor does it go in any direction when it ceases, nor does it persist in a store when it has ceased, but

on the contrary, not having been it is brought into being owing to the lute, the lute's neck and the man's appropriate effort, and having been, it vanishes—so too all material and immaterial states, not having been, are brought into being; having been they vanish."[34]

Although a similar view is expressed in early Buddhism,[35] it should be remembered that in early Buddhism existence was not commuted in terms of moments, as in the Theravāda and Sautrāntika schools. In early Buddhism it was meant as an answer to the metaphysical question that implied the existence of the effect within the cause before it was made manifest. Although these later schools accepted this theory for the same reason, these schools almost denied the connection between cause and effect because of their theory of moments. For early Buddhists it was no problem to establish a connection between a cause and an effect because of their empirical theory of existence. A too strict adherence to the theory of moments, a theory which, in the Indian context, was more metaphysical than empirical, led the Sautrāntikas to this predicament. In the same way David Hume, as a result of his theories of moments and atoms, was compelled to deny any form of causality other than mere antecedence. The Buddhist philosopher Nāgârjuna as well as the Hindu thinker Śaṅkara were quick to take advantage of this weakness in order to justify their own transcendentalist theories.

Just as the identity theory of causality (*satkāryavāda*) of the Sarvâstivādins can be looked upon as a metaphysical theory, so also can the nonidentity theory (*asatkāryavāda*) of the Sautrāntikas, which amounts to a denial of causality. These metaphysical theories, among others, were severely critized by Nāgârjuna. These, then, are some of the results of scholasticism, which emerged with the *parinirvāna* of the Buddha.

In the sphere of religious life, the Hinayāna schools emphasized the doctrine of the Noble Eightfold Path (*ariya aṭṭhaṅgika magga*), while at the same time accommodating the Mahāyāna conception of *bodhisattva*. The gradual path starting from morality (*sīla*), leading to concentration (*samādhi*), and culminating in knowledge or insight (*paññā*) was the theme of Buddhaghosa's famous treatise, "Path of Purity" (*Visuddhimagga*). The attainment of *arahant*-ship was still the goal of the religious life, and the difference between the Buddha and the *arahant* was not emphasized as was done by the Mahāyānists.

Notes

1. I have avoided the use of the name Sthaviravāda because sometimes it is used to refer to other schools of Hinayāna as well. Here Theravāda refers to the Theriya Nikāya of Sri Lanka and South East Asia.
2. P. S. Jaini has made a comprehensive analysis of the development of Abhidharma scholasticism. See the Introduction to his edition of *Abhidharmadīpa*.
3. See *VbhA* 366.
4. *DhsA* 21.
5. *VinA* 5.990
6. See Anuruddha's *Nāmarūpapariccheda*, ed. A. P. Buddhadatta, *Journal of the Pali Text Society* (London: PTS, 1914), p. 5.
7. For detailed descriptions of these categories in the Theravāda Abhidhamma, the reader is referred to Nyanatiloka Mahāthera's *A Guide through the Abhidhamma Piṭaka* (Colombo: Associated Newspapers of Ceylon, 1957), and for a description of the Sarvâstivāda categories, to Stcherbatsky's *The Central Conception of Buddhism and the Meaning of the Word 'Dharma'* (London: Royal Asiatic Society, 1923).
8. *DhsA* 313.
9. *S* 2.3f.; *TD* 2.85a–b.
10. *M* 1.185ff.; *TD* 1.464b.
11. See *Paramatthamañjusā or the Commentary on the Visuddhimagga*, ed. M. Sri Ñānissara Dhammānanda (Colombo: Mahabodhi Press, 1930), p. 367f.
12. John Locke, *An Essay Concerning Human Understanding*, ed. Alexander Campbell Fraser (Oxford: The Clarendon Press, 1894), vol. 1, p. 392.
13. *Dhs* 585.
14. See *Abhidhammâvatāra* of Buddhadatta, ed. A. P. Buddhadatta, in *Buddhadatta's Manuals* (London: PTS, 1915), vol. 1, p. 1.
15. Ibid., p. 17.
16. See my article "Schools of Buddhism in Early Ceylon," *Ceylon Journal of the Humanities* (Peradeniya: University of Ceylon), 1 (1970):159–190. It is significant that the *Abhidhamma Piṭaka* of the Theravādins makes no mention of either the theory of atoms or the theory of moments. They are certainly not found in either the Pali Nikāyas or the Chinese Āgamas. In his commentary on the *Dhammasaṅgani*, Buddhaghosa makes a very important remark regarding the theory of moments. He says: "Herein, the continued present (*santatipaccuppanna*) finds mention in the commentaries (*aṭṭhakathā*); the enduring or long present

(*addhāpaccuppanna*) in the discourses (*sutta*). Some say that the thought existing in the momentary present (*khaṇapaccuppanna*) becomes the object of telepathic insight" (*DhsA*, p. 421). According to this statement, it was *some people* (*keci*) who spoke about the momentary present; it was found neither in the discourses nor in the commentaries preserved at the Mahāvihāra which Buddhaghosa was using for his own commentaries in Pali. This may be taken as substantial evidence for the view that the doctrine of moments was not found in Theravāda Buddhism as it was preserved at the Mahāvihāra in Sri Lanka. In the same way, the theory of atoms was for the first time suggested by Buddhaghosa and came to be accepted as an important theory in the Theravāda tradition after him.

17. *AD* 139; *ADV* p. 104.
18. *VbhA*, p. 7.
19. See *Sakv*, p. 33.
20. See *S* 2.94, 96; *TD* 2.81c.
21. *VbhA*, pp. 25–26.
22. *Abhs* pp. 16f.
23. *ADV* p. 32. See Jaini's Introduction to *AD*, p. 75.
24. *ADV* p. 47f.
25. Ibid.
26. See *Sarvadarśanasaṃgraha*, ed. V. S. Abhyankar (Poona: Bhandarkar Oriental Research Institute, 1951), p. 36.
27. See *Vijñaptimātratāsiddhi*, ed Sylvan Lévi (Paris: Champion, 1925), p. 16.
28. Ibid., p. 7.
29. See my article "Dinnāga's Theory of Immaterialism," *Philosophy East and West*, 20 (1970):121–128.
30. See *ADV*, pp. 259f.
31. *Sakv*, p. 362.
32. *Abhidharmakośavyākhyā*, ed. Pralhad Pradhan (Patna: K. P. Jayaswal Research Institute, 1967), 5.27ab.
33. *Śikṣāsamuccaya*, ed. C. Bendall (St. Petersburg: The Imperial Academy of Sciences, 1879–1902), p. 229.
34. *Vism*, p. 630.
35. See *M* 3.25.

Selected Readings

PRIMARY SOURCES

Abhidhammatthasaṅgaha of Anuruddha, ed. T. W. Rhys Davids,

Journal of the Pali Text Society London: PTS, 1884; tr. S. Z. Aung and C. A. F. Rhys Davids, *Compendium of Philosophy*, London: PTS, 1910.

Abhidhammâvatāra of Buddhadatta, ed. A. P. Buddhadatta, *Buddhadatta's Manuals*, vol. 1, London: PTS, 1915.

Abhidharmadīpa with *Vibhāṣāprabhāvṛtti*, ed. P. S. Jaini, Patna: K. P. Jayaswal Research Institute, 1959. This work presents the standpoint of the Vaibhāṣika school of Sarvâstivāda.

Abhidharmakośa and vyākhyā of Vasubandhu, ed. Pralhad Pradhan, Patna: K. P. Jayaswal Research Institute, 1967; *Sphuṭârthâbhidharmakośavyākhyā* of Yaśomitra, ed. U. Wogihara, 2 vols., Tokyo: The publishing Association of Abhidharmakośavyākhyā, 1932–1936; The Chinese version of the *Abhidharmakośa and vyākhyā* translated by Hsüan Tsang has been rendered into French by L. de la Vallée Poussin, *L'Abhidharmakoṣa de Vasubandhu*, 6 vols., Paris: Paul Geuthner, 1923–1935. These treatises represent the Sautrāntika standpoint.

Atthasālinī of Buddhaghosa, ed. E. Müller, London: PTS, 1897; tr. Pe Maung Tin, *The Expositor*, 2 vols., London: PTS, 1920–1921.

Kathāvatthu, ed. A. C. Taylor, 2 vols., London: PTS, 1894–1897; tr. S. Z. Aung and C. A. F. Rhys Davids, *Points of Controversy*, 2 vols., London: PTS, 1915.

Nāmarūpapariccheda of Buddhadatta, ed. A. P. Buddhadatta, *Journal of the Pali Text Society*, London: PTS, 1914.

Visuddhimmagga of Buddhaghosa, ed. C. A. F. Rhys Davids, 2 vols., London: PTS, 1920–1921; tr. Bhikkhu Nānamoli, *Path of Purification*, Colombo: Semage, 1964; tr. Pe Maung Tin, *The Path of Purity*, 3 vols., London: PTS, 1922, 1928, 1931.

SECONDARY SOURCES

Conze, Edward. *Buddhist Thought in India*. Pp. 92–116. This is one of the best accounts on the Abhidharma doctrines.

Guenther, H. V. *Philosophy and Psychology in the Abhidhamma*. Lucknow: Buddha Vihara, 1957. A good comparative study of the Theravāda and Sarvâstivāda traditions.

Karunadasa, Y. *Buddhist Analysis of Matter*. Colombo: Government Press, 1967. This analysis is based mostly on the Theravāda Abhidhamma.

Mookerjee, Satkari. *Buddhist Philosophy of Universal Flux*. Calcutta: University of Calcutta Press, 1935. A good account of the Sautrāntika standpoint in Buddhist philosophy.

Nyanaponika Thera. *Abhidhamma Studies*. Kandy: Buddhist Publications Society, 1965.

Nyanatiloka Mahathera. *A Guide Through the Abhidhamma Piṭaka.* Colombo: The Associated Newspapers of Ceylon, 1949. A useful summary of the contents of the seven books of the Theravāda *Abhidhamma Piṭaka.*

Rhys Davids, C. A. F. *Buddhist Psychology*. London: George Bell & Sons, 1914.

Sogen, Yamakami. *Systems of Buddhistic Thought.* Calcutta: University of Calcutta Press, 1934.

Stcherbatsky, T. I. *The Central Conception of Buddhism and the Meaning of the Word 'Dharma'*. London: Royal Asiatic Society, 1923. This work is an exposition of the Sarvâstivāda Abhidharma.

Takakusu, J. *The Essentials of Buddhist Philosophy*. Honolulu: University of Hawaii Press, 1956.

Chapter Ten
Development of Mahāyāna

While on the one hand, scholasticism gradually grew up and matured, giving rise to the three major philosophical schools mentioned above, on the other hand, certain aspects of popular religion developed and found expression in the basic teachings of Mahāyāna, bringing about radical changes in the religious life and aspirations of the followers.

It was pointed out in chapter 8 that Mahāyāna is the culmination of the speculation concerning the nature of the Buddha. This speculation was prevalent even during the Buddha's lifetime. In the *Aṅguttara-nikāya*, in answer to the question Who is a Buddha? the Buddha declared himself to be neither a god nor a *gandhabba* nor a *yakkha* nor a man.[1] It is possible to interpret this statement as implying that his is a transcendental existence, completely different from any form of existence known to man. But the real implication of the statement seems to be that, since the Buddha has eradicated craving for and grasping after the things of the world, he cannot be described in terms of those who are in possession of them. Hence the Buddha is represented as saying:

> As a result of which there would be birth as a god, or a *gandhabba* traversing the air, that by which one would attain the state of a *yakkha* or of a man, such defiling tendencies (*āsavā*) of mine are exhausted, destroyed, and rendered useless. Like the beautiful lotus which is unsmeared by water, even so am I untainted by the world. Hence, O Brahman, I am a Buddha.[2]

This is the status of a person who has completely eradicated craving of any sort. Such a person, as pointed out in chapter 7, is one who, even though he experiences pleasurable and painful sensations when coming into contact with the world, is able to remain unmoved by them. It is a state to be attained by utmost human endeavor and striving, understanding and renunciation. This was Buddhahood attained by a human being—Siddhattha Gotama.

There is no doubt that the information found in the Pali Nikāyas and the Chinese Āgamas is the earliest available with regard to any doctrine in Buddhism. The material pertaining to the conception of the Buddha found in the Nikāyas and the Āgamas may, therefore, be contrasted with the legends in the Pali commentaries and the available Buddhist Sanskrit literature. The gradual development of the conception of the Buddha from a historical personality to the status of a cosmic principle can be clearly seen in these texts. But there cannot be any denial that even in the Pali Nikāyas and the Chinese Āgamas this conception has far outgrown its original form.

The earliest conception of the nature of the Buddha was that of a human being. He was born to a well-to-do *kṣatriya* family and was nurtured with all the comforts such a family could provide. As a youth he left his weeping parents, renouncing all the wealth associated with his family, and adopted the life of asceticism, a movement which seems to have been in its ascendency at this time. After associating with some of the leading ascetics of his day and gaining mastery of the techniques of *yoga*, he attained enlightenment at the age of thirty-five. Having attained enlightenment and having founded an order, he spent the rest of his life traveling and preaching in the lands of Magadha and Kosala. Finally, he passed away at the age of eighty, having spent the last few days in sore afflication due to an illness, which he endured with super human courage.

His message had a profound effect on every aspect of life. To the ordinary religious-minded man who was dissatisfied with the existing religion, which advocated piety founded on animal sacrifices, his teachings on morality based on broad ethical principles intended to promote the happiness and well-being of every human being and animal, came as a welcome shower after a long drought. His social philosophy based on equality of men brought solace to those who were harassed by the social stratification justified by belief in divine creation. To the ascetics who had stopped halfway (*antarāvosānam āpanna*), his teachings on spiritual matters offered meaning and significance to the life of asceticism. Finally, to the philosopher engaged in endless diatribes, speculating on the nature of Ultimate Reality while engrossed in his own likes and dislikes, the Buddha's antimetaphysical attitude paved the way for the attainment of right understanding.

The effects of these teachings were so great that in no time he gained a large number of followers from all walks of life. In fact, a Jaina called Dīghatapassī who was an immediate follower of Nigaṇṭha Nātaputta, a senior contemporary of the Buddha, advised Nātaputta not to send another of his disciples, Upāli, to approach or confront the Buddha because the Buddha was supposed to possess the 'magical power of converting' (*āvaṭṭanī māyā*) people to his way of thinking.[3] A person who was able to elicit such respect even from his opponents, was no doubt highly venerated and adored by his own followers. This indeed was one of the most important factors that contributed to the development of the conception of Buddha.

Although the appellative Buddha was used specifically to refer to Siddhattha Gotama, and means 'enlightened one', we occasionally find the term being used to refer to other *arahant*s as well, especially in the phrase *buddhânubuddha*, 'enlightened after the enlightened one'.[4] It certainly reflects the fact that even the *arahant*s were considered to be 'enlightened ones'. In fact, in the *Saṃyutta-nikāya* the Buddha pointed out that there is no difference between him and his disciples who have attained freedom (*vimutti*). The only distinction he claimed for himself was that of a *teacher* who pointed out the path leading to that freedom. This distinction was indeed sufficient for Ānanda, who had not by that time attained freedom, to glorify the Buddha in the following manner:

> There is no one monk entirely and completely endowed with those qualities with which the Lord, the *arahant*, the all-enlightened, was endowed. For the Lord was the producer of the unproduced path, the preacher of the path that had not been originated [earlier], the knower, the cognizer, the perceiver of the path. But now the disciples are the followers of the path, being endowed with it afterwards.[5]

This is the portrait of the Buddha as a teacher (*satthā*). The respect he elicited from his followers as a teacher was responsible for his elevation to the status of a 'god' or a 'Brahmā' even during his lifetime. The *Majjhima-nikāya* contains several accounts of the knowledge and powers attained by the Buddha at his enlightenment. These consist of the four stages of meditative rapture and the three categories of higher knowledge. These were attained even by the *arahant*s. They are included in the list of attainments which are given as the fruits of being a monk (*sāmañña-phala*). The *Sāmaññaphala-suttanta*[6] includes in this list all the supernormal powers, the working of miracles, the feats of levitation, the sixfold extrasensory knowledge, and so forth, all of which can be attained by one who practices concentration (*samādhi*). The Buddha seems to have denied that he possessed omniscience (*sabbaññutā*) which was attributed to him during the period represented by the post-canonical literature. This power, however, was claimed by Nigaṇṭha Nātaputta, the leader of the Jainas, who, according to his followers, claimed that he was all-knowing (*sabbaññū*) and all-seeing (*sabbadassāvī*), and professed that he had complete knowledge and insight (*ñāṇadassana*) and that this knowledge and insight were continually present even when he was walking, standing, sleeping, or awake.[7] The Buddha was asked by a wandering ascetic whether he too could be described as possessing such powers, but the Buddha denied this. What he claimed was only the threefold knowledge (*tisso vijjā*) consisting of (1) clairvoyance (*dibbacakkhu*) or the knowledge of the arising and passing away of human beings (*sattānaṃ cutûpapātañāṇa*), (2) knowledge of one's past births (*pubbenivāsânussatiñāṇa*), and (3) knowledge of the arising and passing away of the cankers or defiling tendencies (*āsavakkhayañāṇa*)—all of which knowledge was attained by the *arahant*s as well. But the respect and veneration that the disciples held for their teacher led to the development of the conception of the Buddha, and the doctrine of his omniscience did finally become the accepted view.

It was pointed out in chapter 3 that the main discovery that the Buddha made when he attained enlightenment was the uniformity of the causal law (*dhammatā*). Referring to this discovery, the Buddha is represented as saying:

> Whether the Tathāgatas were to arise in this world, or whether the Tathāgatas were not to arise in this world, this fact or element [of causality], this causal status, this causal orderliness, this relatedness remains. That the Tathāgata understands and realizes; having understood and realized, he declares it, preaches it, makes it known, establishes it, reveals it, analyses it and shows it up saying: "Look."[8]

Causal uniformity (*dhammatā*), then, is the truth concerning the nature of the world. The function of the Buddha was to understand this and make it known, so that the people could fashion their lives according to this truth. This means that there may have been other people in the past who discovered the same truth and that others in the future may also discover it. This certainly left room for recognition of Buddhas of the past as well as of the future, and, in fact, the *Mahāpadāna-suttanta* refers to six previous Buddhas.[9]

Freedom from the normal causal process and the attainment of the state in which the supernormal causal process is operative (see chapter 7) is achieved as a result of renunciation and the elimination of the defiling tendencies (*āsavakkhaya*). This was the unproduced path which the Buddha produced. And this discovery is aptly compared to the discovery of an ancient path (*purāṇam añjasaṃ*), hidden and covered by a dense forest, which led to a bygone kingdom (*purāṇaṃ rājadhāniṃ*). In the same way, the Buddha discovered this ancient path trodden by the previous Buddhas (*pubbakehi sammāsambuddhehi anuyātaṃ*).[10]

In the *Mahā-hatthipadopama-sutta* the Buddha declared, "He who sees causality (*paṭiccasamuppāda*) sees the *dhamma*, and he who sees the *dhamma* sees causality."[11] Then again in the *Itivuttaka*, the Buddha is represented as saying, "A monk sees the *dhamma* and seeing the *dhamma* he sees me [i.e., the Buddha]."[12] These two statements are combined in the *Ārya-śālistamba-sūtra*,[13] a later composition based on the material found in the early discourses, to give the simple equation: causality = *dhamma* = Buddha. What is meant in the early discourses is that because causality (*paṭiccasamuppāda*) is the essence of the *dhamma* (teaching), an insight into the causal law provides an understanding of the *dhamma*. Without an understanding of the causal law, one is unable to put an end to the normal causal pattern and hence unable to free oneself from the bonds of existence. Therefore, a knowledge of the *dhamma* is essential to realize the freedom from defiling tendencies (*āsavā*) that had been attained by the Buddha. Hence the Buddha's statement, "He who sees the *dhamma* sees me." It is true that causality represents a cosmic principle. But to identify this cosmic principle with the Buddha or Buddhahood on the basis of the Buddha's statement quoted above would seem unwarranted, as this leads to metaphysics which the Buddha himself rejected.

Within this framework, Siddhattha Gotama is but one of many Buddhas, a representation, as it were, of the type Buddha. Thus many of the developed doctrines of Mahāyāna could possibly be *logically deduced* from the statements found in the early discourses. But the real impetus to such speculations was given by the incident related in the *Mahā-parinibbāna-suttanta* as discussed in chapter 8.

It is evident that the faithful followers wanted the Buddha to continue without passing away. They seem to be reluctant to believe that such a great person as the Buddha who was looked upon as the 'god of gods' (*devâtideva*) could die. The immortality (*amata*) he spoke of would be meaningless for them unless he could survive bodily death. Hence the theory set forth in the Buddhist Sanskrit texts that the Buddha did not actually pass away and that his *parinirvāṇa* is, *inter alia*, merely a means of conforming to the ways of the world (*lokânuvartana*) in order to inculcate the truth of impermanence of worldly things.

A transcendental conception of the Buddha seems to have emerged with greater force with the development of the conception of past Buddhas and the consequent belief that Siddhattha Gotama was no other than the representation of Buddhahood. Hence, even in some of the discourses included in the Nikāyas and the Āgamas, we find transcendence attributed to the Buddha, not only after his enlightenment, but even when he was aspiring toward enlightenment (*bodhisatta*) and seeking the truth (*kiṃkusalagavesi*), nay, even before he was actually born. Thus we find the idea that the *bodhisatta* descends "mindful and conscious" from the Tusita heaven, stays visible as a thread through a precious stone when he is in the mother's womb, and is received by the gods at his birth.[14] Even his conception was different from that of normal human beings. He was conceived by his mother, Mahāmāyā, at a time when she had observed the higher precepts, one of which is the practice of celibacy, thus hinting at a kind of virgin birth, like that of the Christ according to Biblical legends.

The legends in the *Lalitavistara* go even a step further in describing these events. Although it does not set out the Mahāyāna doctrines as definitely as do the other treatises such as the *Saddharmapuṇḍarīka*, a Sarvâstivāda text subsequently accepted by the Mahāyānists, yet the miraculous aspect of the life of the Buddha is emphasized, providing new material and relating so many novelties that occasionally the narrative is interrupted to extol the merits of faith (*śraddhā*), through fear that such a description might cause the followers to doubt its validity.

Thus, in these initial stages of the development of Mahāyāna, two doctrines were evolving. The first is the doctrine of the plurality of Buddhas leading to a conception of transcendental monism as represented by terms like *tathatā* and *dharmakāya* in the later Mahāyāna texts. The second is the doctrine of a 'being aspiring to enlightenment' (*bodhisattva*) which is a development based on an earlier conception. In the earliest sections of the discourses (*sutta*), the term *bodhisatta* was used to denote the career of Siddhattha Gotama from birth to enlightenment, but its meaning was extended to refer to the time when he remained in the Tusita heaven before entering the mother's womb. This was again extended, in an attempt to inculcate the doctrines of *karma* and rebirth, to include all the previous lives during several aeons up until the time he made a decision to become a fully enlightened one (*sammāsambuddha*). These doctrines are found in the literature belonging to several schools—the *Buddhavaṃsa* and the *Jātaka-nidāna-kathā* of the Theravādins, the *Mahāvastu* of the Lokuttaravādins, as well as the *Lalitavistara*, originally of the Sarvâstivādins. These are the foundations of the fully developed Mahāyāna as embodied in the *Prajñāpāramitā* and the *Saddharmapuṇḍarīka-sūtras*.

Although a transcendentalist conception of Buddha as well as an extended conception of *bodhisattva* developed within the three traditions—Theravāda, Sarvâstivāda, and Lokuttaravāda (Mahāsāṅghika)—a deliberate attempt to lower and condemn the status of the early *arahant*-ideal is not found until we come to the *Saddharmapuṇḍarīka*, 'The Lotus of the True Doctrine'. Realization of the dangers associated with a completely transcendental conception of Buddha and with neglect of the historical personality, led the Theravādins to reject some of the ideas expressed on this subject during the time of King Asoka, as is evident from the *Kathāvatthu* 'Points of Controversy'.[15] This rejection by the Theravādins of the transcendence of Buddha displeased those who attempted to popularize this ideal. The tone in which the *arahant*-ideal is criticized in the *Saddharmapuṇḍarīka* bears ample testimony to this fact.

At the very beginning of this work belonging to the Mahāyāna school, the Lord tells Śāriputra that only the Tathāgatas (i.e., Buddhas) can explain things. A Tathāgata's knowledge surpasses that of all other beings, and he declares that he addresses all the disciples and *pratyeka-buddhas*, all those who are established in nirvana and have been released from the series of births and deaths. "This," as pointed out by E. J. Thomas, "is a direct challenge to the older teaching."[16]

Some of the monks in the assembly were not only puzzled but got up and left the assembly,[17] an incident that goes counter to the Mahāyā-nist conception of the Buddha's 'skill in means' (*upāyakauśalya*), so much emphasized in the *Saddharmapuṇḍarīka* itself. Thomas opines that this incident might quite well have happened at a Mahāyāna meeting in which there were some Sarvâstivādins present.[18] The statement of the Buddha that the meeting had been cleared of rubbish and that it was fortunate that the proud ones (referring to the *arahants*), were gone, certainly reflects the antagonism that had developed between the two factions, the so-called Mahāyāna and Hinayāna. The purpose of the appearance of a Buddha in the world is to reveal the *tathāgata* knowledge. The Buddha then made one of his most important declarations, as far as the Mahāyānists are concerned. He said, "By means of one career only I teach beings the doctrine, namely, the Buddha-career. No second or third career exists."[19] But it was because of his skill in means (*upāyakauśalya*) that the Buddha expounded the Buddha-career as being threefold. One whole chapter is devoted to setting forth this theory of skill in means, which was so essential for the Mahāyānists to accommodate the teachings of the early discourses and not appear to be introducing a completely new doctrine.

It is in the fourth chapter of the *Saddharmapuṇḍarīka* that we come across an entirely new conception of the Buddha which illustrates very vividly the psychology behind the Mahāyāna doctrines. Earlier, when Śāriputra heard the Buddha almost condemning the *arahant*-ideal, he was astonished and feared that it was the Māra, the Evil One, speaking. But he also heard the Buddha say that he (Śāriputra) would become a Buddha. The Buddha revived in him the knowledge that in the past he had made the vow of a *bodhisattva* to become a perfectly enlightened one (*samyaksambuddha*), and he promised its fulfillment. This incident is made the topic of discussion in the fourth chapter of the *Saddharmapuṇḍarīka*, where many of the early disciples, such as Subhūti, Mahā-kātyāyana, Mahā-kāśyapa, and Mahā-maudgalyāyana, all of whom had attained nirvana, were amazed and struck with wonder on hearing the prediction of the Buddha that Śāriputra, who had attained nirvana, would in the future become a perfectly enlightened one. The disciples say:

> Lord, we are old, aged, advanced in years, honored as seniors in this assemblage of monks. Worn out by old age, we fancy

> that we have attained nirvana; we make no efforts, O Lord, for supreme and perfect enlightenment; our strength and exertion are inadequate to it. . . . Hence, O Lord, we are unable, in spite of the Lord's preaching, to realize the fact that all is empty (*śūnya*), without characteristic (*animitta*), and undetermined (*apraṇihita*). We have conceived no longing after the teachings of the Buddha, divisions of the Buddha-fields, the sports of the *bodhisattva*s or *tathāgatas*. For, by having fled out of the triple world, O Lord, we imagined having attained nirvana, and we are decrepit from old age. Hence, O Lord, though we have exhorted other *bodhisattva*s and instructed them in supreme and perfect enlightenment, we have, in doing so, never conceived a single thought of longing.[20]

Here, no doubt, is an attempt to distinguish between *arahant*ship and Buddhahood, between nirvana and supreme and perfect enlightenment (*samyaksambodhi*). Even the *arahant*s who earlier were not recognized as being different from the Buddha as far as their attainments were concerned, confess that they are inferior in their aspirations, inferior in a sense to the *bodhisattva*s who have neither attained nirvana nor achieved supreme and perfect enlightenment, but who are ordinary human beings except for the fact that they aspire to attain supreme and perfect enlightenment. This distinction between the *arahant* and the Buddha, therefore, represents a further extension of the difference between the pupil and the teacher (*satthā*), as mentioned at the beginning of this chapter.

But once the Buddha was raised to such a status, that status could be preserved and amplified only by devaluing the *arahant*-ideal, which the remaining part of the fourth chapter of the *Saddharma-puṇḍarīka* attempts to do. The distinction between the Buddha and the *arahant*s is further illustrated by the story of a wealthy man's son who, after being lost for some time, was unable to recognize his own father and, as a result of his low disposition which he developed during the long period of poverty, was, even when invited, unable to enjoy the wealth. In the same way, the *arahant*s, not being able to realize the true nature of Buddhahood, continue to be satisfied with the teachings pertaining to the 'aggregates' (*skandha*), 'gateways' (*āyatana*), and 'elements' (*dhātu*)—categories recognized in the Abhidharma—and do not understand such teachings as that on 'emptiness' (*śūnyatā*), like the son who clears the heap of rubbish in his father's garden, not being able to recognize his own father and therefore not in a position to enjoy the wealth consisting of gems, gold, and so forth. Like the son of the rich man, the *arahant*s are of low disposition or inclination (*hīnâdhimukti*), and the Buddha, like the rich man, is aware of his own exalted power (*udāra-sthāmatā*). The simile suggests another characteristic attributed to the Buddha in the developed Mahāyāna doctrines. From the status of a teacher (*satthā*, Sk. *śāstṛ*) he was raised to that of a father figure (*pitṛ*), providing protection for all those who are of inferior disposition and are tormented by the suffering inherent in the world. In fact, the monks themselves are shown as claiming that they are his pseudo-sons (*putra-pratirūpakā*), not real sons like the *bodhisattva*s. Thus the conception of Buddha in the Mahāyāna caters to the psychological needs of ordinary people who are faced with the hazards of existence, and, in a way, it is similar to the conception of God in many of the theistic religions which emphasize the conception of a father figure.[21] This, therefore, may be taken as the culmination of the religious trend initiated by the Mahāsāṅghikas, who took up the cause of the ordinary man and his religious aspirations.

In the short space available here it is not possible to examine in detail the development of the conception of Buddha. Later Mahāyāna texts like the *Sukhāvatīvyūha-sūtra* and the *Amitâyurdhyāna-sūtra* continued to develop the conception of Buddha on these lines, combining the conception of gods and heaven (*sagga*, Sk. *svarga*) in early Buddhism with the conception of Buddha, and producing parallels to the Christian conceptions of God and Heaven, but without contributing to a theory of creation or attributing any such function as the creation of the world to the Buddha. It is this conception of 'Pure Land' (Chinese, *ching-tu*, Japanese, *jodo*) that dominated the religious life of many of the people in the Far Eastern countries where Buddhism flourished.

The development of the conception of Buddha and the conception of *bodhisattva* seem to have reached a dead end in the *Prajñāpāramitā* literature. This is evident from the nature of the problems faced by the compilers of texts like the *Vajracchedikā Prajñāpāramitā* (popularly known in the West as "Diamond Sutra" or "Diamond Cutter"). The term *prajñāpāramitā* means 'perfection of wisdom', and the literature so designated is devoted to an elucidation of the nature of the highest knowledge or perfect and supreme enlightenment (*samyaksambodhi*).

As pointed out earlier, according to the *Saddharmapuṇḍarīka*, the aim of the Buddha's appearance in this world was to reveal the Buddha-knowledge. This knowledge is such that

> it is impossible to explain it; it is unutterable; nor is there such a being in this world to whom this doctrine could be explained or who would be able to understand it when explained, with the exception of the *bodhisattvas* who are of firm resolve. As to the disciples of the 'knower of the world' [i.e., the *arahants*], those who have done their duty and received praise from the Sugatas [i.e., the Buddhas], who have exhausted the defilements and have arrived at the last stage of bodily existence, the Buddha-knowledge lies beyond their sphere.[22]

It is the nondual (*advaya*) knowledge, free from discrimination (*nirvikalpa*). He who realizes it becomes one with the realization. Buddha is the embodiment of that knowledge. It is the Buddha's *dharma*-body (*dharma-kāya*), the real body as opposed to the *nirmāṇa-kāya*, which is his apparitional or mind-made body. (See chapter 12 for a discussion of the doctrine of the 'three bodies'—*trikāya*.) It is identical with the Ultimate Reality (*paramârtha-satya*), the 'suchness' (*tathatā*). It is inexpressible (*anirvacanīya*) and beyond logical analysis (*atarkâvacara*). Hence the famous set of quatrains from the *Vajracchedikā*:

> Those who by my form (*rūpa*) did see me,
> And those who followed me by voice;
> Wrong the efforts they engaged in,
> Me those people will not see.
>
> From the *dharma* should one see the Buddhas,
> For, the *dharma-bodies* are the Guides [i.e., the Buddhas].
> Yet *dharma*'s true nature should not be discerned,
> Nor can it, either, be discerned.[23]

This doctrine of *dharma-kāya* represents the apex of the movement toward the development of absolutism which began immediately after the Buddha's passing away. The whole of the *Vajracchedikā* is devoted to an analysis of the phenomenal world in terms of this noumenal reality. The statements in this text may at first seem baffling to students. For example, it is said:

> What do you think, Subhūti, if a son or daughter of good family had filled this world system of a thousand million worlds with the seven treasures, and then give it to the *tathāgatas*, Arhats, Fully Enlightened Ones, would that son or daughter of good family on the strength of that beget a great heap of merit?
>
> Great, O Lord, great, O Well-Gone, would the heap of merit be which that son or daughter of good family would beget on the strength of that. And why? What was taught by the *tathāgata* as 'heap of merit', as no-heap that has been taught by the *tathāgata*. Therefore the *tathāgata* teaches, 'heap of merit, heap of merit'.[24]

The implications of this passage are as follows: One can speak of a 'heap of merit' acquired by a person who practices charity. But in actual fact, there is nothing that can be grasped as a 'heap of merit'. The so-called 'heap of merit' is nonsubstantial, is empty (*śūnya*). Hence the statement that it is no-heap (*a-skandha*). But it is only for the purpose of instruction that the Buddha speaks of a 'heap of merit'. The repetition of the phrase as 'heap of merit, heap of merit' seems to show that it is merely a convention (*vyavahāra*), a term or a mode of description, without any Ultimate Reality.

But what of Ultimate Reality? That indeed is indescribable.

> What do you think, Subhūti, is there any *dharma* which has been fully known by the *tathāgata* as 'the utmost, right and perfect enlightenment' or is there any *dharma* which has been demonstrated by the *tathāgata*?
>
> No. As I understand the Lord's teaching, there is not any *dharma* which has been fully known by the *tathāgata* as 'the utmost, right and perfect enlightenment', and there is no *dharma* which has been fully known or demonstrated by the *tathāgata*,—it is not to be seized, it is not to be talked about, it is neither *dharma* nor no-*dharma*.[25]

The basic theme of the *Prajñāpāramitā* literature is to be found here. On the one hand, there is the indescribable Ultimate Reality, on the other, empty phenomenality. The reconciling of these two, the *paramârtha* or Ultimate Reality and the *saṃvṛti* or phenomenality, was one of the most difficult problems faced by the compilers of the *Prajñāpāramitā* literature. It was, in fact, a dead end of speculation regarding the Absolute. In the *Mūla-madhyamaka-kārikā*, Nāgârjuna made an attempt to provide a philosophical basis for the doctrines in the *Prajñāpāramitās*. While in the *Prajñāpāramitās* we find an attempt to demonstrate the unreality of the phenomenal from the standpoint of the noumenal, in the *Mūla-madhyamaka-kārikā* the dialectic is employed to prove the unreality of the phenomenal without making any reference to the noumenal. In the latter there is no discussion of the noumenal except once when Nāgârjuna was compelled to refer to it in order to defend himself against the objections raised by the opponents of the theory of emptiness (*śūnyatā*).[26] It is only in the *Mahā-prajñāpāramitā-śāstra* that Nāgârjuna discusses the conception of *dharma-kāya*.

The other concept which seems to have come to a dead end in the *Vajracchedikā* is that of the *bodhisattva*. According to early Buddhism as well as later Mahāyāna thought, beings are subject to suffering in this world because of ignorance (*avijjā*) and craving (*taṇhā*) which lead to grasping (*upādāna*). By eliminating ignorance and by developing insight into the nature of things, one is able to eliminate craving and thereby, grasping. A person who has no grasping will be freed from suffering in this world as well as from continued rebirth (*punabbhava*). Such a person is called one who has attained *nibbāna*. But a *bodhisattva*, according to the Mahāyāna definition, is one who has postponed the attainment of nirvana in order to continue in *saṃsāra* in the hope of helping all beings to cross over the flood of existence. He continues to exist in *saṃsāra* for countless aeons aspiring to attain the supreme and perfect enlightenment, since only a being who has attained the supreme and perfect enlightenment, according to the *Saddharmapuṇḍarīka*, can help others. The *Vajracchedikā* says:

> Here, Subhūti, someone who has set out in the vehicle of *bodhisattva* should produce a thought in this manner: "As many beings as there are in the universe of beings, comprehended under the term, *beings*,—either egg-born, or born from a womb, or moisture-born, or miraculously born; with or without form; with perception, without perception, or with neither perception nor nonperception—as far as any conceivable universe of beings is conceived: all these should

> by me be led to nirvana, into that realm of nirvana which leaves nothing behind."[27]

This is the aspiration and the goal of the life of a *bodhisattva.* But the *Vajracchedikā* goes on to say:

> If in a *bodhisattva*, the perception of a 'being' should take place, he could not be called a '*bodhi-being*'. And why? He is not to be called a '*bodhi*-being', in whom the perception of a self or a being would take place, or the perception of a living soul or a person.[28]

Or else,

> Not by a *bodhisattva* who is established on something should a gift be given, nor by one who is established anywhere should a gift be given. Not by one who is established in form (*rūpa*) should a gift be given, nor by one who is established in sounds, smells, tastes, tangible objects or mental objects.... For a being who gives gifts without establishing himself on anything, his heap of merit is not easy to measure.[29]

Thus, while on the one hand the *bodhisattva* should be one who is possessed of understanding or wisdom and therefore not led by belief in the real existence of souls or persons, on the other hand he should not have any kind of interest or motivation, whether good or bad, when practicing virtues such as generosity. In other words, he should be one who has completely destroyed ignorance (*avidyā*) and grasping (*upādāna*). Then only could he lead a life of true selfless service. Then only could he do his duty for duty's sake. And this, of course, is the same position achieved by the *arahant* (see chapter 6). It is certainly the noblest ideal to which one can aspire. But it should not be forgotten that a person who has eliminated ignorance and craving has also put an end to rebirth. After his death he is not able to continue in this *saṃsāra* or recurring cycle of existences in order to help others. He attains nirvana. Hence, the purpose of following the *bodhisattva*-ideal, that is, to help others during a number of lives, seems to be completely defeated.

For several reasons the *bodhisattva*-ideal developed and became popular in later Buddhism. It was an ideal presented to everyone, lay followers as well as monks and nuns. The developments consequent on the death of the Buddha were referred to earlier. One was the emergence of the scholastic trend, and the other was the reaction to this scholasticism prompted by an attempt to cater to the religious aspirations of ordinary men and women. With the development of scholasticism the originally strong zeal for spiritual advancement on the part of the monks gradually waned. They lived a cloistered life, devoting themselves to the study of the *dhamma* (*pariyatti*) rather than living it. Moreover, compared with the more organized religions such as Hinduism, Buddhism accommodated very few rituals connected with lay life. This, coupled with the cloistered life adopted by the monks, created a certain vacuum in the religious life of the ordinary followers. The result was the emergence of the *bodhisattva*-ideal accompanied by devaluation of the *arahant*-ideal.

Altruism or selfless service is a fascinating ideal. Sacrifice of one's own happiness for the weal of others is generally recognized as a noble ideal in any society. The Utilitarian ethical principles are sometimes criticized as being hedonistic. Altruism was, no doubt, the basis of the *bodhisattva*-ideal. For this reason, the *bodhisattva* offered himself as prey to a hungry tigress to prevent her from eating her own cubs. The *Bhagavadgīta* presented a similar altruistic ideal. But, as pointed out earlier, the fulfillment of such an ideal becomes impossible unless the individual has completely eradicated craving. Selfishness has to be replaced by selflessness. This indeed was the old ideal of an *arahant* found in early Buddhism. Starting as a layman, the *bodhisattva* finally ended up an *arahant*. This shows how the Mahāyānists, by rejecting the *arahant*-ideal as low and inferior and by presenting a more exalted ideal of selfless service, came around full circle to accepting the old ideal as enunciated in early Buddhism. According to the Sixth Patriarch, Hui-nêng, "If you wish to convert an ignorant person, then you must have expedients."[30] This is to say that, to help others achieve freedom, one must be free oneself.

Notes

1. *A* 2.38; *TD* 2.28a–b.
2. Ibid.
3. *M* 1.375; *TD* 1.628f.

4. *Thag* 679, 1246.
5. *M* 3.8; cf. *TD* 1.654a.
6. *D* 1.69ff.; *TD* 1.107ff.
7. *M* 1.482.
8. *S* 2.25; *TD* 2.48b.
9. *D* 2.1ff.; *TD* 1.16ff.
10. *S* 2.104ff.; *TD* 2.80.
11. *M* 1.191; *TD* 1.467a.
12. *It* 91.
13. *Ārya-śālistamba-sūtra*, restored from quotations and Tibetan and Chinese translations by L. de la Vallée Poussin, *Théorie des Douze Causes*, p. 70.
14. *M* 3.118ff.; *TD* 1.469ff.
15. *Kathāvatthu*, ed. A. C. Taylor (London: PTS, 1894), pp. 221ff.
16. *History of Buddhist Thought*, p. 181.
17. *Sdmp*, p. 36.
18. Ibid.
19. *Sdmp*, p. 37.
20. Ibid., pp. 95f.
21. Cf. J. O. Wisdom, "Gods," in *Logic and Language*, ed. Antony Flew (New York: Doubleday, 1965), pp. 195f.
22. *Sdmp*, pp. 29f.
23. *Vajra*, p. 56; translated by Conze, p. 89.
24. Ibid., p. 33; tr., p. 70.
25. Ibid., p. 32; tr., pp. 69f.
26. See *MK* 24.8.
27. *Vajra*, pp. 28f.; tr., p. 66.
28. Ibid., p. 29.
29. Ibid.
30. *The Platform Sutra of the Sixth Patriarch*, tr. Philip B. Yampolski (New York and London: Columbia University Press, 1967), p. 161.

Selected Readings

PRIMARY SOURCES

Buddhavaṃsa, ed. R. Morris, London: PTS, 1882.

Jātaka-nidāna-kathā, ed. V. Fausboll, London: PTS, 1877; tr. T. W. Rhys Davids, *Buddhist Birth Stories*, London: PTS, 1880.

Lalitavistara, ed. S. Lefmann, 2 vols., Halle: Buddhandlung des Waisenhouses, 1902–1908; tr. P. Foucaux, *Annales du Musée Guimet*, vol. 6, Paris: Musée Guimet, 1884.

Mahāvastu, ed. É. Senart, 3 vols., Paris, 1882–1897; tr. J. J. Jones,

The Mahāvastu, 3 vols., *SBB*, xvi, xviii, xix, London: PTS, 1949, 1952, 1956.

Saddharmapuṇḍarīka-sūtra, ed. U. Wogihara and C. Tsuchida, Tokyo: The Seigo Kenkyu-kai, 1958; tr. H. Kern, *The Saddharma-puṇḍarīka or the Lotus of the True Law*, *SBB*, xxi, Oxford: The Clarendon Press, 1884.

Vajracchedikā Prajñāpāramitā, ed. and tr. Edward Conze, *Serie Orientale Roma* 13, Rome: Istituto italiano per il Medio ed Estremo Oriente, 1957.

SECONDARY SOURCES

Conze, Edward. *Buddhist Thought in India*. Pp. 195–237.

Dayal, Har. *The Bodhisattva Doctrine in Buddhist Sanskrit Literature*. London: Kegan Paul, Trench & Trübner, 1932.

Dutt, Nalinaksa. *Aspects of Mahāyāna Buddhism and Its Relation to Hīnayāna*. London: Luzac, 1930.

Eliot, Charles. *Hinduism and Buddhism*. Vol. 2. London: George Allen & Unwin, 1930.

McGovern, W. M. *Introduction to Mahāyāna Buddhism*. London: Kegan Paul, Trench & Trübner, 1922.

Suzuki, D. T. *Outlines of Mahāyāna Buddhism*. London: Luzac, 1907.

Thomas, E. J. *History of Buddhist Thought*. Pp. 166–211.

Chapter Eleven
Mādhyamika Transcendentalism

Mādhyamika is one of the most widely studied schools of Buddhism. Studies by Western, Indian, and Far Eastern scholars are too numerous to mention. One of the most authoritative and widely acclaimed analyses of Mādhyamika thought is T. R. V. Murti's *The Central Philosophy of Buddhism*,[1] where the author compares Mādhyamika thought with that of Immanuel Kant in Western philosophy. This study is largely based on Nāgârjuna's *Mūlamadhyamakakārikā* and Candrakīrti's commentary on it, the *Prasannapadā Mādhyamikavṛtti*.

According to our analysis of early Buddhism and the subsequent development of Buddhist thought, the theory of an Absolute came into existence only after the Buddha's demise and reached its culmination in the *Prajñāpāramitā* literature. The origin of dialectical consciousness which finally culminated in the full-fledged Mādhyamika dialectic, as pointed out in chapter 10, was the conflict between noumenal reality and phenomenality that is very vividly depicted in the *Prajñāpāramitās*. On the other hand, the two Buddhist schools Sarvâstivāda and Sautrāntika, *inter alia*, contributed to the emergence of the Mādhyamika school when they presented metaphysical theories in their attempt to explain the nature of the phenomenal world. The *Mūlamadhyamakakārikā* of Nāgârjuna is devoted mostly to a refutation of the metaphysical theories of these two schools, and, as we have seen, the Theravāda school of Ceylon had little or no direct influence on the development of Buddhist schools in India.[2]

The *Mūlamadhaymakakārikā* begins with a statement and a refutation of each of the four metaphysical theories of causality presented by the Buddhist schools, as well as the non-Buddhist schools current during Nāgârjuna's time. They are: (1) self-causation or self-production (*svata utpatti*), (2) external causation or production by external factors (*parata utpatti*), (3) both self- and external causation (*dvābhyām utpatti*), and (4) noncausation (*ahetuta utpatti*).[3]

In chapter 9 it was pointed out that the Buddhist school of Sarvâstivāda as well as the non-Buddhist school of Sāṅkhya presented an identity theory of causality (*satkāryavāda*), and this is the first of the four theories mentioned by Nāgârjuna. It was the theory found in the *ātma*-tradition, the Sarvâstivādins themselves falling into this category as a result of their conception of 'substance' (*svabhāva*), although they claimed that they belonged to the *anātma*-tradition. This becomes evident from Nāgârjuna's own analysis. After enumerating the four theories of causation, Nāgârjuna examines the first. He refers to the theory of causal correlations (*pratyaya*) which was formulated by the Abhidharma schools and later also by the Yogâcāra school,[4] implying that it was the first of the four causal theories, namely, self-causation (*svata utpatti*). This is further confirmed by the third quatrain, where he points out that "the substance (*svabhāva*) of the existents (*bhāva*) is not to be found in the different causal factors or correlations (*pratyaya*)."[5] This certainly was a criticism of the identity theory of causality (*satkāryavāda*) presented by the Sarvâstivādins, for it is they who insisted on the identity of cause and effect based on substance or 'inherent nature' (*svabhāva*). But according to Murti, the identity theory of causality (*satkāryavāda*) criticized by Nāgârjuna is that of the Sāṅkhya school. For him, it was the Vaibhāṣikas, a school of Sarvâstivādins, who presented the nonidentity theory of causality (*asatkāryavāda*). But the Sāṅkhya school did not present a theory of causal correlations (*pratyaya*) of the like criticized by Nāgârjuna. For these reasons it is clear that the identity theory presented and criticized by Nāgârjuna is none other than the causal theory of the Sarvâstivādins.

For Nāgârjuna, 'substance' (*svabhāva*) was a metaphysical principle, just as 'self' or 'soul' (*ātman*) of the Upaniṣads was for the Buddha. Candrakīrti, elaborating on Nāgârjuna's criticism, points out that if the 'substance' or 'own nature' of the effect were to be found in the cause, production would be rendered meaningless (*vaiyarthya*),[6] for there would then be mere self-duplication, not the emergence of a more prominent factor which is not already existent. A seed would produce only another seed, not a tree, which is of a different nature. It is possible to counter this criticism by maintaining that the tree is found in the seed in *potential* form and that it becomes actual later on; in other words, there is a difference in state, but identity of 'substance'. The views expressed by the four Sarvâstivāda teachers (see chapter 9) seem to be directed toward just such a solution of the problems inherent in a theory of self-causation. But this, according to Candrakīrti, is self-contradictory, for it is not possible for an entity to be partly actual and partly potential; it would then not be one, but would contain two opposite natures.

Having criticized the theory of 'substance' (*svabhāva*), which was the basis of the identity theory of causality (*satkāryavāda*), Nāgârjuna goes on to refute the nonidentity theory (*asatkāryavāda*). He points out that in the absence of 'substance' or 'own nature' (*svabhāva*) there cannot be 'other nature' or 'otherness' (*parabhāva*).[7] Thus the nonidentity theory of causality would be meaningless unless one accepts a theory of 'substance' (*svabhāva*); one can speak of 'other nature' only if one recognizes 'own nature'. This shows that, as far as Nāgârjuna is concerned, the rejection of self-causation (*svata utpatti*) is not tantamount to accepting external causation (*parata utpatti*). Similarly, the rejection of the identity theory of the Sarvâstivādins (and of Sāṅkhya) does not lead to acceptance of the nonidentity theory of the Sautrāntikas (or of the Vaiśeṣikas). For him, both are metaphysical theories (*dṛṣṭi*). Hence he adopted the dialectical approach in his refutation of these theories.

This was the *prāsaṅgika* or *reductio ad absurdum* method which was vehemently advocated by Candrakīrti. As Murti has pointed out, "*Prasaṅga* is not to be understood as an apagogic proof in which we *prove* an assertion *indirectly* by disproving the opposite. *Prasaṅga* is disproof simply, without the least intention to prove any thesis."[8] This is true as far as Nāgârjuna's analysis of phenomenality is concerned. But rejection of all theses pertaining to phenomenality was believed to lead to the conception of the Absolute or Ultimate Reality (*paramârtha*), which the early Mahāyānists considered indefinable (*anirvacanīya*, see chapter 10).

As examples of the apagogic proof, Murti takes the Sāṅkhya proof of the identity theory (*satkāryavāda*) by disproving the opposite, nonidentity theory (*asatkāryavāda*), and also the Buddhist proof of momentariness (i.e., the momentary as the efficient) by disproving the permanent. He says:

> Such proofs, however plausible they may appear, fail to carry any conviction. For, the disproof of the opponent, even if it is cogent, does not necessarily mean the establishment of one's position as true. For, both the opponent's view as well as one's own may be false. The

> apagogic proof can have cogency and compulsion in spheres where by the nature of the subject matter, such as in mathematics, we so completely possess the field *in concreto* that the alternatives are narrowed down to two, and by rejecting one, we indirectly prove the other. *It must fail with regard to empirical facts and especially with regard to the suprasensuous* [italics mine]. For, we not only lack any sensuous intuition of the latter, but we do not also have an adequate representation of it. It would be circular reasoning to arrive at this very knowledge through the apagogic proof, which, to be cogent, does itself presuppose this intuition. The *reductio ad absurdum* of the Mādhyamika does not establish any thesis. It accepts a particular thesis *hypothetically*, and by eliciting its implications shows up the inner contradiction which has escaped the notice of the opponent.[9]

This was the dialectical method adopted by the so-called Prāsaṅgika school of Mādhyamika, which found its advocates in teachers like Āryadeva, Buddhapālita, Candrakīrti, and Śāntideva. But it is rather significant that this position was not accepted wholeheartedly by some of the other Mādhyamika teachers, especially Bhāvaviveka. Realizing the difficulties inherent in the above position, Bhāvaviveka believed in advancing a counter thesis or one's own thesis (*svatantra*). This was the Svātantrika school of Mādhyamika, which unfortunately did not come into prominence for reasons that will be discussed at the end of this chapter.

The close relationship between Mādhyamika thought and the teachings of the *Prajñāpāramitās* is undeniable. According to Murti,

> The Mādhyamika system is the systematized form of the śūnyatā doctrine of the *Prajñāpāramitā* treatises; its metaphysics, spiritual path (*ṣaṭpāramitānaya*) and the religious ideal are all present there, though in a loose, prolific garb. With the *Prajñāpāramitās* an entirely new phase of Buddhism begins. A severe type of Absolutism established by the dialectic, by the negation (*śūnyatā*) of all empirical notions and speculative theories, replaces the pluralism and dogmatism of earlier Buddhism.[10]

From this it becomes evident that, with the development of absolutistic metaphysics, not only speculative metaphysics but even empirical notions came to be negated. Thus, in a sense, the absolutism of the *Prajñāpāramitās* became the Mādhyamika thesis. Nāgârjuna is credited with having written the *Mahāprajñāpāramitā-śāstra* before compiling the *Mūlamadhyamakakārikā*, the Mādhyamika treatise *par excellence*, thus showing his indebtedness to the *Prajñāpāramitā* absolutism. Murti, while maintaining that the *Prajñāpāramitās* revolutionized Buddhism, has at the same time made a persistent attempt to show that they are not innovations. He says that

> they can and do claim to expound the deeper, profounder teachings of the Buddha. The fourteen avyākṛta (inexpressibles) of Buddha receive their significant interpretation here. The dialectic that is suggested in Buddha is the principal theme here.[11]

Murti's views regarding the teachings of the Buddha and Nāgârjuna may be summarized thus: The Buddha as well as Nāgârjuna accepted a suprasensuous Ultimate Reality, an Absolute (*paramârtha*) which is inexpressible in terms of concepts. The causal theories such as self-causation (*sayaṃ kataṃ* = *svata utpatti*) and external causation (*paraṃ kataṃ* = *parata utpatti*) must fail with regard to empirical facts and especially with regard to the suprasensuous.

According to our analysis of early Buddhism as embodied in the Pali Nikāyas and the Chinese Āgamas, the Buddha did not accept a suprasensuous or extraempirical reality which is inexpressible. The pre-Buddhist causal theories, such as self-causation and external causation, were rejected, not because they failed with regard to the suprasensuous, but because they were based on certain metaphysical assumptions which emphasized certain aspects of experience to the neglect of others (see appendix 1). Moreover, it would be unfair to attribute to the Buddha the *reductio ad absurdum* (*prasaṅga*) method, for, having rejected the metaphysical theories, he did not remain silent, saying that Ultimate Reality is indescribable or inexpressible, but presented his own thesis in unmistakable terms. And this *thesis* is the *pratītyasamutpāda* or 'dependent arising' or simply, causality. It is an empirical theory about the world, including ordinary men as well as the enlightened ones.

Moreover, in early Buddhism there is no dialectical analysis of the pre-Buddhist theories of causality, as there is in the Mādhyamika system of Nāgârjuna. In early Buddhism the rejection of these theories is based on an appeal to experience (see appendix 1).

Finally, it was pointed out that early Buddhism does not contribute to a theory of absolutism; it does not recognize a transcendental transempirical reality which is at the same time ineffable (*anirvacanīya*). *Nibbāna* is not a transcendental reality in the sense in which transcendence was understood in later Buddhism. We have attempted to explain the gradual development of the absolutist tendency within Buddhism after the death of the Buddha. If what has been said here regarding the early doctrines is true, then the *Prajñāpāramitās* certainly represent a 'revolution' (*viparyāsa*!) in Buddhism. The revolution consists of the adoption of the transcendentalist standpoint, which is opposed to the empirical approach of early Buddhism.

This change of emphasis from the empirical to the transcendental is very clearly seen from the manner in which 'concepts' and 'propositions' were evaluated in the two traditions, early Buddhism and Mādhyamika. Let us first examine the former.

The term *sammuti* is used in the earliest texts to denote 'concept'. It is derived from $\sqrt{mn}$ (*mṇ*), 'to think', and when prefixed with *sam* (meaning 'together with'), the word conveys the idea of 'convention', 'agreement', and so on. It is a convention which is used to designate, to refer to something; hence, it is also called 'designation' (*paññatti*, *vohāra*). We will refer later to a statement of the Buddha regarding an instance of overstepping the limits of convention (see appendix 1). Such confusions with regard to the use of concepts and terms, sometimes prompted by one's own inclinations, have led to the formulation of many of the metaphysical concepts and theories. According to the Buddha, by avoiding such confusions and not allowing one's inclinations to interfere with the use of concepts, it is possible to understand the truth, to see things as they are (*yathābhūtaṃ*). For the Buddha, it is our likes and dislikes—our prejudices—that distort our perception and understanding, and also our description and definition of reality. It is, thus, not the concept (*sammuti*) that distorts or 'covers' the real nature of the object which it purports to designate, but the manner in which each individual, driven by his inclinations, attempts to see or grasp *what he wants to see or grasp* with the concepts. Thus the term 'self' (*ātman*), which is used to refer to the psychophysical personality, especially when speaking reflexively, is taken to refer to an immortal, permanent, and sometimes transcendental 'self'. Thus we have different 'points of view' (*dṛṣṭi*) regarding which there is no unanimity. But if one were able to use concepts without attachment and prejudice, without bias or inclination, then it would be possible to avoid many of the conflicts. This indeed was the 'conflict in reason' that the Buddha tried to resolve, especially as is evident from the discourses in the *Sutta-nipāta*.

But for Nāgârjuna, the 'conflict in reason' was of a different sort. For him, as for all the later Buddhist schools, a 'concept' was something that conceals or covers the real nature of the object. Hence the earlier term *sammuti* appears as *saṃvṛti*, which has a completely different connotation in the developed metaphysic. The new term is derived from *sam* and √*vṛ*, 'to cover', 'to obstruct'. The term *saṃvṛti*, unlike *sammuti*, would therefore mean 'something that covers'.[12] A concept, in this sense, would be like an outer shell that covers the kernel, the real nature. The so-called Ultimate Reality (*paramârtha*) comes to be concealed by the 'concept' (*saṃvṛti*). It is *revealed* to the individual only on the development of the highest intuition.[13] Thus, reality cannot be resolved into concepts; it is indescribable or indefinable (*anirvacanīya*, a new term coined by the later Buddhists). The noumenal or the 'thing-in-itself' (*tattva*) cannot be grasped by concepts. It transcends conceptual description (*nirvikalpa*), is transcendent or self-existent (*apara-pratyaya*).[14] This is seen to justify Nāgârjuna's view that there is no difference whatsoever between the phenomenal (*saṃsāra*) and the transcendental (*nirvāna*),[15] for the reality of *saṃsāra* or the world is identical with the Absolute.

If concepts cannot reveal the nature of reality, neither can propositions. Propositions can merely state the relative or the conventional, not the Ultimate Reality or truth. It should be remembered that the Mādhyamikas recognized two levels of reality only, the conventional (*saṃvṛti*) and the ultimate (*paramârtha*), unlike the Yogâcārins who accepted three levels, the conceptual (*parikalpita*), the relative (*paratantra*), and the ultimate (*pariniṣpanna*) (see chapter 12). Therefore, according to the Mādhyamikas, since reality is indefinable, all propositions fail with regard to empirical facts. Not only the non-Buddhist theories, but even the Buddhist theories of causality, *karma*, and so forth, were rejected. Buddhism, after the Buddha, it was pointed out, not only developed a theory of absolutism, but also propounded metaphysical theories in explanation of causality, *karma*, etc. Thus, it stands to the credit of the Mādhyamikas that, although they contributed to a theory of absolutism, they were able to eliminate metaphysical assumptions from the domain of philosophy.

It is only in the matter of eliminating metaphysics that early Buddhism compares with Mādhyamika thought. Still, they differ with regard to the manner in which metaphysics was rejected. While early Buddhism appealed to experience in order to eliminate metaphysics, Mādhyamika thought depended entirely on an appeal to the dialectic and the transcendental. Because of this transcendentalist approach of the Mādhyamikas, they differ considerably from early Buddhists. Belief in a transcendental reality or an Absolute has no place in early Buddhism. The *Sutta-nipāta* says:

> Apart from sense data, no diverse and eternal truths exist in this world. Having organized one's reasoning with regard to metaphysical assumptions, [the sophist] spoke of two things, truth and falsehood.
>
> (*Na h'eva saccāni bahūni nānā,*
> *aññatra saññāya niccāni loke;*
> *takkañ ca diṭṭhīsu pakappayitvā,*
> *saccaṃ musā ti dvayadhammam āhu.*)[16]

The problems faced by Nāgârjuna and by the later Mādhyamikas as a result of the adoption of the transcendental point of view is very clearly stated by Nāgârjuna himself, anticipating the objections raised by the opponents:

> If everything is empty, there is no origination or destruction. That would be to accept the nonexistence of the four Noble Truths.
>
> In the absence of the four Noble Truths, there would neither be understanding [of suffering], nor elimination [of the cause of suffering], nor cultivation [of the path leading to cessation of suffering], nor realization [of the cessation of suffering].
>
> If these are nonexistent, then also the four noble 'fruits' do not exist. In the absence of the four noble 'fruits', there would not be those who have attained the fruits nor those who have attained the path [leading thereto].

> In the absence of these eight types of people, there would be no Order. From the nonexistence of the Noble Truths, the true *dharma* also does not exist.
>
> Without the *dharma* and the Order, how can there be Buddha? Consequently, what you assert also destroys the Three Treasures [i.e., the Buddha, the *dharma*, and the Order].[17]

In answer to this objection, Nāgârjuna, for the first and last time in the *Mūlamadhyamakakārikā*, refers to the two levels of truth and maintains that the Ultimate Reality (*paramârtha*) cannot be communicated without resorting to the conventional (*saṃvṛti*), and that without understanding the Ultimate Reality one cannot realize nirvana. Furthermore, on the basis of his own interpretation of causality, Nāgârjuna gives an ingenious explanation of the problem raised by the opponent. Causality, according to Nāgârjuna, is pure relativity, and this relativity is synonymous with emptiness (*śūnyatā*). Therefore he maintains:

> Since there is no *dharma* whatever which is not causally conditioned [i.e., not relative], no *dharma* whatever exists which is not empty.
>
> If all existence is not empty [i.e., if it is not causally conditioned], there is neither origination nor destruction. You must therefore wrongly conclude that the four Noble Truths exist.[18]

The argument is clear. Every *dharma* is relative. Hence every *dharma* is also empty. There is no *dharma* that is not relative. Therefore, there is no *dharma* that is not empty. If there is any *dharma* that is not empty, it cannot be causally conditioned. Therefore, if one accepts nonemptiness (*aśūnyatā*), one also accepts nonrelativity, and as a result one has to reject origination and destruction. If one does not accept origination and destruction, one cannot accept the four Noble Truths. Nāgârjuna argues that it is not the acceptance of emptiness (*śūnyatā*), but its rejection, that makes it difficult to speak of the four Noble Truths. This is interesting dialectic.

The important question is this: Was Nāgârjuna prepared to accept origination (*utpāda*) and destruction (*vyaya*) as facts? It would seem that according to his statements in the *Ratnāvalī*, Nāgârjuna would assert origination and destruction and hence the causal principle: "When this exists, that exists, as 'long' exists, when 'short' exists. On the arising of this, that arises, as light arises on the arising of a lamp."[19] But this very same causal principle is invalidated in the *Mūlamadhyamakakārikā* when he maintained, "Since existence (*sat-tā*) of things that are nonsubstantial is not evident (*na vidyate*), [the theory] that 'when this exists, that exists,' is not possible."[20] What makes him assert both existence and arising in one context, and deny both in another? The only possible explanation seems to be that from the worldly point of view (*saṃvṛti*) both existence and arising are valid, but from a transcendental point of view (*paramârtha*) both are invalid. This is an extremely faithful presentation of the basic teachings of the *Prajñāpāramitā* literature.

But the 'nondiscriminated' (*a-prapañcita*) experience of the *yogin* was so important for the Mādhyamikas that they considered all worldly reality (*lokasaṃvṛti*) to be 'conceptual' (*savikalpika*), not empirical, and hence adopted the most effective method of refuting all concepts, namely, the dialectical approach.

By adopting this dialectical approach, the Mādhyamikas were able to uphold the sole reality of the Absolute, which they termed variously *tathatā*, *dharmakāya*, *tathāgata*, *tattva*, and *satya*. Hence the realization of this Ultimate Reality was presented as the goal of the religious life. The only way to attain this realization is by becoming a Buddha, a fully and perfectly enlightened one (*samyak-sambuddha*). It is the only path (*mārga*). To become a Buddha, one must adopt the life of a *bodhisattva*. Only a person of low disposition aspires to *arahant*ship. By providing a philosophical basis for the Mahāyāna ideal in this manner, Nāgârjuna attained preeminence as a Mahāyāna thinker.

We have already referred to the subsect of the Mādhyamikas —the school of Bhāvaviveka which came to be known as the Svātantrika Mādhyamika. In spite of Nāgârjuna's superiority in the field of logic and dialectic, his theory of emptiness (*śūnyatā*) seems to have been rather unpalatable to the ordinary man as well as to the philosopher. In fact, the Mādhyamikas had difficulty avoiding the criticism that they represented a nihilistic standpoint (*nāstika dṛṣṭi*). Nāgârjuna's reluctance to present an empirical theory contributed to this criticism. Although in early Buddhism causality was presented as an empirical theory, the transcendentalist approach adopted by

Nāgârjuna prevented him from considering causality as a counter-thesis to the causal theories advocated by other philosophers, both Buddhist and non-Buddhist.

Bhāvaviveka seems to have dreaded this situation, and he held the view that one should have a thesis to refute another. He seems to have felt that causality (*pratītyasamutpāda*), as the cornerstone of the Buddha's teaching, should be accepted as the empirical reality of the phenomenal world and as the thesis with which to counter the heretical or metaphysical theories. But this position could not be maintained in an atmosphere in which absolutism reigned supreme. It is this very dilemma—the recognition that causality is the central teaching of the Buddha with regard to the phenomenal world, on the one hand, and the difficulty of recognizing such an empirical reality in the face of the transcendental, on the other—which led the Mādhyamikas to raise causality (*pratītyasamutpāda*) to the level of the transcendental, as is evident from the following description:

> I salute the perfectly enlightened one, the foremost of all teachers, who proclaimed the principle of causality (*pratītyasamutpāda*) [which leads to] the pacification of obsessions and is blissful, which neither disappears nor appears, neither has an end nor is eternal, neither undifferentiated nor differentiated, moves neither hither nor thither.[21]

Notes

1. T. R. V. Murti, *The Central Philosophy of Buddhism* (London: George Allen & Unwin, 1955).
2. Ibid., p. 69.
3. *MK* 1.1.
4. Ibid., 1.2.
5. Ibid., 1.3.
6. *MKV*, p. 14.
7. *MK* 1.3.
8. *The Central Philosophy of Buddhism*, p. 131.
9. Ibid.
10. *The Central Philosophy of Buddhism*, p. 83.
11. Ibid.
12. *MKV*, pp. 492–493.

13. This seems to be the implication of Candrakīrti's statement at *MKV* p. 350, where he maintains that "[concepts like] aggregates, elements, and spheres are not obtained at the time of the perception of emptiness by the *yogin*."
14. *MK* 17.9.
15. Ibid., 25.19.
16. *Sn* 886.
17. *MK* 24.1–6.
18. Ibid., 24.19–20.
19. *Ratnāvalī*, ed. G. Tucci, *Journal of the Royal Asiatic Society* (New Series, 1934), p. 318.
20. *MK* 1.10.
21. *MKV*, pp. 3 f.

Selected Readings

PRIMARY SOURCES

Catuḥśataka of Āryadeva, Sanskrit and Tibetan texts with copious notes from the commentary of Candrakīrti, reconstructed and edited by Vidhushekhara Bhattacarya, Calcutta: Visva-Bhāratī Book-Shop, 1931.

Karatalaratna of Bhāvaviveka, restored from Chinese translation into Sanskrit by N. Aiyaswami Sastri, Santiniketan: Visva-Bhāratī, 1949; tr. into French by L. de la Vallée Poussin, "Le Joyau dans la Main," *Mélanges Chinois et Bouddhiques*, 2 (1932–1933): 68–138.

Mūlamadhaymakakārikā of Nāgârjuna, Sanskrit text and translation by Kenneth K. Inada, Tokyo: Hokuseido Press, 1970. *Mūlamadhyamakakārikās . . . de Nāgârjuna avec la Prasannapadā* (*Mādhyamikavṛtti*), ed. L. de la Vallée Poussin, St. Petersburg: The Imperial Academy of Sciences, 1903.

Vigrahavyāvartanī of Nāgârjuna, with Nāgârjuna's own commentary, ed. E. E. H. Johnston and Arnold Kunst, *Mélanges Chinois et Bouddhiques*, 9 (1951): 99–152.

SECONDARY SOURCES

Conze, Edward. *Buddhist Thought in India.* Pp. 238–249.

Dasgupta, S. N. *A History of Indian Philosophy*. Vol. I. Pp. 138–145.

de la Vallée Poussin, L. "Reflections sur le Mādhyamika." *Mélanges Chinois et Bouddhiques*, 2 (1933): 1–59.

Kalupahana, David J. *Causality: The Central Philosophy of Buddhism.* Pp. 147–162.

Murti, T. R. V. *The Central Philosophy of Buddhism*. London: George Allen & Unwin, 1955.
Robinson, R. H. *Early Mādhyamika in India and China*. Madison: University of Wisconsin, 1967.
Streng, F. J. *Emptiness. A Study in Religious Meaning*. Nashville: Abingdon Press, 1967.
Takakusu, J. *The Essentials of Buddhist Philosophy*. Pp. 96ff.
Thomas, E. J. *History of Buddhist Thought*. Pp. 212–229.

Chapter Twelve
Yogâcāra Idealism

Just as the "critical philosophy" of Immanuel Kant paved the way for Hegelian Idealism, even so the critical philosophy of Nāgârjuna may be said to have contributed to the systematized form of absolute Idealism of Vasubandhu, although Idealism as such was not unknown earlier. Idealism developed gradually from the second century A.D., and reached its culmination with the writings of Asaṅga and Vasubandhu. The *Sandhinirmocana-sūtra* and the *Laṅkâvatāra-sūtra* represent the earlier unsystematic phase of Yogâcāra thought, while the more systematic form is found in Vasubandhu's *Vijñaptimātratā-siddhi*, which consists of two parts: (1) *Viṃśatikā*, 'Twenty Verses', together with his own commentary, and (2) *Triṃśikā*, 'Thirty Verses', with commentary by Sthiramati. Other treatises of note are Asaṅga's *Abhidharmasamuccaya* and *Mahāyānasaṅgraha*, and Maitreyanātha's *Mahāyānasūtrâlaṅkāra* and *Madhyântavibhāga*. Hsüan Tsang's *Ch'eng wei shih lun* (*Vijñaptimātratāsiddhi*) represents chiefly the views of Dharmapāla who lived during the sixth century. In addition to these is the encyclopedic work, the *Yogâcārabhūmi-śāstra*.

Doctrinally, the Sautrāntikas are considered to be the precursors of Yogâcāra Idealism. In fact, tradition has it that Vasubandhu, the chief exponent of Yogâcāra, was a Sautrāntika but was converted to the new faith by his older brother Asaṅga. The Sautrāntika theory of representative perception leads logically to Idealism. The Sautrāntikas, as mentioned earlier (see chapter 10), held that an object does not come into contact with the sense organ directly, because the object is without any duration. They upheld the inferability of the object (*bāhyârthânumeya*). This indeed is good supporting evidence for an idealistic theory which holds that the external object is a mere mental fabrication (*manomaya*). The Mādhyamikas, too, contributed in great measure to the development of Yogâcāra Idealism. Their ruthless analysis of concepts leading to the view that these do not designate any reality or that they are empty of content or that they do not reveal the nature of phenomena was welcomed by the Yogâcārins. While denying that the external object has any reality, the Yogâcārins differed from the Mādhyamikas in maintaining that the mind or consciousness is real. Since the Absolute (*paramârtha*) was looked upon as being nondual (*advaya*) and nonconceptual (*nirvikalpa*) and as transcending worldly experience, the Yogâcārins maintained that it is realized in the highest state of yogic rapture where there is undiscriminated consciousness without subject-object dichotomy. Hence the name Yogâcāra, which means 'practice of *yoga*'. While the Mādhyamikas had little to say of *yoga* or *dhyāna*, the Yogâcārins emphasized it. They advocated a ruthless withdrawal from everything by following the traditional method of *yoga*.

Although an absolute form of Idealism is found in the *Sandhinirmocana-sūtra* and the *Laṅkâvatāra-sūtra* as well as in the works of Asaṅga and Maitreyanātha, a philosophical justification and a clear statement of the Yogâcāra philosophy is found in the famous work of Vasubandhu. The *Viṃśatikā* of the *Vijñaptimātratāsiddhi* is devoted to a refutation of the Realist's position and a philosophical justification of the Idealist's standpoint. It is mainly a polemical work. The *Triṃśikā* is devoted to a systematic treatment of the basic teachings of the Idealists. It is rather surprising that, although these two treatises supplement each other and, in fact, constitute one whole, the early Chinese scholars concentrated their attention on the second part only. Thus, Hsüan Tsang's *Ch'eng wei shih lun* contains the second part and not the first. Because of the philosophical importance of both parts of Vasubandhu's treatise, this work will serve as the *locus classicus* of the present chapter.

Vasubandhu begins his work by stating the basic premise of the Idealists that everything "is ideation only" (*vijñaptimātram*), and, in his own commentary on this statement, he maintains that the whole concept of the 'three worlds' is mere ideation, quoting it as a statement of the Buddha himself. For Vasubandhu, 'mind', 'thought', 'consciousness', and 'ideation' are synonyms. The external object is merely an appearance, like the perception of hair in the sky or double vision on the part of one whose sight is impaired by an ailment. He then proceeds immediately to enumerate four kinds of objection a Realist would raise against his theory:

1. If the external object does not exist in reality but is a mental projection only, then it is not possible to account for its spatial determination (*deśa-niyama*). That is, an object is seen to cover or

occupy a certain space, and if it is only mind-made it will be perceived as existing, not in a particular place, but in every place to which we direct our mind. Thus the occupation of space by an object, which is part of our sense experience, would be meaningless if the object is a mere mental projection.

2. In the same way, an object is perceived only at a particular time, not always; for example, it may be perceived when one is looking at it, not when one is not looking at it. If an object is mind-made, then such temporal determinations (*kāla-niyama*) will be without satisfactory explanation.

3. The indetermination of the perceiving stream of consciousness (*santāna-aniyama*) could not be explained if one were to deny the real existence of the external object. If the object is a mental projection, it can be determined in terms of (= be seen by) that stream of consciousness (= that individual), and may not be available to another perceiving stream of consciousness (= another individual). In other words, an object cannot serve as a common object of perception for several individuals. Since not every object is determined in this manner, there must be real external objects.

4. If the object is only a mental representation, fruitful activity (*kṛtya-kriyā*) caused by the objects cannot be explained. Hunger is not satisfied by taking imaginary food. In the same way, water, clothes, poison, weapons, and so on, have their causal activities or efficiencies which cannot be explained in terms of imaginary objects.

In his refutation of these arguments, Vasubandhu does not resort to an analysis of the epistemological problems associated with the realist position. It was left to his pupil Dinnāga to lay bare such epistemological questions. To this we shall come later. Vasubandhu seems to have been interested in refuting the realist thesis by using metaphysical or dialectical arguments only, and thereby justifying the existing form of absolute Idealism which for him appeared to be more compatible with the basic teachings of Mahāyāna. He bases his arguments merely on dream experience and the experience of infernal beings. Taking in turn each of the objections raised by the Realist, Vasubandhu examined them in the light of these experiences.

1. In dreams people experience the existence of objects at particular places, and not everywhere. Spatial determination is to be

had in dream experience. But a dream object is a mental fabrication only, not something existing in reality. Hence, Vasubandhu asks why this could not be the case in ordinary sense experience.

2. An object of dream experience is also temporally determined. It is perceived at a particular time only, not always. The same could be true of ordinary everyday experiences which may not have real objects.

3. In order to refute the argument concerning the indetermination of the perceiving stream of consciousness, Vasubandhu takes up the experiences of the denizens of hell and points out that all these beings, including the infernal guards, perceive the river of pus into which the evil-doers are thrown. Vasubandhu's assumption seems to be that the river of pus, nay even hell itself, are mental constructions not existing in reality, and that, though these are mental projections, they are objects of common experience not particularly limited to one person.

4. As for the last objection of the Realist, Vasubandhu points out that fruitful activity, too, results from unreal dream objects, for the sight of a dream tiger causes real fear and an erotic dream is followed by consequences which are physically real.

The basic assumption behind all these arguments seems to be that it is not possible to find any definite proof for the nonillusory or veridical nature of sense experience. The recognition of the superiority and transcendence of yogic intuition contributed greatly to this view. From the standpoint of the highest yogic rapture, wherein is to be found a form of undiscriminated pure consciousness, sense experience characterized by subject-object discrimination appears illusory, in the same way that dream experience is found to be illusory from the standpoint of waking consciousness. Hence consciousness is the only reality.[1]

Vasubandhu then proceeds to explain why the Buddha spoke of the twelve 'gateways' (*āyatana*) representing the subjective and objective aspects of experience. He points out that in actual fact consciousness manifests itself as subject and object. It arises out of its own seed and then manifests itself as an external object. Therefore, the Buddha, according to Vasubandhu, spoke of the two bases of cognition, internal and external, with the sole intention of disciplining the ordinary people, just as he spoke of the 'beings of spontaneous birth' (that is, the gods), not because such beings existed in reality, but because the belief in the existence of such beings could be utilized to regulate the lives of ordinary people (see chapter 6). From here, Vasubandhu tries to justify one of the most important claims of the Mahāyānists. He points out that reality was analyzed by the Buddha into twelve 'gateways' (*āyatana*) of cognition in order to eliminate the belief in an eternal and unchanging 'self' (*ātman*). This is the theory of the nonsubstantiality of the individual (*pudgala-nairātmya*), which was upheld by the Hīnayānists. But by denying the reality of the external object, the Mahāyānists claimed that they supersede the Hīnayānists because they advocate the nonsubstantiality of the *dharmas* (*dharma-nairātmya*) as well. This criticism of the Mahāyānists may be considered valid as far as some of the later schools of Buddhism are concerned, for the Sarvâstivādins as well as the post-Buddhaghosa Theravādins, in a sense, accepted the substantiality of the *dharmas* (see chapter 9).

Next, Vasubandhu takes up the different atomic theories presented by the realist schools. In the Abhidharma schools as well as in some of the Hindu schools, the external object was analyzed in terms of material atoms (*paramâṇu*, see chapter 9). Vasubandhu adduced dialectical arguments to refute these atomic theories.

The net result of all these speculations was the view that perception cannot guarantee the existence of external objects, because the awareness of them does not seem to be very different from that of dream experience. Memory, too, is not helpful in that it implies the perception of consciousness itself, or rather what is found in the stream of consciousness. Anticipating objections from the opponent, Vasubandhu maintains that before we are fully awake we cannot know that dream objects are unreal. Things seen in a dream are as real to the dreamer as any object is to a person who is awake. The unreality of dream objects is realized only when a person is awake. The difference between dream consciousness and waking consciousness is that in the former, a person's mind is overwhelmed by torpor (*middha*). Similarly, compared with a person in the highest state of yogic concentration, worldly people are slumbering in ignorance. So long as they remain in this state of ignorance they do not realize that the world of sense experience does not exist in reality. Highest knowledge yields the realization that reality is pure and undiscriminated consciousness. This, of course, leads Vasubandhu to deny not only the validity and possibility of sense perception, but also of extrasensory perception. For example, in telepathy (see chapter 2) one is said to perceive the nature and functioning of another's mind (*para-citta*). If this is possible, here again there will be dichotomy of subject (i.e., one's own mind, *sva-citta*) and object (i.e., another's mind, *para-citta*), and this dichotomy is false. This is absolute Idealism. And like Nāgârjuna, Vasubandhu, with the intention of justifying the Mahāyāna doctrine of 'one vehicle' (*eka-yāna*), insisted that this highest knowledge is attained with the realization of Buddhahood.

In the *Triṃśikā*, Vasubandhu gives a systematic exposition of the Idealist philosophy which, along with Mādhyamika thought, became extremely popular in the Far Eastern countries where Buddhism found a congenial home.

The false belief in 'self' (*ātman*) and 'real elements' (*dharma*), according to the *Triṃśikā*, is due to the evolution of consciousness (*vijñāna-pariṇāma*), which in turn is due to its inherent power (generated by ignorance). This evolving consciousness undergoes a threefold modification or transformation as: (1) the resultant (*vipāka*), (2) egocentric mental operation (*manana*), and (3) ideation or consciousness of external objects (*viṣaya-vijñapti*).

The first of these is represented by the *ālaya-vijñāna*, 'store consciousness'. It is called 'resultant' (*vipāka*) because it represents the germination of the seeds (*bīja*), which are the dispositions (*vāsanā*) of good and bad actions and which have attained maturity (*paripāka*). Thus the *ālaya* is the receptacle of all the dispositions (*vāsanā*), which, as seeds, ripen and produce their fruits. It is the basis of all the conscious and unconscious processes. When it evolves, it develops touch or contact (*sparśa*), mental activity (*manaskāra*), feeling (*vedanā*), sensation (*saṃjñā*), and volitional activity (*cetanā*). The difference between the 'store consciousness' of the Vijñānavādins and the 'unconscious process' (*bhavaṅga*) of the Abhidharmikas is that, according to the latter, the vibrations in the unconscious are produced by external stimuli, while the former believe that the transformations are initiated by the ripening of seeds within the 'store consciousness'. This is the first transformation.

The second transformation is the evolution of *manas* or 'mentation', the seventh consciousness according to the Yogâcāra list, and different from *mano-vijñāna*, 'mind-consciousness', which is one of the six types of sense consciousness having their respective objective supports (*ālambana*). According to the *Triṃśikā*, "Depending upon the store consciousness and having it as the support, the consciousness called *manas*, which has the nature of cogitation, functions." It is associated with four types of defilements: perception of self (*ātma-dṛṣṭi*), confusion with regard to the self (*ātma-moha*), self-pride (*ātma-māna*), and self-love (*ātma-sneha*). This is the second transformation, in which *manas* comes to be associated with the false belief in a 'self'.

The third transformation consists of the evolution of the consciousness of the sixfold object—form (*rūpa*), sound (*śabda*), odor (*gandha*), taste (*rasa*), tangible object (*spraṣṭavya*), and concepts or ideas (*dharma*). Although consciousness of external objects is recognized, this consciousness is not produced by the activity of the external objects; they are mere mental projections. The perception of a 'self' (*ātman*) and of material bases of external objects (*dharma*, i.e., material elements, according to the Abhidharma), is due to false imagination (*parikalpita* or *abhūta-parikalpa*). These have no reality whatsoever.

The discrimination (*vikalpa*) of consciousness into subjective and objective aspects is caused by factors inherent in the store consciousness (*ālaya-vijñāna*). Since it is consciousness itself that appears as the subject and the object and since consciousness is the sole reality, this subject-object discrimination (*vikalpa*) carries more reality than the consciousness of the 'self' or 'real external objects', which are but falsely imagined (*parikalpita*). While the 'self' and the 'object' have no real existence, the consciousness which appears as subjective and objective aspects has relative existence (*paratantra*). This discrimination also appears to be unreal as perfect knowledge is attained, and consciousness appears in its true nature without any discrimination whatsoever. This, according to the Yogâcārins, is the Ultimate Reality (*pariniṣpanna*). Thus, unlike the Mādhyamikas who recognized two levels of reality only, the conventional (*saṃvṛti*) and ultimate (*paramârtha*), the Idealists recognized three levels of reality or nature (*svabhāva*).

Existence (*saṃsāra*) is explained in terms of the 'store consciousness'. The evolution or transformation of this 'store consciousness' is without beginning (*anâdikālika*). The cyclic evolution takes place in the following manner: As the seeds mature in the 'store consciousness', the second transformation, or the evolution of *manas*, takes place. Then comes the third transformation—the evolution of the perceptive consciousness (*pravṛtti-vijñāna*), consisting of subject-object discrimination. This perceptive consciousness leads to activity or behavior (*karma*), good, bad, or indeterminate. As a result, there is accumulation of dispositions (*vāsanā*), which are stored up in the 'store consciousness' and serve as the seeds for the repeated evolution of *manas* and the sixfold perceptive consciousness. The complete stopping of this process is achieved with the attainment of enlightenment. This enlightenment comes with the realization that everything is mere ideation (*vijñaptimātram*) or mere consciousness (*cittamātram*). The realization that all is mere ideation (*vijñaptimātram*) is not alone sufficient for the attainment of freedom. He who grasps an object and says, "This is *vijñaptimātra*," has not reached *vijñaptimātra*. While realizing that everything is *vijñaptimātra*, one has to eliminate all forms of grasping. Thus, the *Triṃśikā* says:

> When consciousness is without an objective support, then consciousness is established in *vijñaptimātra*, since in the absence of anything to grasp, there is no grasping.
>
> When [he] is without thought, without objective support, his knowledge is supramundane. There is 'turning away' from the object, through the abandonment of the two kinds of weaknesses [i.e., the belief in a 'self' and the belief in 'real elements'].
>
> That is the realm without defiling tendencies (*āśrava*), inconceivable, good, permanent, happy with released body; this is what is called the *dharma* [-body] of the great Sage.[2]

It is significant that *vijñaptimātra* or the ultimate undifferentiated reality is equated with the *dharma* of the Buddha. The attainment of this state involves the practice of the career of a *bodhisattva* for countless aeons, fulfilling the six perfections (*pāramitā*) and acquiring omniscience (*sarvâkārajñatā*). This state is Buddhahood, and, according to the *Triṃśikā*, it is the *dharma* of the great Sage. Thus, with the attainment of enlightenment, a *bodhisattva* becomes, "not merely *a* Buddha, but Buddha." He becomes one with the Ultimate Reality. As Maitreya has said, "On the pure stage there is neither oneness nor plurality of Buddhas; there is no oneness owing to their formerly having had bodies, nor is there plurality because like space they have now no bodies."[3] It is this kind of metaphysical speculation which seems to have contributed to the conception of the three bodies (*trikāya*) of the Buddha, one of the most prominent doctrines in Mahāyāna. While accepting the unity or oneness of Buddhahood or Ultimate Reality which is represented by the *dharma*-body (*dharma-kāya*), the Mahāyānists had to account for the different individuals who have completed their careers as *bodhisattvas* and have taught the doctrine. Mere merging with an Ultimate Reality and losing all identity appeared frightening. Hence those who have realized the unity of Buddhahood were considered as existing in a state of bliss, freed from all illusion and relative truth. This is the 'body of enjoyment' (*sambhoga-kāya*), through which the Buddhas are able to provide instruction in the doctrine to the various divine assemblies. In the early discourses of the Mahāyāna, the Buddhas are described as existing in different worlds preaching to the various assemblies. Lastly, the 'transformation-body' (*nirmāṇa-kāya*) represents the historical Buddha.

In contrast to the absolute form of Idealism discussed above, a theory of Immaterialism, comparable with that of George Berkeley in Western philosophy, was propounded by Dinnāga who was a pupil of Vasubandhu. Dinnāga is looked upon as the foremost of the Buddhist logicians, and his *Pramāṇasamuccaya* is rated as the greatest work on Buddhist logic. While his logical theories are presented in the *Pramāṇasamuccaya*, his ontological speculations are embodied in a very short but extremely important treatise, the *Ālambanaparīkṣā*, 'Examination of the Object'.

The *Vijñaptimātratāsiddhi* of Vasubandhu represents a systematization of the metaphysical Idealism embodied in the early Yogâcāra texts like *Sandhinirmocana-sūtra* and *Laṅkâvatāra-sūtra*, but there is no fresh evaluation of the ideas found in these early texts. As mentioned earlier, Vasubandhu employed metaphysical or dialectical arguments against the reality of the phenomenal world. Absolute Idealism reached its culmination with the writings of Vasubandhu. But his successors had to meet the criticisms made by the opponents of this school; hence Dinnāga's interest in logic and metaphysics. Without taking for granted the existing idealistic framework, Dinnāga undertook a fresh evaluation of the epistemological basis of Idealism, which finally led him to the formulation of a philosophy very similar to that of Berkeley, without, of course, Berkeley's final conclusions (as for example, the conception of God). This new philosophy is to be found in the *Ālambanaparīkṣā*.

Comparing Vasubandhu and Dinnāga, it may be said that the former, adopting a transcendentalist approach, denied the efficacy and even the possibility of sense experience, while the latter denied, in Berkeleyan fashion, the substantial reality of matter. According to Dinnāga, it is consciousness itself that appears in the form of an external object and it is this external object that serves as the object condition (*ālambana-pratyaya*). From time immemorial this objective aspect and the force which transforms consciousness into the subject-object relationship, that is, the sense organ, have been, and continue to be, mutually conditioned. But, unlike Vasubandhu, Dinnāga does not posit the metaphysical principle of 'store consciousness' (*ālaya-vijñāna*) in order to account for the source of this subject-object discrimination. Moreover, Dinnāga evaluates sense experience in its own light and, unlike Vasubandhu, does not attempt to evaluate sense experience in the light of a transcendental consciousness such as *vijñaptimātra*. Hence he does not seem to have contributed to a theory of transcendental or universal illusion (*mukhyavibhrama*). This is evident from his definition of perception (*pratyakṣa*). While Vasubandhu, following Asaṅga, defined perception as being "devoid of mental construction (*kalpanâpoḍha*) and nonillusive (*abhrānta*)," Dinnāga accepted the first part of the definition and dropped the second, implying thereby that illusiveness is not a universal characteristic of sense perception. Furthermore, he spoke of an element of fact or object (*artha*) which is external (*bāhya*) and which has a distinctive character (*svalakṣaṇa*), showing thereby that he denied only the materiality, and not the externality, of the object of sense experience. It is therefore possible to conclude that an examination of the epistemological problems inherent in a realist as well as an idealist theory of perception led Dinnāga to accept a theory of Immaterialism, which was the first of its kind in the history of Indian philosophy.

Notes

1. See *Vijñaptimātratāsiddhi*, *Viṃśatikā* 16–18.
2. *Vijñaptimātratāsiddhi*, *Triṃśikā* 28–30.
3. *Mahāyānasūtrālaṅkāra*, ed. Sylvan Lévi (Paris: Champion, 1907), 9.26.

Selected Readings

PRIMARY SOURCES

Ālambanaparīkṣā, restored from Chinese and Tibetan by N. A. Sastri, Adyar Library Series 32, Adyar: Adyar Library, 1942.

Vijñaptimātratāsiddhi, *Viṃśatikā* and *Triṃśikā*, with Sthiramati's commentary, ed. S. Lévi, Paris: Librairie Ancienne Honoré Champion, 1925; tr. into French, S. Lévi, *Matériaux pour l'Étude du Système Vijñaptimātra*, Paris: Paul Geuthner, 1932. Dharmapāla's version, translated into Chinese by Hsüan Tsang, *TD* 1585; tr. into French, L. de la Vallée Poussin, *Vijñaptimātratāsiddhi. La Siddhi de Hiuan-Tsang. Bouddhica* 1, 5, Paris: Librairie Orientaliste Paul Geuthner, 1928–1929.

SECONDARY SOURCES

Conze, Edward. *Buddhist Thought in India*. Pp. 250–260.

Dasgupta, S. N. *History of Indian Philosophy*. Vol. 1. Pp. 145–151.

Kalupahana, D. J. "Dinnāga's Theory of Immaterialism." *Philosophy East and West*, 20 (1970): 121–128.

Sharma, C. *Dialectic in Buddhism and Vedānta*. Benares: Nand Kishore & Bros., 1952.

Stcherbatsky, T. I. *Buddhist Logic*. Vol. 1. Leningrad: The Academy of Science of the USSR, 1930.

Suzuki, D. T. *Studies in the Laṅkâvatāra-sūtra*. London: George Routledge & Sons, 1930.

———. *Philosophy of Yogâcāra*. Bibliotheque du Muséon. Louvain: Bareau du Muséon, 1904.

Thomas, E. J. *History of Buddhist Thought*. Pp. 230–248.

Appendix I
Metaphysics and the Buddha

So far we have been using the term *metaphysical principle* to refer to certain concepts found in the pre-Buddhist traditions, without giving an adequate account of what the Buddha meant by metaphysics, or what he included in this category, or even the Buddha's attitude toward such concepts. The discussion of this problem was deliberately postponed because it was thought that only after examining the main doctrines of Buddhism would it be possible to determine exactly which type of theory was included in this category. This was all the more necessary since the Buddha did not consider as metaphysical all the questions that a modern philosopher would classify in this way, for example, the questions pertaining to causation (*paṭiccasamuppāda*) and causal uniformity (*dhammatā*).

In addition to the few minor propositions that the Buddha occasionally referred to as being metaphysical, there is a set of major questions which he always considered metaphysics proper. The former were propositions regarding causation presented by the pre-Buddhist thinkers, and the latter included the ten (sometimes fourteen) undeclared or unanswered (*avyākata*, Sk. *avyākṛta*) questions.

Let us consider the set of propositions regarding causality which the Buddha viewed as metaphysical. In the *Samyutta Nikāya*,[1] a person called Acela Kassapa poses the following questions:

1. Is suffering caused by oneself? (*sayaṃ kataṃ dukkhaṃ*, self-causation of suffering)
2. Is suffering caused by another? (*paraṃ kataṃ dukkhaṃ*, external causation of suffering)
3. Is suffering caused by both self and another? (*sayaṃ kataṇ ca paraṃ katañ ca*, a combination of self-causation and external causation)
4. Is suffering caused neither by oneself nor by another? *asayaṃkāraṃ aparaṃkāraṃ adhiccasamuppannaṃ*, indeterminism or noncausation)

To all these questions, the Buddha's reply was: "Do not (say) so" (*mā h' evaṃ*), instead of a denial, which is generally expressed as: "It is not so" (*no h' etaṃ*). His reluctance to accept the first proposition (self-causation of suffering) was prompted by his awareness that it leads to a belief in eternalism (*sassata*). The second was avoided because it was thought to lead to annihilationism (*uccheda*). The third, combining both theories mentioned above, carried with it both implications, eternalism and annihilationism. And the fourth was a denial of causation altogether.

Why did the Buddha believe that self-causation leads to the belief in eternalism? He found that those who advocated self-causation posited an eternal or unchanging 'self' or 'soul' and tended to ignore the importance of any other factor that contributed to the arising of suffering or the production of its effect. They were so engrossed in belief in a 'self' (*ātman*) that they failed to emphasize the causal efficiency of factors other than the 'self'. This, as pointed out in chapters 1 and 3, was the theory of causation put forward by the Upaniṣadic thinkers. On the other hand, the Materialists, who rejected the Upaniṣadic theory of 'self' (*ātman*) and adopted a non-substantialist (*anātman*) standpoint, went to the other extreme of denying altogether the causal efficiency of human volition or human responsibility. This was probably due to a kind of prejudice against the idealist metaphysics of the Upaniṣadic thinkers. Since the materialist theory, too, was prompted by certain prejudices and inclinations, it also does not represent the true nature of things.

Just as the Upaniṣadic theory did not seriously consider certain important factors of experience in explaining causation, so did the Materialists overlook the efficacy of individual volition and hence rejected certain aspects of experience. These are what the Buddha called individual or partial truths (*paccekasacca*).[2] The Jaina theory of causation, which combined these two theories, also carried with it a belief in a 'self' (*ātman*) or determinism (*niyata*) as well as the absence of a 'self' implied by their indeterminism (*aniyata*). According to the Buddha, the combination of two metaphysical theories will not produce a satisfactory or even an empirical theory.

This, no doubt, was the raison d'être of an entirely new term—*paṭiccasamuppāda*, 'dependent arising'—to refer to causality. Because people are bound by their own approaches, attachments, and inclinations (*upāya-upādāna-abhinivesa-vinibandha*),[3] as mentioned above, no form of logic or reasoning could convince them of the truth of the theory of 'dependent arising' (*paṭiccasamuppāda*). This certainly was the reason why the Buddha maintained that the doctrine of causality presented by him is beyond the sphere of logical reasoning, and not because it is an extraempirical theory which cannot be described in empirical terms. In the *Ariyapariyesana-sutta* he says:

> It occurred to me that I have discovered this *dhamma*, profound, difficult to see, difficult to comprehend, peaceful, excellent, beyond the sphere of logic, subtle and to be understood by the wise. These people are devoted to their likes (*ālaya*), deeply engrossed with their likes, and nourished by their likes. For those who are devoted to their likes, engrossed with their likes, and nourished by their likes, this fact, namely, relativity (*idappaccayatā*) or causality (*paṭiccasamuppāda*) is difficult to comprehend.[4]

It may also be said that the pre-Buddhist theories, while prompted by the different inclinations, likes, and dislikes of those who formulated them, were also based on a priori reasoning directed at showing what reality ought to be rather than explaining what is given in experience.

The *Udāna* relates the well-known anecdote in which the people who hold differing metaphysical views are compared with those who are blind from birth (*jaccandha*).[5] A group of blind people is taken to examine an elephant. Each person is allowed to touch some part of the animal, and each one is then questioned as to what an elephant is like. The one who felt the animal's head said that an elephant is like a huge pot. The person who felt the ear said that it is like a winowing basket. The one who left the tusk maintained that it is like a ploughshare. And so on. The moral of the story is that persons belonging to different schools of thought are *conditioned* to think in accordance with the teachings of those schools and are blind to other facts.

Sixty-two metaphysical views (*diṭṭhi*) are discussed in the *Brahmajāla-suttanta*.[6] Many of these can be subsumed under one or the other of the ten undeclared (*avyākata*) problems. These ten are as follows:

1. The world is eternal (*sassato loko*)
2. The world is not eternal (*asassato loko*)
3. The world is finite (*antavā loko*)

4. The world is infinite (*anantavā loko*)
5. The soul is identical with the body (*taṃ jīvaṃ taṃ sarīraṃ*)
6. The soul is different from the body (*aññaṃ jīvaṃ aññaṃ sarīraṃ*)
7. The *tathāgata* exists after death (*hoti tathāgato parammaraṇā*)
8. The *tathāgata* does not exist after death (*na hoti tathāgato parammaraṇā*)
9. The *tathāgata* both exists and does not exist after death (*hoti ca na ca hoti tathāgato parammaraṇā*)
10. The *tathāgata* neither exists nor does not exist after death (*neva hoti na na hoti tathāgato parammaraṇā*)

It will be noticed that the first two pairs of propositions refer to the duration and the extent of the world, the third, to the nature of the soul, and the last four, to the state of the dead saint.

The first two propositions about the world may, in a way, represent the two opposite views about the nature of the world—the view of the eternalists (*sassatavādī*), who believed that the real nature of the world (as well as the soul) is eternality or permanence, and the view of the Materialists, who maintained that the world is not eternal (*asassata*). A similar paradoxical situation is seen in the third and the fourth alternatives. The questions whether the world is eternal or not, finite or not, according to the Buddha, cannot be decided on the basis of the knowledge available to man. But man will not rest content with such uncertainties regarding the nature of the world. In fact, as pointed out earlier (see chapter 6), the quest for certainty was one of the major incentives to lead the religious life. Hence, from the earliest times attempts have been made to find solutions for these problems, and the different solutions are embodied in the various religions that have emerged.

In the absence of direct evidence, man, in his attempt to acquire knowledge regarding the origin and extent of the universe as well as its nature, has fallen back on speculation determined to a very great extent by a priori principles. Both in the West (cf. Parmenides) and in the East (cf. Aghamarśaṇa and Uddālaka), philosophers adopted the principle of sufficient reason to provide answers to these questions. Such speculations were very much colored by the philosophers' own likes and dislikes. Morris Lazerowitz, commenting on the nature of metaphysics, has remarked: "Like a dream, a metaphysical theory is a production of the unconscious and has both sense and motivation.

We enjoy it or are repelled by it; it gives us pleasure or pain, a feeling of security or one of danger; but its meaning is hidden from us."[7] The discourses of the Buddha included in the *Aṭṭhakavagga* of the *Sutta-nipāta*, one of the earliest portions of the canon, emphasize this fact. The essence of the argument contained in this section is aptly summarized in the verse, "How can men abandon their own views which they cherish as they organize them, led by inclinations and engrossed with their likes?—As they understand, so do they speak."[8]

The same can be said of the other propositions. The view that there is an eternal and unchanging psychic principle called the 'self' (*ātman*), different from the body that is ephemeral and subject to change, is implied by the sixth proposition. When it was asked how we could know the existence of such a 'self', the Upaniṣadic thinkers insisted that it is suprasensible (see chapter 1). This answer again may stem from conscious or unconscious motives, such as the desire to perpetuate one's life and personality (*jīvitukāma*, *amaritukāma*, see chapter 5). The opposite theory, the identity of soul and body, was held by the Materialists, who denied the survival of the human personality after death, thereby ignoring certain facts regarding survival which, the Buddha maintained, can be verified through sensory as well as extrasensory experience.

Finally, we have the four propositions regarding the nature of the saint after death. As pointed out in chapter 7, it is not possible to say, from any direct experience, whether or not the saint exists in any transcendental state. (That the saint is not reborn because he has eliminated craving is said to be verified by those who have developed extrasensory perception.[9] Moreover, on attaining enlightenment one realizes that he has put an end to rebirth, etc. See chapter 7.) Hence the attempt on the part of some, who craved eternal life and avoidance of death, to maintain that the saint continues after death but in a different form of existence. On the other hand, the Materialists denied any survival, not only of the ordinary person, but even of the saint. Since no answer based on experience is possible, the Buddha remained silent when pressed for an answer and maintained that the questions as to whether the *tathāgata* exists (*hoti*) or arises (*uppajjati*), does not exist or does not arise, both or neither, do not fit the case (*na upeti*). It is like asking whether unicorns exist or not. It is not that the questions impute to transcendental reality the characteristics of 'existence', 'nonexistence', and the like, which have valid application only within the realm of ordinary experience, as Jayatilleke seems to think.[10]

We have already discussed two of the criticisms leveled by the Buddha against metaphysical theories. The first is that metaphysical theories are based on a priori reasoning without any empirical basis. This is the criticism of metaphysics used by those who adopt the principle of empirical verification. The second criticism is that a metaphysician, in the absence of direct knowledge, attempts to determine in advance what any object of knowledge must be like, without being satisfied with what he knows.

A third hypothesis construes metaphysical statements as meaningless strings of words, sentences which conform to the rules of grammar but are lacking in meaning, even though they are capable of arousing strong emotional responses in the people. (It is this characteristic of metaphysics, that it is capable of arousing strong emotional reactions, which prompted the German philosopher Immanuel Kant to include it as a regulative principle.) This is the Logical Positivist criticism of metaphysics and is found in the early Buddhist texts. Meaningless statements are here referred to as *appāṭihīrakataṃ*,[11] and the commentator was very definite in upholding this meaning of the term, using the word *niratthakaṃ*, 'meaningless', in explanation of *appāṭihīrakataṃ*.[12] As the Logical Positivists themselves maintain, these metaphysical statements are meaningless because they are not verified in experience. As mentioned in chapter 2, the empiricist attitude of early Buddhism is stated in no unmistakable terms in the *Sabba-sutta* of the *Saṃyutta-nikāya*. Here the Buddha addresses the monks in the following manner:

> Monks, I will teach you 'everything'. Listen to it. What, monks, is 'everything'? Eye and material form, ear and sound, nose and odor, tongue and taste, body and tangible objects, mind and mental objects. These are called 'everything'. Monks, he who would say: "I will reject this *everything* and proclaim another *everything*," he may certainly have a theory [of his own]. But when questioned, he would not be able to answer and would, moreover, be subject to vexation. Why? Because it would not be within the range of experience (*avisaya*).[13]

The implication of the discourse is that our direct perception is based on the six spheres of experience and the corresponding objects.

These are called the twelve 'gateways' (*āyatana*). To speculate on the nature of reality by going beyond these twelve 'gateways' would lead to conflict and disagreement, to vexation and worry, because one would here go beyond the limits of experience (*visaya*). According to our analysis, even extrasensory perception can be included under the twelve 'gateways' (*āyatana*) (see chapter 2). What is directly perceived by both sensory and extrasensory perception is causality as it operates in all spheres—physical, psychological, moral, and spiritual. There is no transcendent reality or Being or 'self' that is given as the object of such direct perception.

In modern philosophy we come across another approach to the problem of metaphysics—an approach adopted by Ludwig Wittgenstein, Gilbert Ryle, and a large number of British and American philosophers—which asserts that traditional metaphysics is based on a superficial understanding of ordinary linguistic usage. Similar criticism of metaphysics by the Buddha is evident from the early Buddhist texts. It is clearly seen in the Buddha's analyses of the concept of 'self' and of the propositions regarding the nature of the saint after death.

The Buddha attributed the belief in a 'self' to a mistaken understanding of ordinary language. Once, when the Buddha made a very impersonal statement explaining the causality of the human personality with the words, "There are four kinds of food or nutriment for the sustenance of beings who are born and for assisting those who are to be born, namely, gross material food, contact, volition, and consciousness," a monk named Moliya Phagguna raised the question: "Lord, who feeds on consciousness?" (*ko nu kho bhante viññāṇâhāraṃ āhāretîti*).[14] Here, even when the Buddha's view was presented in a very impersonal, causal statement, Moliya Phagguna converted that statement into an ordinary linguistic expression, and, following the grammatical structure of that statement, implied the existence of a being, an agent in the ultimate sense. On another occasion, when the Buddha explained the causal process consisting of twelve factors, a monk raised the questions: "What, O Lord, is decay and death? Of whom is this decay and death?"[15] Thereupon, the Buddha insisted that these were misleading questions (*no kallo pañho*), because "if one were to say 'What is decay and death?' and 'Of whom is decay and death?' or if one were to say decay and death is one thing and this decay and death belongs to another, these [questions] are the same [in meaning], only the wording is different." What the Buddha expressly stated here is that, following the grammatical structure of the sentence, one should not assume the existence of a subject ontologically different from the attributes (see chapter 7). This is repeated with regard to all the factors referred to in the twelvefold formula of causation.

On several occasions the Buddha analysed the nature of linguistic conventions and pointed out their uses and limits. In one of the famous passages from the *Saṃyutta-nikāya*, an example of overstepping the limits of linguistic convention is described:

> There are these three linguistic conventions or usages of words or terms which are distinct, have been distinct in the past, are distinct in the present, and will be distinct in the future, and which are not ignored by the wise brahmans and recluses. Which three? Whatever material form (*rūpa*) there has been, which has ceased to be, which is past and has changed, is called, reckoned, and termed 'has been' (*ahosi*), and it is not reckoned as 'it exists' (*atthi*) or as 'it will be' (*bhavissati*). . . . [Same repeated for the other four aggregates —feeling, perception, disposition, and consciousness.] Whatever material form has not arisen, nor come to be, is called, reckoned, or termed 'it will be' (*bhavissati*), and it is not reckoned as 'it exists' (*atthi*) or as 'it has been' (*ahosi*). . . . Whatever material form has arisen and has manifested itself, is called, reckoned, or termed 'it exists' (*atthi*), and it is not reckoned as 'it has been' (*ahosi*) nor as 'it will be' (*bhavissati*).[16]

This probably was the Buddha's criticism of the Substantialists' conception of reality, referred to elsewhere,[17] according to which 'everything exists' (*sabbaṃ atthi*); that is, the substance of everything or the 'self' which, by definition, is eternal (*sassata*), exists throughout the past, present, and future. It is this selfsame theory that was advocated by the later Buddhist schools like Sarvâstivāda (see chapter 9). The Buddha's advice in this connection was that "one should not cling to dialectical usage nor go beyond the limits of linguistic convention" (*janapadaniruttiṃ nâbhiniveseyya sāmaññaṃ nâtidhāveyya*).[18]

Finally, it may be said that the Buddha, in order to avoid metaphysical questions, occasionally adduced the argument from pragmatism or relevance. The *Culla-Māluṅkyaputta-sutta* points out that the solutions to these questions do not lead to well-being and do not contribute to the higher religious life, to renunciation, dispassion, cessation, pacification, insight, enlightenment, or *nibbāna*.[19]

Thus, early Buddhism regarded questions pertaining to the origin and extent of the universe, the nature of the 'soul' or 'self', and the state of the saint after death, as being metaphysical. The Sarvâstivāda conception of 'substance' or 'self-nature' (*svabhāva*), which was an attempt to see the underlying reality of momentary experiences, would also be in the category of metaphysics. Mahāyāna speculation regarding the Buddha or the Absolute may be included in the same category. But problems such as causal uniformity and survival of the human personality, which are considered metaphysical in modern philosophy, were not looked upon as such in early Buddhism.

Notes

1. *S* 2.18 ff.; *TD* 2.86a.
2. *Sn* 824.
3. *S* 2.17.
4. *M* 1.167; *TD* 1.777a.
5. *Ud*, pp. 66 ff.
6. *Ḋ* 1.12 ff.
7. *The Structure of Metaphysics* (London: Routledge and Kegan Paul, 1955), p. 26.
8. *Sn* 781.
9. *S* 1.122.
10. *Early Buddhist Theory of Knowledge*, p. 293.
11. *D* 1.193 ff.; 239, 241 ff.; *M* 2.33, 41.
12. *Papañcasūdani, Majjhimənikāya-aṭṭhakathā*, ed. I. B. Horner (London: PTS, 1933), 3.237.
13. *S* 4.15; *TD* 2.91a–b.
14. *S* 2.13; *TD* 2.102a.
15. *S* 2.61; *TD* 2.99c.
16. *S* 3.70 ff.
17. *S* 2.17; *TD* 2.81a.
18. *M* 3.230, 234.
19. *M* 1.426 ff.; *TD* 1.704 ff.

Selected Readings

PRIMARY SOURCES

Brahmajāla-suttanta (*D* 1.1ff.); 'The Perfect Net' (*SBB* 2.1ff.); *TD* 1.88ff.

Poṭṭhapāda-suttanta (*D* 1.178ff.); 'The Soul Theory' (*SBB* 2.244ff.); *TD* 1.109ff.

Tevijja-suttanta (*D* 1.235ff.); 'On Knowledge of the Vedas' (*SBB* 2.300ff.); *TD* 1.104ff.

Culla-Māluṅkyaputta-sutta (*M* 1.426ff.); 'Lesser Discourse to Māluṅkyā (putta)' (*MLS* 2.97ff.); *TD* 1.704ff.

Aggi-Vacchagotta-sutta (*M* 1.483ff.); 'Discourse to Vacchagotta on Fire' (*MLS* 2.162ff.); *TD* 2.245ff.

Niruttipatha-sutta (*S* 3.70ff.); 'Mode of Reckoning' (*KS* 3.62ff.).

Diṭṭhi-saṃyutta (*S* 3.202–224); 'Kindred Sayings on Views' (*KS* 3.164–176); cf. *TD* 2.42ff.

Udāna. Jaccandha-vagga (*Ud* 62ff.); 'Jaccandha' (*Minor Anthologies of the Pali Canon*, 2.74ff.)

Sutta-nipāta. Aṭṭhaka-vagga (*Sn* 766ff.); 'Book of Octads' (R. Chalmers, *Buddha's Teachings*, Harvard Oriental Series 37, Cambridge, Mass.: Harvard University Press, 1932, pp. 184ff.)

SECONDARY SOURCES

Jayatilleke, K. N. *Early Buddhist Theory of Knowledge*. Pp. 470–476.

Murti, T. R. V. *The Central Philosophy of Buddhism*.

Ñāṇananda, Bikkhu. *Concept and Reality in Early Buddhist Thought*.

Appendix 2
Reflections on the Relation between Early Buddhism and Zen

We have traced the development of Buddhist thought in the five major schools of Indian Buddhism—the three Sthaviravāda or Hinayāna schools (Theravāda, Sarvâstivāda, and Sautrāntika) and the two Mahāyāna schools (Mādhyamika and Yogâcāra). With the introduction and gradual evolution of Buddhist thought in the Far Eastern countries, especially China and Japan, several schools emerged, each of which may in one way or other be related to one or both of the Mahāyāna schools. Two of the most popular of these schools which have survived to this day in the Far East are Zen and Jodo. Zen (Chinese, Ch'an) is generally described as a Chinese adaptation of Mādhyamika-Yogâcāra syncretism. Jodo (Chinese, Ching-tu) is based on Indian Buddhist texts like *Sukhāvatīvyūha* and *Amitâyur-dhyāna* which represent the popular side of Mahāyāna Buddhism.

The form of Buddhism that has become most popular in the West, especially in America, is Zen. Moreover, unlike Jodo, Zen has a definite philosophical basis and has influenced the philosophical, religious, and aesthetic life of the Chinese and Japanese to such an extent that a text on Buddhist philosophy would appear incomplete without a discussion of at least some aspects of it. This appendix is not intended as an exposition of the basic tenets of Zen. On the contrary, it is an attempt to evaluate the relationship of Zen to early Buddhism, included here especially because my analysis of early Buddhism differs greatly from those given by many scholars who have written on Zen Buddhism and the Buddha.

Two of the scholars whose writings on Zen Buddhism have been received with much respect in the West are D. T. Suzuki and Heinrich Dumoulin. While granting that their analyses of Zen teachings are authoritative and comprehensive, the relationship they infer between early Buddhism and Zen appears unacceptable. These two scholars present slightly different views regarding the connection between early Buddhism and Zen. While Dumoulin favors the view that the basic teaching of the Buddha—the theory of an Absolute, an Ultimate Reality—runs through the entire fabric of Buddhist philosophy including Zen, Suzuki adopts the classical Mahāyāna theory (expressed by the simile of the Lotus) that the Mahāyāna doctrines are found in germinal form in the words of the Buddha and that it took a few centuries for them to unfold, and that the so-called Hīnayāna schools failed to understand the full implications of the Buddha's teachings.

Referring to the conception of nirvana in the "ancient collection of hymns," Dumoulin says:

> Nirvana is regarded as consummate salvation, supreme blessedness, the haven of peace and isle of deliverance. Could such figures be veils without substance, enshrouding nothingness? Or do they not rather conceal a positive core? Attention was called to this contradiction in the teachings of the Buddha, and he was asked whether the Perfected One would or would not exist beyond death. Buddha declined to answer this question, apparently because it is theoretical in nature and its solution is irrelevant to the one thing required, namely, the achievement of salvation. He was therefore accused of philosophical agnosticism. It is possible, however, that the Buddha did not wish to express himself regarding life in the beyond, since our conceptual language is not adequate to that purpose. Regarding the "other shore," the immortal sphere removed from death, nothing can be expressed with certainty in human words. That realm is accessible only in mystic ascent.[1]

Having presented this account of early Buddhism, Dumoulin goes on to connect the threads as follows:

> Nāgârjuna, probably in the second century A.D., built up his philosophy of the MiddleWay (mādhyamika) in the Sūtras of TranscendentalWisdom, which have as their apex intuitive enlightenment. Revered as a Bodhisattva throughout all Mahāyāna Buddhism, Nāgârjuna is reckoned among the patriarchs by both mystical schools, the Tantrist Shingon and Zen, and is regarded as the most important link in the long chain of witnesses since Shakyamuni. The chief elements in

> the doctrine of Transcendental Wisdom—negativism, paradox, religious experience in the intuitive cognition, the comprehension of things in their thusness—all flowed from the *Prajñāpāramitā Sūtras* through Nāgârjuna into Zen, embedding themselves deeply in its substance.[2]

This linking up of the *Prajñāpāramitās*, Mādhyamika, and Zen with the Buddha himself was done, no doubt, by the Zen masters themselves. Such attributions are based on the belief that the basic teachings of the Buddha remained unchanged until the time of Zen.

In this book an attempt has been made to show that the basic teachings of the Buddha underwent rather significant changes and that these changes were prompted by the needs and aspirations of the followers, as well as by historical circumstances. Changes which were initiated immediately after the Buddha's death may not have been felt much at that time. But one hundred years later the differences resulting from these changes would have reached considerable magnitude, without the followers being aware at any stage that this process was taking place. It was for this reason that each of the schools advocating divergent doctrines claimed that it truly represented the Buddha-word. Not only the Mahāyāna conception of the Absolute, but even the theories of momentariness, atomism, causality, substance, and so forth, presented by the so-called Hīnayānists, differed from the teachings of early Buddhism. In the case of Mahāyāna Buddhism, we see how Absolutism, which was alien to early Buddhism, developed by gradual stages after the passing away of the Buddha and how, as a result of this development, the *Prajñāpāramitās* were faced with the problem of reconciling the Absolute and the phenomenal. Nāgârjuna attempted to resolve this problem philosophically, or rather, dialectically. The Yogâcārins attempted to solve it by emphasizing withdrawal from the phenomenal by the traditional method of yogic meditation. Zen, it may be held, represents yet another method of reconciling this conflict.

The later Buddhists, who presented divergent theories, also attempted to trace their doctrines to the basic tenets of the Buddha. When they realized that there was some difference between the Buddha's teachings as embodied in the discourses (*sūtra*) and their own, they tried very hard to trace their doctrines to the Buddha himself. This is seen in the *Saddharmapuṇḍarīka-sūtra* as well as the *Kathāvatthu*. Hence many of the interpretations of early Buddhism were not done independently but in the light of the doctrines that developed much later. The Mahāyānists as well as the Hīnayānists, both classical and modern, have tried to *see the germs* of their doctrines in early Buddhism. In this attempt to trace their origins, these later schools of thought either ignored the basic differences between their schools and early Buddhism or disregarded the doctrines of other schools as not representing the true word of the Buddha. Following is a statement from Suzuki explaining the relationship between Mahāyāna and early Buddhism:

> To be accurate, the fundamental ideas of the Mahāyāna are expounded in the Prajñāpāramitā group of Buddhist literature, the earliest of which must have appeared at the latest within three hundred years of the Buddha's death. The germs are no doubt in the writings belonging to the so-called primitive Buddhism. Only their development, that is, a conscious grasp of them as the most essential in the teachings of the founder, could not be effected without his followers' actually living the teachings for some time through the variously changing conditions of life. Thus enriched in experience and nurtured in reflection, the Indian Buddhists came to have the Mahāyāna form of Buddhism as distinguished from its primitive or original form.[3]

This interpretation of early Buddhism is based on acceptance of the superiority of Mahāyāna to other forms. Indeed, it is the view embodied in the Mahāyānist conception of the "three swingings of the Wheel of the Law" (*tridharmacakrapravartana*) mentioned in the *Sandhinirmocana-sūtra*,[4] and which served as the basis of the conception of the 'lotus' (*puṇḍarīka*) gradually unfolding itself during several centuries. The multipetaled lotus, according to this view, did not blossom forth in its inexhaustible fullness until the passage of some centuries. To justify this conception, it became necessary to devalue even the ideal of freedom (*vimutti*) described in the early discourses of the Buddha. This, as pointed out in chapter 10, was the basic theme of the "Discourse on the Lotus of the True Doctrine" or *Saddharmapuṇḍarīka-sūtra*. Thus the Mahāyānists criticized the so-called Hīnayānists on the grounds that the latter presented theories, such as the 'substantiality of elements' (*dharma-svabhāva*), which were contrary to the Buddha's doctrine of nonsubstantiality (*anāt-*

man). But they themselves did not realize that they too were upholding theories, for example, Absolutism, which cannot be attributed to the Buddha.

If one were to keep this fact in mind when attempting to understand the relationship between early Buddhism and Zen, the Zen doctrines would appear in a completely different perspective. It should be noted that Zen Buddhism replaced the Mādhyamika and Yogâcāra schools which were extremely popular in China. Although Zen may have developed as a result of the Mādhyamika-Yogâcāra syncretism, yet there is much in Zen Buddhism that represents a rejection of some of the basic tenets and practices of these two schools. Why did this happen? Was it that Mādhyamika and Yogâcāra forms of Buddhism were modified by the Chinese in the light of the indigenous Taoist tradition? Could Chinese Buddhism have been influenced by some other, perhaps not very popular tradition which still survived in China? A careful study of the innovations brought about by Zen Buddhism in the religious and philosophical atmosphere in which it arose shows a remarkable similarity to those brought about by the Buddha himself in the environment in which he lived. Let us examine these innovations briefly.

Bodhidharma is credited with having founded the school of Zen Buddhism. Zen (Chinese, Ch'an) means *dhyāna*, or meditation, and the famous stanza, which was attributed to Bodhidharma but was actually formulated much later when Zen had reached a high point of development and maturity, is taken as a statement of the essential doctrines of Zen. It runs thus:

> A special tradition outside the Scriptures;
> No dependence upon words and letters:
> Direct pointing at the soul of man;
> Seeing into one's own nature and the attainment of
> Buddhahood.[5]

The "special tradition" referred to here is based on both Mādhyamika and Yogâcāra ideas. The Mādhyamika analysis of concepts as being inadequate to denote reality probably led to rejection of the scriptural tradition. In this connection, the Zen tradition seems to have gone beyond the Mādhyamikas in rejecting completely the scriptural tradition, for the Mādhyamikas, while considering the concepts to be inadequate to represent reality, upheld the value of the 'conventional' (*saṃvṛti*) for an understanding of the 'ultimate' (*paramârtha*) (see chapter 11). "Direct pointing at the soul of man," and "seeing into one's own nature," appear to echo the Yogâcāra method. It was pointed out that during the early period of Chinese Buddhism the most popular schools were Mādhyamika and Yogâcāra. The philosophical teachings of the Mādhyamikas, especially their conception of *śūnyatā* or 'emptiness', were generally acceptable to the intellectual elite who were mostly Taoist. The practice of meditation, a characteristically Indian practice although something similar may have been found in the indigenous tradition, was followed with enthusiasm by the Chinese. The development of these two traditions may have culminated in the doctrines of Zen Buddhism.

In spite of the fact that Mādhyamika philosophy was antimetaphysical, antispeculative, and antischolastic, there was a great upsurge in scholastic activity as a result of the enthusiasm with which the new teachings were received in China. Teams of scholars devoted the greater part of their time to translating texts and compiling commentaries. Not only the entire collection of *sūtras* (discourses) and *śāstras* (philosophical treatises), but also all the commentarial works were rendered into Chinese. In addition, the Chinese themselves compiled their own commentaries. Nearly five hundred years of such scholastic activity must have led to a realization of the futility of the endeavor, and the Zen reaction was very similar to that which was taking place in the other parts of the Buddhist world. For example, in Ceylon, then the center of Theravāda Buddhism, there was a lengthy controversy as to whether 'learning' (*pariyatti*) was the root or foundation of the dispensation or whether it was 'practice' (*paṭipatti*).[6] It is indeed very similar to the change the Buddha himself attempted to effect in his own day. In a discourse included in the *Aṅguttara-nikāya*, the Buddha refers to four types of individuals and compares them with different types of rain clouds (*valāhaka*):

1. One who recites (*bhāsitā*) but does not practice (*no kattā*), like a rain cloud that thunders (*gajjitā*) but does not rain (*no vassitā*)
2. One who practices (*kattā*) but does not recite (*no bhāsitā*), like the rain cloud that rains (*vassitā*) but does not thunder (*no gajjitā*)

3. One who neither recites nor practices (*n'eva bhāsitā no kattā*), like the rain cloud that neither thunders nor rains (*n'eva gajjitā no vassitā*)
4. One who both recites and practices (*bhāsitā ca kattā ca*), like the rain cloud that thunders and rains (*gajjitā ca vassitā ca*)[7]

The first of these is further explained as one who studies the texts, consisting of prose compositions (*sutta*), mixtures of prose and verse (*geyya*), explanations (*veyyākaraṇa*), verse compositions (*gāthā*), and so on, but who does not understand 'unsatisfactoriness' (*dukkha*), its cause, its cessation, and the path leading to its cessation. This no doubt was an allusion to some of the brahmans of the Buddha's day who were accused by the Buddha of being mere reciters of Vedic hymns, who did not make any attempt to understand their meaning or to live according to an understanding of them. The Buddha condemned this kind of textual study. Moreover, according to the *Alagaddūpama-sutta*,[8] a study of the *dhamma* confined to mere textual analysis will not lead man to enlightenment. Neither should proficiency in the *dhamma* be used as a means of stricture on others (*upārambhânisaṃsā*) or for the sake of escaping reproach (*itivādappamokkhânisaṃsā*). Such a study of the doctrine is comparable to holding a poisonous snake by the tail. If a poisonous snake is held by its tail, it turns around and bites the man who holds it, thereby causing even his death. Even so, the *dhamma* wrongly studied leads to misery and frustration. The Buddha's advice was to understand the meaning of the *dhamma*, to bear in mind the spirit of it, and to live accordingly. *Dhamma* is for the sake of crossing over (*nittharaṇa*) and not for the sake of grasping (*gahaṇa*).[9] The Buddha's condemnation of such scholastic activity was certainly known by his later disciples who read some of these discourses, either in Pali or in Chinese. The aversion to scholastic activity is no doubt symbolically represented by the legend of the Sixth Patriarch's (Hui-neng's) complete illiteracy. This attitude of the Zen masters compares well with those of some of the Theravāda teachers who insisted on the practice of the Buddhist life rather than mere scholastic activity, and also of the Buddha, as explained above.

In addition to this, another change brought about by the Buddha was followed by the Zen masters. The practice of meditation, as pointed out earlier, was widely prevalent during the Buddha's day. The ascetics Ālāra Kālāma and Uddaka Rāmaputta, among others, were deeply involved in *yoga* and the meditative raptures attained by such means. As the Buddha saw them, they did not progress beyond attaining to the various raptures (*dhyāna*), and, as mentioned in the *Ariyapariyesana-sutta*,[10] he left these ascetics dissatisfied. Although unsatisfied with the mere ability to attain to the trances, the Buddha is said to have used this knowledge and the powers of the mind to prevent the influx of evil tendencies (*āsava*). He utilized the powers of mental concentration to put an end to grasping (*upādāna*) after developing insight into the nature of things of the world (*dhamma*), and thus he became one who had overcome 'unsatisfactoriness' (*dukkha*). He practiced mental concentration not only during *yogic* meditation, but at all times, even as he went about his everyday activities.

A study of the early history of Buddhism in China reveals the extent to which the Chinese Buddhists were engrossed in the practice of meditation. Tradition has it that Bodhidharma, the first patriarch who emphasized the practice of meditation, remained seated for nine years before the wall of a monastery until his legs withered away. This legend points, perhaps, to the importance attached to meditation during the early period of Buddhism. Or it may have been an attempt to show the futility of practicing meditation for its own sake. It reminds one of the six years of utter austerity practiced by Siddhârtha Gautama before his enlightenment. Moreover, before the introduction of Buddhism into China, India witnessed the emergence of an independent school of *yoga*, based on the *Yoga-sūtras* of Patañjali (about the second century B.C.). The writings of Patañjali led to a popularization of the techniques of *yoga*. The Buddhist counterpart of this school is the Yogâcāra school. Judging from the popularity of the Yogâcāra school of Buddhism in China, it is tempting to conclude that the practice of *yoga*, too, was popular in the early period of Chinese Buddhism. (Even in the Theravāda tradition this emphasis on meditation came to prevail at one stage, as is evident from a special treatise devoted to the techniques of *yoga*.[11]) The attitude of the Zen masters toward meditation is better understood against this background.

The important question is, How can we explain the attitudes of the Zen masters with regard to scholasticism and meditation? Do they represent a Chinese reaction to the absolutism of Mahāyāna and meditational practices emphasized by the Yogâcāra school? Were they the result of the influence of indigenous Taoist tradition only? Or, were the Chinese Zen masters influenced by another Buddhist tradition? In this connection it is interesting to note that almost all the discourses in which the Buddha rejected scholasticism and emphasized the limitations of meditation are found in the Chinese Āgamas. It would be difficult to believe that the great Chinese Buddhist patriarchs were ignorant of the contents of these discourses. The Mahāyānists recognized the fact that the Āgamas represented the earliest discourses of the Buddha.

Yet it is possible to raise the question, if the Zen patriarchs knew of the existence of the discourses that contained the Buddha's approval of ideas which the Zen masters were themselves presenting, why did they not quote these discourses in support of these doctrines which they were trying to attribute to the Buddha himself? It should be remembered that although such Indian Mahāyānists as Nāgârjuna quoted from the early discourses, yet they believed that these discourses, being the property of the Hīnayānists, really represented the Hīnayāna standpoint. They do not seem to have distinguished between the discourses of the Buddha included in the Pali Nikāyas and the Chinese Āgamas on the one hand, and the *Abhidharma Piṭaka* of the Hīnayānists on the other. (This probably was due to the attempt of the Hinayānists to show identity between the Nikāyas and the Abhidharma.[12]) Hence, they had their own *sūtras* that incorporated the Mahāyāna doctrines—*sūtras* like the *Laṅkâvatāra* and the *Saddharmapuṇḍarīka*.

The discourses of the Buddha, which were translated during the earliest period of Chinese Buddhism by scholars like An Shih-kao, pertained either to the system of mental culture (*dhyāna*) or to the explanation of numerical categories such as the six 'gateways' (*āyatana*), the five aggregates (*khandha*), the four psychic powers (*iddhi*), the five powers (*bala*), and the four states of mindfulness (*satipaṭṭhāna*).[13] No doubt, the early Chinese Buddhists considered the entire collection of discourses as representing the *locus classicus* of Hīnayāna.

Moreover, the *Saddharmapuṇḍarīka*, in its chapter "The Skill-in-Means," lays down the Mahāyāna view that the discourses of the Buddha, consisting of the twelve limbs (*aṅga*), were preached to disciples who were slow of wit and lacking in any power of comprehension of the deeper truths of Buddhism. But the *sūtras* of Mahāyāna —the *Vaipulya-sūtra*—were preached to the Bodhisattvas who were quick-witted and had higher aspirations. This tradition was sufficient to prevent the Zen masters who were enthusiastic Mahāyānists from quoting the discourses of the Nikāyas or Āgamas.

Unlike the Buddha who could reject the pre-Buddhist doctrines and modes of life if they did not conform to his philosophy, the Zen masters were restricted by their Mahāyāna background and had to achieve the two goals discussed above, namely, rejection of speculation and restriction of the use of meditation, within the Mahāyāna framework. While the Buddha could reject the non-Buddhist metaphysical speculations regarding the nature of Ultimate Reality and adopt the powers gained by mind control for regulating his life, the Zen masters had to grapple with the metaphysical speculations of the Mahāyānists, especially of the Mādhyamika-Yogâcāra syncretism, for they could not abandon this framework, it being Buddhist and not non-Buddhist. It is evident that the conception of an underlying reality, an Absolute, indescribable and indefinable, is at the back of all Zen practices. The nature of the *kōan* explicates this concept.

It has been mentioned that Zen represents the culmination of two trends, the Mādhyamika and the Yogâcāra. In spite of reciprocal influences, the two trends appear to have retained their salient features, thus giving rise to two different forms of Zen. The school of Zen which emphasized 'gradual enlightenment' was perhaps inspired by the Yogâcāra tradition with its emphasis on the gradualness of the path of meditation aimed at developing the highest form of illumination. The Zen school upholding 'sudden illumination' seems to have been influenced by the Mādhyamika conception of 'emptiness' (*śūnyatā*). These two trends may be traced back to the two disciples of the Fifth Patriarch, Hung-jên. Hung-jên had two disciples, Shên-hsiu and Hui-neng. According to the *Platform Sūtra* of Hui-neng, Hung-jên ordered his disciples each to compose a verse in order to reveal to the master their degree of enlightenment. His purpose was to find a successor to whom he could entrust the patriarchal insignia. Shen-hsiu composed the following verse and wrote it on the wall of the pillared hall of the monastery:

> The body is the Bodhi-tree,
> The mind is like a clear mirror.
> At all times we must strive to polish it,
> And must not let the dust collect.[14]

This verse, no doubt, presents the Yogâcāra philosophy in a nutshell. The mind is pure by nature (*prabhāśvara*) and is defiled by the inflowing cankers (*āśrava*). Therefore, it should be constantly cleaned by wiping off the particles of dust settling on it. And this is achieved through constant meditation.

The legend says that the other disciples read these lines with admiration and believed that the question of succession was thereby settled. But the Fifth Patriarch, Hung-jên, was not completely satisfied and privately informed Shen-hsiu that the verse showed no sign of enlightenment. Should this be taken as a hint that Hung-jên did not favor the Yogâcāra teachings on which the theory of gradual enlightenment was based?

The legend continues: At this time, a boy of little or no education named Hui-neng was living in the monastery. He had come from South China, having heard of the fame of Hung-jên, and begged the master to accept him as a disciple. Although Hung-jên recognized this boy's extraordinary intuitive and intellectual capacities, he did not admit him to the circle of disciples. Instead, he was allowed to work in the monastery splitting firewood and grinding rice. The boy heard of Shên-hsiu's verse, and, because he was illiterate, he asked to have it read for him twice. Thereupon, he composed another verse and had it written on the wall:

> The *bodhi* originally has no tree.
> The clear mirror also has no stand.
> From the beginning not a thing is.
> Where is there room for dust?[15]

Compared with the earlier verse, this one shows definite traces of Mādhyamika thought, especially the doctrine of 'emptiness' (*śūnyatā*). The fact that Hung-jên may have been well disposed toward Mādhyamika rather than Yogâcāra thought is further suggested by the fact that he secretly summoned Hui-neng to his room by night and conferred upon him the patriarchal insignia; but he ordered Hui-neng to flee south across the Yangtse, for he feared the envy of Shên-hsiu and other disciples.

This legend may be taken to represent the schism between northern and southern sects of Chinese Zen, and the two verses clearly depict the doctrinal standpoints of the two sects, the northern sect influenced by Yogâcāra ideas and the southern inspired by

Mādhyamika ideas. These two sects were probably the forerunners of the two main streams of Zen that flourished later in both China and Japan. The Ts'ao-tung sect, which advocated 'silent illumination' and which probably was inspired by the northern sect and its Yogâcāra ideas, came to be known as the Sōtō sect of Japanese Zen. The other is the Lin-chi sect which emphasized the *kōan* exercises as the way to enlightenment and seems to be based on the teachings of the southern sect, as is evident from the influence of Mādhyamika ideas on the *kōan*. This is the Rinzai sect of Japanese Zen.

Some of the *kōan*, referred to in many of the treatises in Zen, are as follows:

1. A monk named Tung-shan asked, "Who is the Buddha?" The answer: "Three chin of flax."

2. Yun-men once asked, "When not a thought is stirring in one's mind, is there any error here?" The answer: "As much as mount Sumeru."

3. When Ming, the monk, overtook the fugitive, Hui-neng, he wanted Hui-neng to give up the secret of Zen. Hui-neng replied: "What are your original features which you had even prior to your birth?"

4. A monk asked Chao-chou: "What is the meaning of the First Patriarch's visit to China?" The answer: "The cypress tree in the front courtyard."

5. When Chao-chou came to study Zen under Nan-ch'uan, he asked: "What is the Way (or the *tao*)?" Nan-ch'uan replied: "Your everyday mind, that is the Way."

6. When P'ang, the old Zen adept, first came to Ma-tsu in order to master Zen, he asked: "Who is he who has no companion among the ten thousand things of the world?" Ma-tsu replied: "When you swallow up in one draught all the water in the Hsi Ch'iang, I will tell you."

7. The Buddha preached for forty-nine years, and yet his broad tongue never moved once.

It appears from these examples that, although the *kōan* does not represent an expression of the inexpressible, yet it points in that direction. The paradox expressed in (7) certainly represents a transcendental conception of the Buddha such as one might find in the *Vajracchedikā Prajñāpāramitā*. "In almost all the *kōan*," says Dumoulin, "the striking characteristic is the illogical or absurd act or word. . . . The *kōan* are one great mockery of all the rules of logic"[16] If this is so, they not only reflect the philosophy of the Mādhyamikas who insisted on the inability of concepts to denote reality, but even go beyond the Mādhyamikas in rejecting all kinds of logic, including that of the Mādhyamikas.

Suzuki interprets the *kōan* differently. He maintains:

> Technically speaking, the *kōan* given to the uninitiated is intended to "destroy the root of life," "to make the calculating mind die," "to root out the entire mind that has been at work since eternity," etc. This may sound murderous, but the ultimate intent is to go beyond the limits of intellection, and these limits can be crossed over only by exhausting oneself once for all, by using up all the psychic powers at one's command. Logic then turns into psychology, intellection into conation and intuition. What could not be solved on the plane of empirical consciousness is now transferred to the deeper recesses of the mind.[17]

A similar view is expressed by C. G. Jung who, in his foreword to Suzuki's *Introduction to Zen Buddhism*, states his belief that the *kōan* is intended as a means to "the final break-through of unconscious contents to the conscious."[18] These two interpretations of Zen *kōan* are no doubt psychological and are based on awareness of the indebtedness of Zen to Yogâcāra, which contains speculation on the unconscious (for example, the *ālaya-vijñāna*, which is comparable to Jung's own theory of the 'collective unconscious'). Basically, they represent an attempt to break away from speculative metaphysics.

Another doctrine generally associated with Zen that is attributed to the influence of the indigenous Chinese tradition is the doctrine of sudden enlightenment or *satori*. Even though a large number of instances of monks and nuns attaining sudden enlightenment have been reported in the *Thera*- and *Therī-gāthās* (included in the Pali Nikāyas), it is generally believed that 'sudden enlightenment' as a theory is a product of Chinese influence. Such originality could be attributed to Zen Buddhism only if one were to overlook the existence of the well-developed theories of 'gradual enlightenment' and 'sudden enlightenment' in the early Mahāyāna tradition. The *Abhisamayâlaṅkāra-prajñāpāramitā-upadeśa-śāstra* of Maitreya contains a chapter on gradual enlightenment and another on sudden enlightenment; this fact alone is sufficient to show that *satori* is not a contribution of the Chinese to Buddhism.[19]

When Buddhism was introduced into China, it had already split into several different schools of thought, and it was natural, therefore, for an indigenous teacher like Hui-neng, or even his predecessors in the Zen tradition, to attempt to see an underlying unity in these divergent systems. Thus, while propounding the teachings of the southern school of Zen Buddhism, which emphasized 'sudden enlightenment', Hui-neng almost denies the distinction between the two methods of realising nirvana.[20] It is difficult to imagine that a teacher like Hui-neng could remain ignorant or unaware of the original discourses of the Buddha, which were available in Chinese translations at that time, although, for obvious reasons, he would have avoided quoting them.

Zen developed in the absolutist background of the *Prajñāpāramitā* literature, which contains statements like the following:

> Here Subhūti, someone who has set out in the vehicle of a Bodhisattva should produce a thought in this manner: "As many beings as there are in the universe of beings, . . . all these should by me be led to nirvana, into that realm of nirvana which leaves nothing behind. And yet, although innumerable beings have thus been led to nirvana, no being at all has been led to nirvana.[21]

A similar absolutist principle is found in Zen, as is evident from some of the *kōan*. Although Mahāyāna emphasized the theory that Ultimate Reality is inexpressible in terms of empirical terminology, yet it embodied much scholasticism. While remaining faithful to the Mahāyāna absolutism, the Zen masters reacted against scholasticism and the recognized forms of conduct. Zen Buddhism differs from early Buddhism with regard to the former and compares well with it in regard to the latter.

Notes

1. *History of Zen Buddhism* (London: Faber and Faber, 1963), p. 14.
2. Ibid., pp. 36f.
3. *Introduction to Zen Buddhism* (New York: Grove Press, 1964), p. 31, note 1.
4. *Sandhinirmocana-sūtra* 7.30.
5. Quoted in Dumoulin's *History of Zen Buddhism*, p. 67.
6. See *Manorathapūraṇī*, *Aṅguttara-nikāya-aṭṭhakathā*, ed. M. Walleser and H. Kopp (London: PTS), 1.92f.
7. *A* 2.102f.; *TD* 2.635a.
8. *M* 1.130 ff.; *TD* 1.763ff.
9. See *Vajra*, p. 32.
10. *M* 1.160ff.; *TD* 1.775ff.
11. See *Yogâvacāra's Manual*, ed. T. W. Rhys Davids, *Journal of the Pali Text Society*, 1896.
12. *Kathāvatthuppakaraṇa-aṭṭhakathā*, ed. J. Minayeff, *Journal of the Pali Text Society*, 1889, pp. 6–7.
13. See E. Zürcher, *The Buddhist Conquest of China* (Leiden: J. E. Brill, 1959), p. 33.
14. *The Platform Sūtra of the Sixth Patriarch*, p. 130.
15. Ibid., p. 133.
16. Dumoulin, *History of Zen Buddhism*, p. 130.
17. *Zen Buddhism*, ed. W. Barrett (New York: Doubleday, 1956), p. 138
18. Ibid., p. 22.
19. *Abhisamayâlaṅkāra-prajñāpāramitā-upadeśa-śāstra*, ed. T. Stcherbatsky and E. Obermiller, *Bibliotheca Buddhica*, 23 (Osnabrück: Biblio Verlag, 1970), pp. 27–32.
20. *The Platform Sūtra of the Sixth Patriarch*, pp. 160–161.
21. *Vajra*, pp. 28–29.

Selected Readings

PRIMARY SOURCES

The Platform Sūtra of the Sixth Patriarch, tr. Philip B. Yampolsky, New York & London: Columbia University Press, 1967.

The Sutra of Hui-Neng, tr. Wong Mou-lam (published together with *The Diamond Sutra*, tr. A. F. Price), Berkeley: Shambala Publications, 1969.

The Zen Teaching of Huang Po on the Transmission of Mind, tr. John Blofeld, New York: Grove Press, 1958.

SECONDARY SOURCES

Benoit, H. *The Supreme Doctrine, Psychological Studies in Zen Thought.* New York: Viking Press, 1955.

Dumoulin, H. *A History of Zen Buddhism.* London: Faber & Faber, 1963.

Luk, Charles. *Ch'an and Zen Teachings.* London: Rider, 1960–1962.

Suzuki, D. T. *Manual of Zen Buddhism.* London: Rider, 1950.

———. *An Introduction to Zen Buddhism.* New York: Grove Press, 1964.

———. *Studies in Zen.* New York: Dell Publications, 1955.

———. *Essays in Zen Buddhism.* 3 vols. New York: Grove Press, 1961.

———. *Zen Buddhism.* Ed. William Barrett. New York: Doubleday, 1956.

Index

Avadāna, 96
avatār (incarnation), 9
Ayer, A. J., 52–53

Bārhaspatya, 12
Being, 'being' (*sat*), 13, 159
Berkeley, George, 151
Bhagavadgītā, 126
Bhāvaviveka, 132, 138, 139
bodhi, 173; -tree, 172
Bodhidharma, 167, 170
bodhisattva, 107, 117–122, 124, 125, 138, 149, 150, 164, 171, 176; ideal, 126
Brahma, 10
Brahmā, 4, 5, 18, 83, 114
Brahmajāla-suttanta, 18, 59, 155
Brahman, 10, 11, 13, 70; -Ātman, 4, 11
Brahmanism, 57
Broad, C. D., 53
Buddha: as a cosmic principle, 113; definition of, 112; as father-figure, 120; as incarnation of Viṣṇu, 9; a Hindu, 9; miraculous aspect of, 117; plurality of, 118; as teacher, 114, 120; transcendental conception of the, 117, 118, 175
Buddhadeva, 104–105
Buddhaghosa, 99, 101, 102, 106, 107
Buddhapālita, 132
Buddhavaṃsa, 96, 118

Candrakīrti, 129–132
Cankī-sutta, 17
Cārvāka, 12
causal: continuity, 104–106; correlations (*pratyaya*), 130; efficiency (*arthakriyākāritva* or *kārtra*) 105, 154; occurrence, 19; orderliness, 115; pattern, 73; principle, 138; process, normal and supernormal, 119; uniformity (*dhammatā*), 26, 153, 161
causality (*paṭiccasamuppāda*, *pratītyasamutpāda*), 26, 36, 53, 64, 69, 101, 104, 133–139, 153–155, 159, 165; = contiguity, 106; corollaries of, 36; a cosmic principle, 116; denial of, 107; = *dhamma*, 116; empiricist theory of, 29; general formula of, 21, 28; of the human personality, 31–33; identity theory of (*satkāryavāda*), 105, 107, 130, 131; beyond logical reasoning, 154–155; Mādhyamika conception of, 137–139; metaphysical theories of, 26, 129, 131; nonidentity theory of (*asatkāryavāda*), 29, 106, 107, 130, 131; not an extraempirical theory, 155; pre-Buddhist theories of, 134; =relativity, 137; Sāṅkhya theory of, 29, 131; Sarvâstivāda theory of, 29, 130, 131; Sautrāntika theory of, 131; universality of, 22; Vaiśeṣika theory of 29, 131. *See also* causation.
causation (*paṭiccasamuppāda*, *pratītyasamutpāda*), 153; =*dhamma*, 64; external (*paraṃ kataṃ*, *parata utpatti*), 26, 27, 29, 46, 129, 131, 133, 153; four characteristics of, 27; through inherent nature (*svabhāva*), 27; Jaina theory of, 154; non-, 129, 153; objectivity of, 28; physical, 27; Sāṅkhya theory of, 105; Sautrāntika view of, 106; self-(*sayaṃ kataṃ*, *svata utpatti*), 26, 27, 129–133, 153, 154; self- and external, 26, 27, 129, 153; twelvefold formula of, 30–33, 160
Central Philosophy of Buddhism, The, 129
cessation (*vyaya*), 13; of perception and feeling (*saññāvedayitanirodha*), 7, 9, 70, 71, 76, 77; state of (*nirodhasamāpatti*), 9, 70–71
Ch'an. *See* Zen
change: empiricist theory of, 37; logical analysis of, 36, 101;

empty (*śūnya*), 120, 123
enlightenment, 16, 20, 32, 33, 57, 78, 98, 113–115, 117, 118, 149, 157, 161, 169, 170, 173; gradual, 172, 173, 176; intuitive, 164; perfect, 95, 120, 121, 123, 124; sudden (*satori*), 175, 176. *See also* illumination
eternalism, 29, 41, 154
Eternalist, 36, 156
ethical judgment, 60; relativity of, 63
ethics, 56, 59, 63, 65; Positivist definition of, 63
evolution, natural, 12
existence (*bhava*), 12, 138, 148; Ājīvika conception of, 12; craving for (*-taṇhā*), 52; disembodied, 52; empirical theory of, 107; future, 73; =immutability, 29; intermediate (*antarā-*), 52; Jaina conception of, 13; relative, 148; three characteristics of, 36; transcendental, 87, 112; transempirical, 88. *See also* *saṃsāra*
experience, 8, 13, 20, 29, 99, 133–135, 143, 155, 158; common, 145; dream, 144–146; everyday, 145; extrasensory, 157; of infernal beings, 144; limitations of, 83; mystical, 9, 38; nondiscriminated (*aprapañcita*), 138; one's own, 20; sense, 144–146, 150, 151, 157, 158; beyond the sphere of (*avisaya*), 24, 158, 159
Experientialist, 8, 16, 18

faith, 95–96, 117
fatalism (*niyativāda*), 12
freedom (*vimukti*, *vimutti*), 26, 56, 58, 59, 61, 64, 72–74, 78, 114, 126, 149; from birth, 57; devaluation of the ideal of, 166; from the normal causal process, 116; through nongrasping (*anupādā*), 18; perfect, 18; from suffering, 58; Upaniṣadic conception of, 10, 70
Freud, Sigmund, 38, 47

Gaṇaka-Moggallāna-sutta, 58
gandhabba, 51
"gateways" (*āyatana*), 145, 146, 159, 171
Ghoṣaka, 104
"gnosis" (*aññā*), 86
God, 19, 65, 121; (*issara* = creator), 18, 21, 26; -head, 7
god(s), 3–5, 65, 98, 121, 145; Vedic conception of, 4
good: definition of, 60–64; relativity of, 63–64

heaven (*sagga*, *svarga*), 41, 65, 66, 121
hell (*apāya*), 41, 48, 65, 66, 145; =unpleasant feelings, 66
henotheism, 4
Hīnayāna, 107, 119, 163, 164, 171
Hīnayānist, 146, 165, 166, 171
Hindu, 8, 9, 41, 44, 82, 88, 146
Hinduism, 9, 126
Hiriyanna, M., 4
Horner, I. B., 61
Hsi Ch'iang, 174
Hsüan Tsang, 142–143
Hui-neng, 126, 169, 172–174, 176
Hume, David, 106–107
Hung-jên, 172–173

idealism, 142; absolute, 142–144, 147, 150; Hegelian, 142; metaphysical, 150; Yogâcāra, 142
Idealist, 143, 147, 151
"ideation only" (*vijñaptimātra*), 143, 149
identity, 51, 105; denial of, 53; of substance, 130
illumination: silent, 174; sudden, 172. *See also* enlightenment
illusion, transcendental (*mukhya-vibhrama*), 151
immaterialism, 150–151

117, 118, 129, 130, 160, 161, 163
Sarvâstivādin, 98, 100, 102–105, 118, 119, 130, 146; neo-, 104
Sāti, 39, 40, 93
satori. *See* enlightenment, sudden
Sautrāntika, 100, 101, 103–107, 129, 142, 163
sceptics, 8
scholasticism, 107, 112, 126, 170, 171, 176; beginnings of, 94, 97
Selā, 39
self, 10, 11, 21, 26, 27, 29, 31, 36, 38–42, 45, 46, 51, 79, 80, 84, 86, 100, 105, 125, 130, 134, 146–149, 154, 157, 159, 161; denial of, 31, 45–46; immanent, 26; individual, 8, 13, 18, 70; inherently pure, 14; knower of, 11; Materialist conception of, 40–41; perception of, 148; reality of, 14; transcendental, 40, 135; true, 9–10; universal, 8, 14, 18, 70; Upaniṣadic conception of, 9–10, 40, 154. *See also* soul
sense: data, 20; impression, 6, 21
Shên-shiu, 172–173
Śikṣāsamuccaya, 106
Siṅgālovāda-suttanta, 59
Shingon, Tantrist, 164
Śiva, 3
skepticism, 19
soul: different from body, 156–157; identical with body, 156–157; immortal, 41–42, 51, 79, 130; immortality of, 10; permanent, 14
speculation (*vīmaṃsā*), 17–18
spirits, departed, 65–66
Sthaviravāda, 163
Sthiramati, 142
'stream-entrant' (*sotâpanna*), 72
Subhūti, 119, 123, 124, 176
substance, 36, 102; (*svabhāva*), 99, 100, 105, 130, 131, 161, 165; criticism of, 130; denial of, 130; of everything, 160; identity of, 130; material, 100; mental, 39, 102; primordial (*prakṛti*), 105
Substantialist, 26, 27, 29, 40, 160; view, 100
substantiality, 146, 166
Sukhāvatīvyūha-sūtra, 121, 163
śūnyatā. *See* emptiness; nonsubstantiality
survival, 12, 22, 23, 49–51, 53, 78, 161; denial of, 157; of the saint, 87. *See also* rebirth
Sūtra of Transcendental Wisdom, 164
Sutta-nipāta, 59, 63, 64, 80, 135, 136, 157
Suzuki, D. T., 163, 164, 166, 175
Svātantrika school, 132, 138
Śvetaketu, 11

tajjīvataccharīravāda, 41
Taoist, 167, 168, 170
tathāgata (saint), 80, 83, 84, 95, 96, 115, 118–120, 123, 138; after death, 156, 157, 159, 161, 164
tathatā (suchness, objectivity), 118, 122, 138
telepathy (*cetopariyañāṇa*), 22, 23, 146
testimony (*parato ghoṣa*), 20
Theragāthā, 33, 175
Theravāda, 82, 95, 97, 98, 100, 107, 118, 129, 163, 168–170; pre-Buddhaghosan, 100; post-Buddhaghosan, 99–101, 146
Theravādin, 103, 106, 118
Therīgāthā, 33, 175
Thomas, E. J., 118–119
Traditionalist(s), 5, 8, 16
trance, 6, 10; validity of yogic, 9–10
transcendence, 117, 134
transcendentalism, 40, 84, 88; Mahāyāna, 103
transmigration, 44; evolutionary, 12. *See also* rebirth; survival
trikāya (three bodies of Buddha), 122, 149
Triṃśikā, 142, 143, 147, 149
truth(s) (*sacca*, *satya*), 75, 116, 134, 135, 154; =causation, 64, 115; conventional (*vohāra*), 99, 137;

About the Author

David J. Kalupahana is professor and chairman of the Department of Philosophy at the University of Hawaii. He has taught at the University of Sri Lanka (formerly University of Ceylon), and has studied as a British Council Research Scholar at the University of London, where he received the Ph.D. degree. This book is largely an outgrowth of his many lectures over the past fifteen years on the subject of Buddhist philosophy.

Dr. Kalupahana is also the author of *History of Indian Philosophy* (in Sinhalese), published in Sri Lanka in 1963, and *Causality: The Central Philosophy of Buddhism*, published in 1975 by The University Press of Hawaii.